THE PURPOSE OF PLAYING

THE PURPOSE
OF PLAYING

SHAKESPEARE AND THE CULTURAL POLITICS
OF THE ELIZABETHAN THEATRE

Louis Montrose

The University of Chicago Press
Chicago & London

Louis Montrose is chairman of the
Department of Literature at the University
of California, San Diego.

The University of Chicago Press, Chicago 60637
The University of Chicago Press, Ltd., London
© 1996 by Louis Adrian Montrose
All rights reserved. Published 1996
Printed in the United States of America
05 04 03 02 01 00 99 98 97 96   1 2 3 4 5

Portions of the Prologue appeared in "New Historicisms," *Redrawing the
Boundaries*, pp. 392–418. © 1992 by The Modern Language Association of
America. All rights reserved. Reprinted by permission. Portions of chapters 1–4
and epilogue appeared in *Helios*, n.s., 7:153–82. Reprinted by permission. Portions
of chapters 8–10 appeared in a different form in *Representations* 2:61–94. © 1983 by
the Regents of the University of California. Reprinted by permission. Portions of
chapter 11 appeared in David L. Smith, Richard Strier, and David Bevington, *The
Theatrical City*, pp. 68–86. © Cambridge University Press 1995. Reprinted by
permission.

ISBN 0-226-53482-0 (cloth)   ISBN 0-226-53483-9 (paper)

Library of Congress Cataloging-in-Publication Data

Montrose, Louis Adrian.
The purpose of playing : Shakespeare and the cultural politics of
the Elizabethan theatre / Louis Montrose.
p.   cm.
Includes bibliographical references (p.   ) and index.
1. Shakespeare, William, 1564–1616—Stage history—To 1625.
2. Shakespeare, William, 1564–1616—Political and social views.
3. Shakespeare, William, 1564–1616. Midsummer night's dream.
4. Theater—Political aspects—England—History—16th century.
5. Theater—Social aspects—England—History—16th century.
6. Great Britain—Politics and government—1558–1603.   7. Political
plays, English—History and criticism.   8. Power (Social sciences)
in literature.   I. Title.
PR3095.M66   1996
792'.0942'09031—dc20   95-35335
                                              CIP

for
Caroline,
in the Lu–Feng spirit

Contents

ACKNOWLEDGMENTS

Although only recently completed, this book has its origins in what sometimes seems to me a prior lifetime. In her continuous concern and attention, Susan Montrose has proven a paragon of constancy in change. I trust that Tom Dunseath and Roy Pearce, teachers and colleagues who nurtured me then, will now accept this belated token of my gratitude. Harry Berger, Stephen Greenblatt, Stephen Orgel, and Robert Weimann have been invariably generous in their support; I have greatly valued both their friendship and their scholarship. Roxanne Lin, Frank Whigham, and Don Wayne have each read versions of material that has taken final form in this book, and each has aided me, by example and by admonition, to improve my work and myself; I am deeply grateful to each of them. David Bevington, Linda Charnes, and Mary Beth Rose have read the manuscript with care and sympathy and have improved it by their criticisms and suggestions. It was possible for me to bring this and other projects to completion while chairing my department thanks to the research assistance of Ben Bertram, Susan Light, and Karen Raber, the administrative assistance of Barbara Saxon, and the collegiality of Michael Davidson; to all, my thanks.

This book is lovingly dedicated to my wife, Caroline Yi-jun Ding, whose companionship has helped me to complete it and to begin anew.

To the Reader

The Purpose of Playing is part of a larger project addressing the politics of representation in the discursive and performative culture of later Elizabethan England. This project addresses the complex, heterogeneous, and ubiquitous discourse in which the relationship between state and subject was constructed and contested. Part One of *The Purpose of Playing* presents an extended discussion of the place of the public and professional theatre within the ideological and material frameworks of Elizabethan culture and society; my emphasis is upon the theatre of Shakespeare and his company, and upon the unstable relationship between the official centers of political and cultural authority in the state, the city, and the church and the unofficial and marginal site of performative authority in the playhouse. Here I consider some of the socioeconomic, political, and religious forces and institutions that shaped the Elizabethan subject's conditions of existence and the Elizabethan theatre's conditions of production. I seek to identify connections among several contemporaneous historical developments: the religious, political, and social policies and attitudes abetting Elizabethan state formation; the enormous growth of London as an administrative, economic, and cultural center; and the institutionalization of a professional, secular, and commercial theatre with a complex relationship to the dynastic state and the royal court, on the one hand, and to the urban oligarchy and the public market, on the other. I begin by considering the role of the professional theatre and of theatricality more generally in the cultural transformation that was concurrent with religious and sociopolitical change; and I conclude by focusing upon the formal means by which Shakespeare's Elizabethan plays, as performed by the company in which he was a sharer, called into question the absolutist assertions of the Elizabethan state.

Part Two applies the themes of Part One to an extended reading of a particular play, *A Midsummer Night's Dream*, at the same time drawing in discussion of many other relevant cultural texts. Here the relationship between the theatre and the state is figured, in part, through the play's reworkings of the gendered political mythology of the monarch, Queen Elizabeth. Thus, throughout Part Two, I give particular attention to the discourse of gender that circulated through Elizabethan culture, and to its imaginative and conspicuous articulation in *A Midsummer Night's Dream*. I construe this discourse as reciprocally related to other modes of cultural, political, and socioeconomic organization and experience. In the second chapter of Part Two, I discuss Elizabethan constructions of the domestic economy and marital relations, and their articulation with gendered discourses of human physiology and classical mythology within Shakespeare's play; in this discussion, my emphasis is upon ideological instability and contradiction. In chapter 3, I explore how *A Midsummer Night's Dream* and some other Elizabethan performance-texts figure the Elizabethan gender system and Queen Elizabeth's anomalous and privileged place within it. In chapter 4, I analyze the interplay among discourses of gender, social status, and theatricality, in order to suggest how dramatic articulations of the relatively loose and sometimes erratic Elizabethan gender system may have mediated the complex and delicate relationship between the popular Elizabethan theatre and the Elizabethan state.

In Parts One and Two of *The Purpose of Playing*, I have intentionally sought a contrast of critical perspective, rhetorical texture, and analytical techniques. Part Two focuses the broad-ranging cultural-historical perspective of Part One upon a canonical dramatic text; the intention has been to give a local habitation and a name to the workings of ideology in cultural production. Here I pursue historicist and materialist concerns through the rhetorical analysis of texts and of intertextuality. Having drawn my dramatic examples in Part One from the genres of tragedy and history, I focus in Part Two upon a comedy that does not display its politics in so explicit a fashion. By addressing the cultural processes discussed in Part One from the exemplary perspective of *A Midsummer Night's Dream*, I do not seek to demonstrate that this particular cultural text is a *summa* of Elizabethan culture. Nor do I argue for the organic unity of either the culture or the text, but rather treat the text as a site of convergence of various and potentially contradictory cultural discourses. In a prologue, I attempt to articulate the analytical principles that shape and direct my critical practice in the rest of the book. This metacritical essay synthesizes my response to, and position within, the theoretical and methodological debates of recent literary and cultural studies. *The Purpose of Playing* is intended as a contribution to the ongoing refiguration of the sociocultural field within which now-canonical Renaissance literary and dramatic works were originally produced. I am concerned to resituate such texts in relationship to other genres and modes of writing, and to resituate discursive practices in relationship to the social and political institutions and processes of early modern England. It is my conviction that by focusing the analytical resources and techniques of literary criticism upon the historical, cultural, and sociopolitical dimensions of texts, we can work toward a mode of critical practice in which formal and ideological considerations are inseparable. By emphasizing this dialectic of text and history, I hope to have produced an effective demonstration that the formal resources of language and of the literary imagination actively shape cultural value, belief, and understanding; social distinction and interaction; and political control and contestation.

·

TEXTS AND HISTORIES

During the course of the 1980s, literary studies in the American academy came to be centrally concerned with the historical, social, and political conditions and consequences of literary production and interpretation. From a multiplicity of sometimes convergent and sometimes incompatible perspectives, the writing and reading of texts, as well as the processes by which they are circulated and categorized, analyzed and taught, are now being construed as historically determined and determining modes of cultural work. What have often been taken to be self-contained aesthetic and academic issues are now being reunderstood as inextricably though complexly linked to other social discourses, practices, and institutions; and such unstable linkages are construed as constituting the ideological field within which individual subjectivities and collective structures are mutually shaped.

In various combinations and with varying degrees of consistency and effectiveness, the intellectual forces identifiable as feminism, cultural materialism, revisionist forms of Marxism, and new historicism or cultural poetics have been engaged in redrawing the boundaries and restructuring the content of English Renaissance studies— and literary studies, more generally—during the past decade and a half.[1] The critical forces that I have here conveniently if simplistically labelled have in common a concern at once to affirm and to problematize the connections between literary and other discourses, the dia-

---

1. For a detailed analysis and critique of the origins, assumptions, and methods of new historicist work, and the relationship of such work to feminist and cultural materialist projects, see my longer study: "New Historicisms," in *Redrawing the Boundaries: The Transformation of English and American Literary Studies*, ed. Stephen Greenblatt and Giles Gunn (New York: Modern Language Association, 1992), 392–418.

lectic between the text and the world. And in recent years, such perspectives have posed a successful challenge to New Critical rhetorical analysis and positivist historical scholarship, which were hitherto the dominant paradigms in Anglo-American literary criticism. At the same time, these newer modes of criticism have variously reacted against and contributed to the intellectual ferment of the past two decades. This ferment, summed up in the word *theory*, has challenged the assumptions and procedures of normative discourses in several academic disciplines. And in our own discipline, it has shaken if not undermined the aesthetic, moral, and ontological principles that prescribed the ideological dispositions of traditional literary studies. The theoretical field of poststructuralism is inhabited by a multiplicity of unstable, variously conjoined and conflicting discourses. Among the principles that some of them share, those of concern to me here are a problematization of the processes by which meaning and value are produced and grounded; a shift from an essential or immanent to an historical, contextual, and conjunctural model of signification; and a general suspicion of closed systems, totalities, and universals.

The now-dominant poststructuralist orientation to social, political, and historical criticism in literary studies is characterized by an anti-reflectionist perspective on cultural work; a shift of emphasis from the aesthetic analysis of verbal *artifacts* to the ideological analysis of discursive *practices;* and an understanding of meaning as situationally and provisionally constructed. Such an orientation requires a sensitivity to both the *instability* and the *instrumentality* of representation. This orientation is pervasively concerned with writing, reading, and teaching as modes of *action*, and it is in this broad sense that its perspective can be characterized as ideological. Traditionally, "ideology" has referred to the articulated principles serving as an agenda for concerted action by a particular sociopolitical movement or group, or, more generally, to the congeries of ideas, values, and beliefs common to any social group. In recent years, this vexed but indispensable term has in its broadest sense come to be associated with the processes by which social subjects are formed, re-formed, and enabled to perform as agents in an apparently meaningful world.[2] Representa-

---

2. In the well-known formulation of Althusser's essay "Ideology and Ideological State Apparatuses," "Ideology is a 'Representation' of the Imaginary Relation-

tions of the world in written discourse participate in the construction of the world: They are engaged in shaping the modalities of social reality and in accommodating their writers, performers, readers, and audiences to multiple and shifting positions within the world that they themselves both constitute and inhabit.

In *After the New Criticism*, Frank Lentricchia has linked "the anti-historical impulses of formalist theories of literary criticism" with monolithic and teleological theories of "History"—visions of history that, in their unity, totality, and inexorability, can be grounded only upon essentialist or metaphysical premises.[3] I assume that among such visions of history belongs not only the great code of Christian figural and eschatological history but also the master-narrative of classical Hegelian Marxism.[4] One of the most powerful recent theoretical challenges to the Marxian master-narrative has come from within the Marxist tradition itself, in the "post-Marxist" analysis of Ernesto Laclau and Chantal Mouffe. In the polemical introduction to *Hegemony and Socialist Strategy*, they write that

> there is not *one* discourse and *one* system of categories through which the "real" might speak without mediations. In operating deconstructively within Marxist categories, we do not claim to be

---

ship of Individuals to their Real Conditions of Existence," a representation that "Interpellates Individuals as Subjects." See Louis Althusser, *Lenin and Philosophy and Other Essays*, trans. Ben Brewster (New York and London: Monthly Review Press, 1971), 127–86; quotation from 162, 170. Also see Terry Eagleton, *Ideology: An Introduction* (London: Verso, 1991).

3. Frank Lentricchia, *After the New Criticism* (Chicago: University of Chicago Press, 1980), xiii–xiv.

4. The latter has been characterized by Fredric Jameson as "history now conceived in its vastest sense of the sequence of modes of production and the succession and destiny of the various human social formations"; this he projects as the "untranscendable horizon" of interpretive activity, subsuming "apparently antagonistic or incommensurable critical operations, assigning them an undoubted sectoral validity within itself, and thus at once cancelling and preserving them." See Fredric Jameson, *The Political Unconscious: Narrative as a Socially Symbolic Act* (Ithaca: Cornell University Press, 1981); quotation from 75, 10. Perhaps we should now add, as a bathetic coda to the history of grand historical narratives, the recent pop theory that, with the collapse of totalitarian Communist regimes in eastern Europe, history as such had suddenly ended—the end having come somewhat short of the Marxian trajectory, in the supposed universal embrace of liberal democracy and consumer capitalism.

writing "universal history," to be inscribing our discourse as a
moment of a single, linear process of knowledge. Just as the era of
normative epistemologies has come to an end, so too has the era
of universal discourses.[5]

Accordingly, "the rejection of privileged points of rupture and the
confluence of struggles into a unified political space, and the acceptance, on the contrary, of the plurality and indeterminacy of the social, seem . . . the two fundamental bases from which a new political
imaginary can be constructed" (152). Similarly, against the monstrous
marriage of unhistoricized formalisms and totalized History, Lentricchia opposes the multiplicity of "histories," history as characterized
by "forces of heterogeneity, contradiction, fragmentation, and difference" (xiv). It seems to me that the various modes of what could
be called poststructuralist historicist and materialist criticism can be
characterized by such a shift from History to histories.

In recent years, as some historians and anthropologists have become increasingly concerned with the cognitive and ideological import of narrative forms and rhetorical strategies, literary theory has
come to exert an unprecedented extra-disciplinary influence in the
humanities and interpretive social sciences. For example, in a discussion of recent controversies in the discipline of history, Lynn Hunt
defines history as "an ongoing tension between stories that have been
told and stories that might be told. In this sense, it is more useful to
think of history as an ethical and political practice than as an episte-
mology with a clear ontological status." And, in the discipline of anthropology, the ambiguous status of the ethnographer as participant-
observer of the alien culture which is his or her object of study has
been reproblematized by a focus on textual and ideological dimensions of ethnographic practice, on the ethnographer's discursive construction of culture.[6] Such developments within the humanities and

5. Ernesto Laclau and Chantal Mouffe, *Hegemony and Socialist Strategy: Towards
a Radical Democratic Politics* (London: Verso, 1985), 3.

6. See Lynn Hunt, "History as Gesture; or, The Scandal of History," in *Consequences of Theory: Selected Papers from the English Institute, 1987–88*, ed. Jonathan Arac
and Barbara Johnson (Baltimore: Johns Hopkins University Press, 1991), 91–107;
quotation from 103. Among the early and influential textualist critiques of anthropology were Roy Wagner, *The Invention of Culture*, rev. and expanded ed. (Chicago:
University of Chicago Press, 1981); *Writing Culture: The Poetics and Politics of Ethnog-
raphy*, ed. James Clifford and George E. Marcus (Berkeley: University of California Press, 1986); *Anthropology as Cultural Critique: An Experimental Moment in the*

interpretive social sciences point toward a potential synthesis of historicist and formalist, materialist and textualist or tropological, interests and analytical techniques; and to the convergence of such disciplinary projects upon the interconnectedness of the discursive and material domains.

The prevailing tendency across the humanities and interpretive social sciences is now to emphasize that a complex dynamic of mutual constitution and transformation characterizes the relationship between the universe of discourse and material life. On the one hand, the social is understood to be constructed in discourse, and on the other, language-use is understood to be always and necessarily dialogical, to be socially and materially determined and constrained. Thus, Fredric Jameson can retheorize a Marxist concept of the social by appropriating a poststructuralist concept of the textual. He writes that History as material necessity—"Althusser's 'absent cause,' Lacan's 'Real'—is *not* a text, for it is fundamentally non-narrative and nonrepresentational; what can be added, however, is the proviso that history is inaccessible to us except in textual form" (*The Political Unconscious*, 82). From a perspective that affirms the processes of *figuration* to be constitutive of society and history, the recent reorientation in literary studies of which J. Hillis Miller and others have complained—the turn from "language as such . . . toward history, culture, society, politics, institutions"—might be better construed as a broadening and deepening of our central scholarly concern with the analysis of discursive forms, strategies, and effects.[7] The academic discipline of literary criticism has for some time been making its traditional analytical strengths meaningful and useful to new transdisciplinary projects of cultural analysis and critique; and it has been doing so by studying the ways in which discursive forms and processes constitute "history, culture, society, politics, institutions."

The poststructuralist orientation to history that has recently emerged in literary studies I characterize chiastically, as a reciprocal concern with the historicity of texts and the textuality of histories.

Human Sciences, ed. George E. Marcus and Michael J. Fischer (Chicago: University of Chicago Press, 1986).

7. See J. Hillis Miller, "Presidential Address 1986. The Triumph of Theory, the Resistance to Reading, and the Question of the Material Base," *PMLA* 102 (1987), 281–91; quotation from 283.

By *the historicity of texts*, I mean to suggest the historical specificity, the social and material embedding, of all modes of *writing*—including not only the texts that critics study but also the texts in which we study them; thus, I also mean to suggest the historical, social, and material embedding of all modes of *reading*.[8] By *the textuality of histories*, I mean to suggest, in the first place, that we can have no access to a full and authentic past, to a lived material existence that is unmediated by the surviving textual traces of the society in question, and, furthermore, that the survival of those traces rather than others cannot be assumed to be merely fortuitous but must rather be presumed to be at least partially consequent upon complex and subtle social processes of selective preservation and effacement. In the second place, those surviving and victorious textual traces of material and ideological struggle are themselves subject to subsequent textual mediations when they are construed as the "documents" upon which those who profess the humanities ground their own descriptive and interpretive texts. As Hayden White and others have forcefully reminded us, such textual histories and ethnographies necessarily, although always incompletely, constitute in their own narrative and rhetorical forms the past or alien cultural actions and meanings—the *History* or *Culture*—to which they offer access.[9]

8. Compare the concept of the *reading formation* elaborated in Tony Bennett, "Texts in History: The Determinations of Readings and Their Texts," in *Post-Structuralism and the Question of History*, ed. Derek Attridge, Geoff Bennington, and Robert Young (Cambridge: Cambridge University Press, 1987), 63–81. Bennett describes a reading formation as

> an attempt to identify the determinations which, in operating on both texts and readers, mediate the relations between text and context, connecting the two and providing the mechanisms through which they productively interact in representing context not as a set of extra-discursive relations but as a set of inter-textual and discursive relations which produce readers for texts and texts for readers. . . . Texts, readers and contexts . . . are variable functions within a discursively ordered set of relations. Different reading formations . . . produce their own texts, their own readers and their own contexts. (74)

The concept of a *reading formation* implicates critics in historically and institutionally situated roles as privileged readers, whose specialized though hardly disinterested knowledge constitutes the past that they undertake to elucidate.

9. See the following works by Hayden White: *Metahistory: The Historical Imagination in Nineteenth-Century Europe* (Baltimore: Johns Hopkins University Press, 1973); *Tropics of Discourse* (Baltimore: Johns Hopkins University Press, 1978); *The*

Refiguration of the relationship between the verbal and the social, between the text and the world, involves a reproblematization or wholesale rejection of some alternative idealist, empiricist, and materialist conceptions: Literature as an autonomous aesthetic, moral, or intellectual order that transcends the shifting and conflicting pressures of material needs and interests; or, as a collection of inert discursive records of "real events"; or, as the superstructural reflection produced by a determining economic base.[10] Recent theories of textuality have argued persuasively that the referent of a linguistic sign cannot be fixed; that the meaning of a text cannot be stabilized. However, writing and reading are always historically and socially sited events, performed *in* the world and *upon* the world by ideologically sited individual and collective human agents. In any actual situation of signification, the theoretical indeterminacy of the signifying process is delimited by the historical specificity of discursive practices, by the operative constraints and resources of the reading formation within which that signification takes place.

A different form of the polarity between freedom and constraint has underwritten much of the work in English Renaissance literary and dramatic studies during the past decade. At the center of much critical practice and polemic has been the nature and scope of the agency available to subjects of the early modern state, and the degree

---

Content of the Form: Narrative Discourse and Historical Representation (Baltimore: Johns Hopkins University Press, 1987).

10. On the problematic figuration of base and superstructure, see the lucid essay, "Base and Superstructure in Marxist Cultural Theory," in Raymond Williams, *Problems in Materialism and Culture* (London: Verso, 1980), 30–49. Williams begins by noting the complexity of the term designating this relationship, namely, "determination":

> There is clearly a difference between a process of setting limits and exerting pressures, whether by some external force or by the internal laws of a particular development, and that other process in which a subsequent content is essentially prefigured, predicted and controlled by a pre-existing external force. Yet it is fair to say, looking at many applications of Marxist cultural analysis, that it is the second sense, the notion of prefiguration, predication or control, which has often explicitly or implicitly been used. (32)

He concludes that "an active and self-renewing Marxist cultural tradition" must break with this figure, taking as a new point of departure a search "not for the components of a product but for the conditions of a practice" (49, 48).

to which contestation of the dominant ideology and its institutions was possible and actualized. The terms in which the problematic of ideology and resistance came to be posed in Renaissance studies were those of an opposition between *subversion* and *containment.* These terms, which appear to be residues of a Cold War ideology that had pernicious consequences in both international and domestic policy, have proven once again to be wholly inadequate instruments of analysis and debate. Nevertheless, they are also significant indicators of a shift of perspective within Anglo-American literary criticism and its ambient political culture. During the 1980s, as the problem of ideology became an acceptable and even a central topic of critical discourse in the American academy, so the emphasis in sociocultural analysis shifted from unity, reciprocity, and consent to difference, domination, and resistance. During the past decade, it is precisely this shift of emphasis from canonicity and consensus to diversity and contestation that has been the focus of the national debate about the direction of the humanities—a debate that has been waged on the campuses and on the best-seller lists, in the public media and in the policy statements and funding priorities of government agencies.

It was within the context of these culture wars—and, perhaps, as a displacement of the issues at stake—that "The New Historicism" was constituted as an academic site of ideological struggle between "containment" and "subversion." The following scenario may provide one version of this struggle: Critics who emphasized possibilities for the effective agency of individual or collective subjects against forms of domination, exclusion, and assimilation energetically contested critics who emphasized the capacity of the early modern state, as personified in the monarch, to *contain* apparently subversive gestures, or even to *produce* them precisely in order to contain them. According to a now-notorious argument in Stephen Greenblatt's essay, "Invisible Bullets," this capacity of the dominant order to generate subversion so as to use it to its own ends marks "the very condition of power." [11] Thus, a generalized argument for the "containment

11. This essay has appeared in three successively revised and enlarged versions: *Glyph* 8 (1981), 40–61; *Political Shakespeare: New Essays in Cultural Materialism,* ed. Jonathan Dollimore and Alan Sinfield (Ithaca: Cornell University Press, 1985), 18–47; and Stephen Greenblatt, *Shakespearean Negotiations: The Circulation of Social Energy in Renaissance England* (Berkeley: University of California Press, 1988), 21–65. The argument for containment becomes somewhat more qualified

of subversion" reduced arguments for the agency of subjects to the illusory and delusive effects of a dominant order. The binary logic of subversion/containment produces a closed conceptual structure; its terms are reciprocally defining and dependent, complementary and complicit.

The putatively Foucauldian New Historicist argument for the dominant's production and containment of subversion is pungently characterized by Frank Lentricchia as "a prearranged theatre of struggle set upon the substratum of a monolithic agency which produces 'opposition' as one of its delusive political effects." [12] However, any strict argument for the containment of subversion that views power as crystallized in the state apparatus is inconsistent with Fou-

---

in successive versions. In *Shakespearean Negotiations*, it is actually subverted by the Introduction that precedes it, in which Greenblatt repudiates the strong form of the containment argument with which his work had become identified. Although without specific reference to the intense debate and critique provoked by that earlier position, he writes of a turn in his thinking:

> I had tried to organize the mixed motives of Tudor and Stuart culture under the rubric power, but that term implied a structural unity and stability of command belied by much of what I actually knew about the exercise of authority and force in the period.
>
> If it was important to speak of power in relation to Renaissance litera-ture—not only as the object but as the enabling condition of representation itself—it was equally important to resist the integration of all images and expressions into a single master discourse. . . . Even those literary texts that sought most ardently to speak for a monolithic power could be shown to be the sites of institutional and ideological contestation. (*Shakespearean Negotiations*, 2–3)

The governing terms of *Shakespearean Negotiations*—circulation, acquisition, nego-tiation—suggest that a vision of the repressive, monolithic power of the state upon cultural production is not being revised as a more complicated model of power/ resistance so much as it is being displaced by a vision of the energizing and liberat-ing effects of emergent market capitalism. Thus, Greenblatt characterizes the re-lationship between William Strachey's account of the Bermuda shipwreck and Shakespeare's *The Tempest* as a "process whereby the Bermuda narrative is made negotiable, turned into a currency that may be transferred from one institutional context to another. The changes do not constitute a coherent critique of the colo-nial discourse, but they function as an unmooring of its elements so as to confer upon them the currency's liquidity" (*Shakespearean Negotiations*, 155). For a more general presentation of the cultural poetics of capitalism, see Stephen Greenblatt, "Towards a Poetics of Culture," in *The New Historicism*, ed. H. Aram Veeser (New York and London: Routledge, 1989), 1–14.

12. Frank Lentricchia, "Foucault's Legacy: A New Historicism?" in *The New Historicism*, ed. Veeser, 231–42; quotation from 234.

cault's own view that volatile and contingent relations of power saturate social space. Foucault emphasizes that

> power's condition of possibility . . . must not be sought in the primary existence of a central point, in a unique source of sovereignty from which secondary and descendent forms would emanate; it is the moving substrate of force relations which, by virtue of their inequality, constantly engender states of power, but the latter are always local and unstable.[13]

For Foucault, power is never monolithic, and power relations always imply multiple sites not only of power but also of resistance, sites that are of variable configuration, intensity, and effectiveness. He writes that

> The strictly relational character of power relationships . . . depends on a multiplicity of points of resistance: these play the role of adversary, target, support, or handle in power relations. . . . Resistances . . . can only exist in the strategic field of power relations. But this does not mean that they are only a reaction or rebound, forming with respect to the basic domination an underside that is in the end always passive, doomed to perpetual defeat. . . . The points, knots, or focuses of resistance are spread over time and space at varying densities. . . . Are there no great radical ruptures, massive binary divisions, then? Occasionally, yes. But more often one is dealing with mobile and transitory points of resistance, producing cleavages in a society that shift about, fracturing unities and effecting regroupings, furrowing across individuals themselves. . . . It is doubtless the strategic codification of these points of resistance that makes a revolution possible, somewhat similar to the way in which the state relies on the institutional integration of power relationships. (95–96)

This subtle, flexible, and dynamic model of power relations may accommodate local instances of a subversion that is produced for containment, but it also acknowledges revolutionary social transformations and any number of other possible modalities of power and resistance. If, on the one hand, ideological dominance can never be monolithic, total, and closed, then, on the other hand, revolutionary upheavals occur relatively rarely; modes and instances of resistance—subversions, contestations, transgressions, appropriations—tend to be local and dispersed in their occurrences, variable and limited in

13. Michel Foucault, *The History of Sexuality,* vol. 1, *An Introduction,* trans. Robert Hurley (New York: Random House, 1978), 93.

their consequences. Thus, one need look no further than Foucault's own work for a compelling demonstration that *subversion/containment* is hopelessly inadequate as an explanatory model for relations of power. The dynamism and specificity of power relations necessitate subtle discriminations among the modalities of resistance and among their various conditions of possibility.

The significance of such binary terms as *containment* and *subversion, dominance* and *contestation,* is in practice always relational and contextual; their configuration, content, and effect are produced in specific and changing conjunctures. Thus, for example, during the 1940s and 1950s, literary-historical scholarship was much concerned to demonstrate the ideological orthodoxy of such canonical authors as Shakespeare. In the anticanonical climate of today's academy, however, it has become fashionable for critics to re-legitimate their favorite canonical literary works by affirming them to be "subversive" of their own canonicity. Frequently, such claims are based upon analyses that are less historical and dialectical than formal and immanent, implying that "subversiveness" is an essence secreted in particular texts or classes of texts. However, as Jonathan Dollimore has pointed out in his Introduction to *Political Shakespeare,*

> Nothing can be intrinsically or essentially subversive in the sense that prior to the event subversiveness can be more than potential; in other words it cannot be guaranteed a priori, independent of articulation, context and reception. Likewise the mere thinking of a radical idea is not what makes it subversive: typically it is the context of its articulation: to whom, how many and in what circumstances; one might go further and suggest that not only does the idea have to be conveyed, it has also actually to be used to refuse authority *or* be seen by authority as capable and likely of being so used. It is, then, somewhat misleading to speak freely and only of "subversive thought"; what we are concerned with . . . is a social *process.* (13)

Crucial here is the concept of a "context of . . . articulation," which encompasses not only the specific social effectivity of a particular notion, formulation, or action but also the historical and social specificity of its subsequent representations—that is, the context of articulation (or, following Tony Bennett, what we might also call the *reading formation*) within which we retrospectively inscribe, identify, and interpret "subversion." Ideology can be said to exist only as it is instantiated in particular cultural forms and practices. All texts are ideologically marked, however multivalent or inconsistent that inscription may be. And if the ideological status of texts in the literary canon is necessarily overdetermined and unstable, it is so precisely as a condition and consequence of their canonicity. If, for example, I characterize *Hamlet* as a "complex" text, I am not reverting to an aesthetics of immanence, unity, and closure; rather, I am describing the transformation of a *text* into an open, changing, and contradictory *discourse* that is repeatedly and cumulatively produced and appropriated within history and within a history of other productions and appropriations. In so culturally sedimented a textual space—an always-occupied space that signifies to a historically and socially sited reader—so many cultural codes converge and interact that ideological coherence and stability are scarcely possible, except by a process of selection and exclusion of the sort that we perform every time we produce a particular "reading" of the text.

Within the context of the containment/subversion debate in English Renaissance literary studies, my own position has been that a closed and static, monolithic and homogeneous notion of ideology must be replaced by one that is heterogeneous and unstable, permeable and processual. Raymond Williams's admirable *Marxism and Literature* theorizes ideology in just such dynamic and dialogical terms.[14] By emphasizing "interrelations between movements and tendencies both within and beyond a specific and effective dominance" (121), Williams clarifies the existence, at any point in time, of residual and emergent, oppositional and alternative values, meanings, and practices. The shifting conjunctures of such "movements and tendencies" may create conceptual sites within the ideological field from which the dominant can be contested, and against which it must be continuously redefined and redefended—and so, perforce, continuously transformed. An ideological dominance is qualified by the specific conjunctures of ethnic, gender, class, professional, age, and other social positions occupied by individual cultural producers; by the heterogeneous positionality of the spectators, auditors, and readers who consume, appropriate, and resist cultural productions; and by the relative autonomy—the specific properties, possibilities, and limitations—of the cultural medium being worked. In other words, suffi-

14. Raymond Williams, *Marxism and Literature* (Oxford: Oxford University Press, 1977).

cient allowance must be made for the manifold mediations involved in the production, reproduction, and appropriation of an ideological dominance: for the collective, sectional, and individual agency of the state's subjects; and for the specific resources, conventions, and modes of production and distribution of the representational forms that they employ. By representing ideology as a dynamic, agonistic, and temporal process—a ceaseless contest among dominant and subordinate positions, a ceaseless interplay of continuity and change, of identity and difference—this concept of culture opens poetics to politics and to history.

Recent invocations of history (which, like power, is a term in constant danger of hypostatization) have sometimes appeared to be responses to—or, in certain cases, nothing more than positivistic retrenchments against—various structuralist and poststructuralist formalisms that have seemed, to some, to put into question the very possibility of historical understanding and historical experience; that have threatened to dissolve history into what Perry Anderson has suggested is an antinomy of objectivist determinism and subjectivist free-play, an antinomy that allows no possibility for historical agency on the part of individual or collective human subjects.[15] Subject, a simultaneously grammatical and political term, has come into widespread use not merely as a fashionable synonym for *the individual* but precisely in order to emphasize that individuals and the very concept of the individual are historically constituted in language and society. Although it continues to thrive in the mass media, in the rhetoric of politicians, and in the hearts and minds of the general population, the freely self-creating and world-creating Individual of so-called bourgeois humanism has, for quite some time, been defunct in the texts of academic theory. Against the beleaguered category of the historical agent, contending armies of theory have opposed the specters of structural determinism and poststructural contingency—the latter tartly characterized by Anderson as "subjectivism without a subject" (54). We now behold, on the one hand, the implacable code, and on the other, the slippery signifier—the contemporary equivalents of predestination and fortune.

Anderson remarks that the "one master-problem around which *all*

15. Perry Anderson, *In the Tracks of Historical Materialism* (Chicago: University of Chicago Press, 1984).

contenders have revolved" on the battlefield of contemporary social theory is "the nature of the relationships between structure and subject in human history and society" (33). Variations on this problematic might juxtapose structure to history or to practice, might oppose system or totality, on the one hand, to strategy or agency, on the other. And, indeed, during the past decade, one such version has characterized the interplay of historical-social-political orientations to English Renaissance literary studies in the form of containment/subversion. However, whether the focus of our analysis is upon late sixteenth-century England or late twentieth-century America, we should resist the inevitably reductive tendency to constitute our conceptual terms in the form of binary oppositions. Rather, we should construe them as conjoined in a mutually constitutive, recursive, and transformative *process.* I have in mind here such recent work in social theory as Anthony Giddens's concept of *structuration:*

> The structural properties of social systems are both the medium and the outcome of the practices that constitute those systems. . . .
> Rules and resources are drawn upon by actors in the production of interaction, but are thereby also reconstituted through such interaction;

Pierre Bourdieu's concept of *habitus:*

> Systems of durable, transposable *dispositions,* structured structures predisposed to function as structuring structures, that is, as principles of the generation and structuring of practices and representations;

and Marshall Sahlins's concept of the *structure of the conjuncture:*

> History is culturally ordered, differently so in different societies, according to meaningful schemes of things. The converse is also true: cultural schemes are historically ordered, since to a greater or lesser extent the meanings are revalued as they are practically enacted. . . .
> By the "structure of the conjuncture" I mean the practical realization of the cultural categories in a specific historical context, as expressed in the interested action of the historical agents.[16]

16. See, respectively: Anthony Giddens, *Central Problems in Social Theory: Action, Structure, and Contradiction in Social Analysis* (Berkeley: University of California Press, 1979), 69, 71; Pierre Bourdieu, *Outline of a Theory of Practice,* trans. Richard Nice (Cambridge: Cambridge University Press, 1977), 72; Marshall Sahlins, *Islands of History* (Chicago: University of Chicago Press, 1985), vii, xiv. Sahlins

With such perspectives in mind, we might entertain the following propositions: that the processes of subjectification and structuration are both interdependent and ineluctably historical; that the apparent systematicity of society is perpetually produced, adjusted, and transformed by means of the interactive social practices of individuals and groups; and that there is no necessary relationship between the intentions of actors and the outcomes of their actions—in other words, that their effectivity is conjunctural or situational and, to varying degrees, contingent.

The possibilities and patterns for action are always socially and historically situated, always limited and limiting. Nevertheless, collective structures may enable as well as constrain individual agency, and they may be potentially enabling precisely when they are experienced by the subject as multiple, heterogeneous, and even contradictory in their imperatives. Such a concept of agency is articulated clearly and concisely by Paul Smith:

> The symbolic realm, the *place* where we are in language and in social formations and which is also the *process* whereby we fit into them, *constructs* the ideological.
>
> ... Resistance does take place, but it takes place only within a social context which has already construed subject-positions for the human agent. The place of that resistance has, then, to be glimpsed somewhere in the interstices of the subject-positions which are offered in any social formation. More precisely, resistance must be regarded as the by-product of contradictions in and among subject-positions. ... Resistance is best understood as a specific twist in the dialectic between individuation and ideological interpellation.[17]

The possibility of social and political agency cannot be based upon the illusion that consciousness is a condition somehow beyond ideol-

---

concludes an earlier monograph with the following chiastic formulation: "The historical process unfolds as a continuous and reciprocal movement between the practice of the structure and the structure of the practice" (*Historical Metaphors and Mythical Realities: Structure in the Early History of the Sandwich Islands Kingdom* [Ann Arbor: University of Michigan Press, 1981], 72). Sahlins recognizes affinities between his own anthropological mediation of structure and history and the work of Bourdieu and Giddens (see *Islands of History*, 29, 51, 152).

17. Paul Smith, *Discerning the Subject* (Minneapolis: University of Minnesota Press, 1988), 25.

ogy. However, the very process of subjectively *living* the confrontations or contradictions *within* or *among* ideological formations may make it possible for us to experience facets of our own subjection at shifting internal distances—to read, as in a refracted light, one fragment of our ideological inscription by means of another. A reflexive knowledge so partial and unstable may, nevertheless, provide subjects with a means of empowerment as agents. Thus, my invocation of the term "Subject" is meant to suggest an equivocal process of *subjectification:* on the one hand, it shapes individuals as loci of consciousness and initiators of action, endowing them with *subjectivity* and with the capacity for agency; and, on the other hand, it positions, motivates, and constrains them within—it *subjects them to*—social networks and cultural codes, forces of necessity and contingency, that ultimately exceed their comprehension or control.

Practitioners of a poststructuralist historical and cultural criticism must be mindful that they, too, are subjects in the same equivocal sense. All academic texts selectively constitute the objects of their literary-historical knowledge, and do so upon frequently unexamined and inconsistent grounds. Integral to any genuinely new historicist project, however, must be a realization and acknowledgment that our analyses and our understandings necessarily proceed from our own historically, socially, and institutionally shaped vantage points. As scholars, we reconstruct the past, but the versions of the past so reconstructed are also the texts that we, as historically sited subjects, have actively fashioned. Thus, a historical criticism that seeks to recover meanings that are in any final or absolute sense authentic, correct, and complete is in pursuit of an illusion. The process by which we comprehend and represent Renaissance texts involves a dialectic between estrangement and appropriation.[18] Such an interpretive process historicizes the present as well as the past, and historicizes the dialectic between them—those reciprocal historical pressures by which the past has shaped the present and the present reshapes the past; it promotes a continuous dialogue between a *poetics* and a *politics* of culture.

18. See Michael McCanles, "The Authentic Discourse of the Renaissance," *Diacritics* 10:1 (Spring 1980), 77–87; Dominick LaCapra, *Rethinking Intellectual History* (Ithaca: Cornell University Press, 1983), 23–71.

PART ONE

DRAMA, THEATRE, SOCIETY, AND THE STATE: FORM AND PRESSURE

CHAPTER ONE

THE REFORMATION OF
PLAYING

The professional drama of Shakespeare's London had its roots in the late medieval civic religious drama; in the religiously and politically polemical drama of the turbulent mid-sixteenth century; and in the hodgepodge of popular entertainments—juggling and clowning, singing and miming, dancing and fencing, cockfighting and bear-baiting—from which it was still in the process of separating itself when Shakespeare began his theatrical career late in the century.[1] "Game" and "play," "gamehouse" and "playhouse" seem to have been used interchangeably well into the sixteenth century.[2] With the building of the Red Lion in 1567 and the more substantial Theatre in 1576, structures specifically intended for dramatic performances were now available to some of the itinerant players. But it was not until 1599 that a company of professional players could boast of having a permanent home of which they themselves were part owners. The company was the Lord Chamberlain's Men; the playhouse was the first Globe, built from the timbers of the dismantled Theatre; and one of the six player-entrepreneurs with a share in the enterprise

---

1. On the relationship of Shakespeare's theatre to the popular traditions of late medieval English culture, see the seminal work of Robert Weimann, *Shakespeare and the Popular Tradition in the Theater: Studies in the Social Dimension of Dramatic Form and Function*, ed. Robert Schwartz (Baltimore: Johns Hopkins University Press, 1978). For an account of the political content of the polemical drama of the early and mid-sixteenth century, and its transformation into the political drama of the late Elizabethan age, see David Bevington, *Tudor Drama and Politics: A Critical Approach to Topical Meaning* (Cambridge, Massachusetts: Harvard University Press, 1968).

2. See Glynne Wickham, *Early English Stages 1300–1660*, 3 vols. in 4 parts (London: Routledge & Kegan Paul, 1959–81), 2:2:141–45.

was William Shakespeare.[3] At the opening of the Globe and the turn
of the century, the drama of the public and professional stage was
reaching an unprecedented level of artistic achievement, social importance, and economic profitability. Nevertheless, from the perspective of long-term historical change, the professional stage-play was
still an emergent cultural form; the commercial playhouse, an emergent sociocultural space; and the profession of player, an emergent
social calling.

These material and ideological innovations could not be made to
conform comfortably to pre-existing places in the traditional scheme
of things. Elements of this shared culture continued to shape and
to delimit the assumptions, beliefs, expectations, and actions of the
inhabitants of late Elizabethan England. The dominant and most
highly articulated form of this worldview was the work of the Tudor
state. This official systematization of nature and society is conveniently summarized in the "Exhortacion concernyng Good Ordre and
Obedience to Rulers and Magistrates." The text of this sermon or
homily was prepared and printed by the state and was intended for
preaching in Elizabethan churches, where (at least, in principle) regular attendance was compulsory:

> Almightie God hath created and appointed all thinges in heaven,
> yearth and waters in a moste excellent and perfect ordre. . . . Every

3. Glynne Wickham is justifiably emphatic on this point: "The first Globe was
the first playhouse built in England exclusively by professional actors and for their
own exclusive use" (*Early English Stages*, 2:2:116). The Curtain and the playhouse
at Newington Butts were constructed at roughly the same time as the Theatre;
following at relatively long intervals were the Rose (1587) and the Swan (1596).
The financing of the Globe (1599) was split 50/50 between James Burbage's two
sons, Cuthbert and Richard, and five of the eight sharers in the Lord Chamberlain's Men, each of whom contributed 10% and became a "housekeeper" in the
new playhouse. One of these five was William Shakespeare. A sixth sharer in the
company was, of course, Richard Burbage himself.

The scholarly foundation for modern studies of the Elizabethan theatre is the
magisterial work of E. K. Chambers, *The Elizabethan Stage*, 4 vols. (Oxford:
Clarendon Press, 1923). For a judicious summary account of the current state of
knowledge and surmise regarding the playhouses (as well as the companies, players,
staging, and audiences), see Andrew Gurr, *The Shakespearean Stage 1574–1642*, 3rd
ed. (Cambridge: Cambridge University Press, 1992); and his important article on the
relationship of the Lord Chamberlain's/King's Men to their Globe and Blackfriars
theatres, "Money or Audiences: The Impact of Shakespeare's Globe," *Theatre Note-
book* 42 (1988), 3–14. For interesting documentary evidence and methodologically

degre of people, in their vocacion, callyng and office, hath appoynted to them their duetie and ordre. Some are in high degre,
some in lowe, some kynges and princes, some inferiors and subjectes, priestes and laimen, masters and servauntes, fathers and
chyldren, husbandes and wifes, riche and poore, and every one
hath nede of other. . . . Where there is no right ordre, there reigneth all abuse, carnall libertie, enormitie, syn and babilonicall confusion.[4]

During the course of the sixteenth century, English society experienced the dislocations of rapid change. And in the means by which it
established and sought to consolidate its authority, the arriviste Tudor
dynasty itself became a major agent or catalyst of such change. The
Tudor state sought to legitimate itself by means of its integration into
a providentially ordered cosmos. But it could not effectively contain
the ideologically anomalous realities of heterodoxy, nor arrest the social flux, that it had helped to set in motion.

The homily's doctrine of a divinely appointed, unchanging, hierarchical, and homological order was a concerted response to unprecedented changes affecting English society in the sixteenth century:
the ramifications of the Tudor dynasty's efforts to concentrate authority and power, both temporal and spiritual, in the person of the monarch; religious controversy and persecution and the sweeping impact
of Reformation policies upon economic, cultural, and spiritual life
at all levels; the combination of population growth, price inflation,
unemployment and underemployment and critical strains upon what
was even in good times little better than a subsistence economy;
transformations in agrarian modes of production and disruptions of
traditional rural communities and values; the expansion of a specu-
lative and entrepreneurial market economy and the development
of radically new financial institutions and investment instruments;
widespread geographic mobility and rapid social mobility; urban so-

---

alert speculation regarding the period and circumstances leading up to the establish-
ment of public playhouses ca. 1576, see William Ingram, *The Business of Playing: The
Beginnings of the Adult Professional Theater in Elizabethan London* (Ithaca and London:
Cornell University Press, 1992).

4. *Certain Sermons or Homilies (1547) and A Homily against Disobedience and Wilful
Rebellion (1570): A Critical Edition*, ed. Ronald B. Bond (Toronto: University of
Toronto Press, 1987), 161. A second edition of the 1547 text appeared in 1559,
almost immediately after the accession of Elizabeth, and this was reprinted frequently during the reign.

cial problems of unprecedented scope, accompanying the spectacularly rapid demographic and economic growth and diversification of London. Furthermore, the technological, socioeconomic, and ideological conjunction of printing, literacy, Protestantism, and entrepreneurial capitalism led to a proliferation in the publication and circulation of vernacular texts, including works of fiction and play texts. Not only writers but also printers, booksellers, editors, translators, redactors, commentators—and, of course, readers and audiences—shared in this increasingly dispersed and diversified process of formulating, glossing, disputing, and revising cultural meanings. The momentous consequence of this decentering of control over the signifying process was a decentering of the sources of cultural authority.

Recent studies in sixteenth-century English social history have emphasized that a major transformation in cultural life took place during the early decades of Elizabeth's reign and that this cultural revolution manifested a complex interaction among religious, socioeconomic, and political processes. In an influential study, Mervyn James has sought to comprehend the Corpus Christi play in its civic context; he construes it as a multidimensional social drama that literally and figuratively incorporated the identities and interests of the distinct and sometimes contentious guilds within an encompassing celebratory and sacramental communal form. James concludes that the destruction of these great collective representations of the social body was concomitant with the consolidation of the Protestant Tudor state. He writes that

> the abandonment of the observance of Corpus Christi, of the mythology associated with the feast, and of the cycle plays . . . arose from the Protestant critique of Corpus Christi, in due course implemented by the Protestant Church, with the support of the Protestant state. . . .
> The decline and impoverishment of gild organizations, the pauperization of town populations, the changing character and role of town societies, increasing government support of urban oligarchies, were all factors tending toward urban authoritarianism. As a result, urban ritual and urban drama no longer served a useful purpose; and were indeed increasingly seen as potentially disruptive to the kind of civil order which the magistracy existed to impose.[5]

5. "Ritual, drama and social body in the late medieval English town" (1983), rpt. in Mervyn James, *Society, Politics and Culture: Studies in Early Modern England* (Cambridge: Cambridge University Press, 1986), 16–47; quotation from 38, 44.

In another important study of the world the Elizabethans had lost, Charles Phythian-Adams emphasizes that,

> for urban communities in particular, the middle and later years of the sixteenth century represented a more abrupt break with the past than any period since the era of the Black Death or before the age of industrialization. Not only were specific customs and institutions brusquely changed or abolished, but a whole, vigorous and variegated popular culture, the matrix of everyday life, was eroded and began to perish. . . .
>
> If the opportunity for popular participation in public rituals was consequently largely removed, that especial meaning which sacred ceremonies and popular rites had periodically conferred on the citizens' tangible environment also fell victim to the new "secular" order.[6]

These admirable works of historical scholarship appear to proceed from a position that sees, in the advent of the early modern Protestant state, the fragmentation and loss of a pre-existing organic community, one that had been infused with the festive and sacramental culture of late medieval Catholicism. This prelapsarian perspective has been challenged recently in the work of Miri Rubin. Of Corpus Christi, she observes bluntly that "a processsion which excluded most working people, women, children, visitors and servants, was not a picture of the community. . . . By laying hierarchy bare it could incite the conflict of difference ever more powerfully sensed in a concentrated symbolic moment."[7] Taking her revisionist point, I wish to characterize the historical shift in question not as one from sacramental civic *communitas* to disciplinary state hierarchy so much as one from a culture focused upon social dynamics within the local community to one that incorporates the local within a national framework and subordinates it to the political and cultural center.

Throughout most of the sixteenth century, the Tudor regime had

---

James emphasizes the centrality of the Feast of Corpus Christi to late medieval urban culture in England, and the dialectical relationship between procession and play.

6. Charles Phythian-Adams, "Ceremony and the citizen: The communal year at Coventry 1450–1550," in *Crisis and Order in English Towns 1500–1700*, ed. Peter Clark and Paul Slack (London: Routledge & Kegan Paul, 1972), 57–85; quotations from 57, 80.

7. Miri Rubin, *Corpus Christi: The Eucharist in Late Medieval Culture* (Cambridge: Cambridge University Press, 1991), 266.

been engaged in a complex process of consolidating temporal and spiritual power in the hereditary ruler of a sovereign nation-state. Consistent with this project, the Elizabethan government was actively engaged in efforts to curtail traditional, amateur forms of popular entertainment and festivity and to suppress polemical and religious drama, including the civic Corpus Christi plays. These policy goals were pursued by the Elizabethan regime from its very inception. A proclamation prohibiting unlicensed interludes and plays, especially those touching upon matters of religion and policy, was issued on 16 May 1559. Those officials authorized to license plays were instructed to

> permit none to be played wherein either matters of religion or of the governance of the estate of the commonweal shall be handled or treated, being no meet matters to be written or treated upon but by men of authority, learning, and wisdom, nor to be handled before any audience but of grave and discreet persons.[8]

The Elizabethan government perceived much of the established popular and religious culture to be tainted by the superstitions and idolatrous practices of the old faith. Because the traditional objects of its loyalties were the local community, the regional nobility, or the Roman church, this culture was regarded by the Protestant Tudor state as a seedbed for dissent and sedition.

A letter dated 27 May 1576 from the Ecclesiastical Commissioners

---

8. See *Tudor Royal Proclamations*, ed. Paul L. Hughes and James F. Larkin, C. S. V., 3 vols. (New Haven: Yale University Press, 1969), 2:115–16; quotation from 115. See Paul Whitfield White, "Patronage, Protestantism, and Stage Propaganda in Early Elizabethan England," *Yearbook of English Studies* 21 (1991), 39–52, for an argument that "the Royal Proclamation of 1559 was not seriously enforced, and that indeed Protestant stage propaganda was practiced into the early 1570s, after which the growing secularism and commercialism of theatre in London brought polemical interludes into disrepute and decline" (40). White adds that, moreover, "such stage propaganda was encouraged, at times organized, by the central administration, and was sponsored and protected by all the traditional organizations responsible for producing drama" (ibid.). If this argument is correct, it demonstrates that from its very inception, the Elizabethan government did not consistently enforce its policy for regulation of the drama, and that this was so in part because it was unable or unwilling to formulate a consistent policy in the first place. As I shall suggest below, this remained the case throughout the reign.

of York to the bailiff and burgesses of Wakefield concisely encompassed most of the concerns at stake for the Elizabethan regime and the Reformed episcopacy. The letter decrees that in the

> plaie commonlie called Corpus Christi plaie ... no Pageant be used or set furthe wherin the Ma[jes]tye of God the Father, God the Sonne, or God the Holie Ghoste or the administration of either the Sacramentes of baptisme or of the Lordes Supper be counterfeyted or represented, or anythinge plaied which tende to the maintenaunce of superstition and idolatrie or which be contrarie to the lawes of god [and] or of the realme.[9]

Under direct pressure from the central government, its royally appointed bishops, and/or local Reformed clerics, performance of the civic religious dramas ceased after 1564 in Norwich, after 1569 in York, after 1575 in Chester, after 1576 in Wakefield, and after 1579 in Coventry. By 1580, the Corpus Christi play was no longer a vital cultural practice in Elizabethan England.[10]

Popular and liturgical practices, ceremonial and dramatic forms were not systematically suppressed by the royal government but were instead selectively appropriated: In court, town, and countryside, they were transformed by various temporal authorities into elaborate and effusive celebrations of the monarchy; they became part of the ideological apparatus of the state. Such ceremonies of power and authority are epitomized by the Queen's occasional progresses to aristocratic estates and regional urban centers; by her annual Accession Day festivities, celebrated at Westminster with pageants and jousts, and in towns throughout England with fanfares and bonfires; and by the annual procession and pageant for the Lord Mayor and Aldermen

9. Transcription printed in Harold C. Gardiner, S. J., *Mysteries' End: An Investigation of the Last Days of the Medieval Religious Stage,* Yale University Studies in English, 103 (New Haven: Yale University Press, 1946), 78. Gardiner notes that the manuscript strikes out "and" and substitutes "or," indicating "that the grievances mentioned in the body of the letter, all of which had reference to matters supposedly 'contrarie to the lawes of God', were not the exclusive grounds on which the plays were objected to; the 'lawes of the realme' extended still further and might well take care of matters not already covered by the 'lawes of God'."

10. See Gardiner, *Mysteries' End;* R. W. Ingram, "Fifteen seventy-nine and the Decline of Civic Religious Drama in Coventry," in *The Elizabethan Theatre VIII,* ed. G. R. Hibbard (Port Credit, Ontario: P. D. Meany, 1982), 114–28.

of London.[11] This strategy of appropriation was already perceptible the day before Elizabeth's coronation, in her ceremonial entry into and progress through the City of London. The stations of the progress occasioned a coherent program of allegorical pageants that confirmed the royal succession; affirmed principles of good government and reformed religion; encouraged the young, female, and virgin prince with citations of biblical precedent and demonstrations of her subjects' loyalty; and sought to impress upon her her financial dependence upon, and reciprocal responsibilities toward, the civic oligarchy that so magnificently welcomed her. The authorized record of the progress, in print within ten days of the event, asserts that one "could not better tearme the citie of London that time, than a stage wherin was shewed the wonderfull spectacle, of a noble hearted princesse toward her most loving people, and the people's exceding comfort in beholding so worthy a sovereign, and hearing so princelike a voice." As the apt theatrical metaphor suggests, this textualized event was remarkable in several respects: The interests of the city's liveried companies and the civic administration were central factors in the

11. On the process by which cultural practices were appropriated and invented in order to aggrandize the Tudor state, see Sydney Anglo, *Spectacle, Pageantry and Early Tudor Policy* (Oxford: Clarendon Press, 1969); Frances Yates, *Astraea: The Imperial Theme in the Sixteenth Century* (London: Routledge & Kegan Paul, 1975), 29–120; Roy Strong, *The Cult of Elizabeth* (London: Thames & Hudson, 1977); Penry Williams, *The Tudor Regime* (Oxford: Clarendon Press, 1979), 293–310, 351–405; Louis Montrose, "'Eliza, Queene of Shepheardes' and the Pastoral of Power," *English Literary Renaissance* 10 (1980), 153–82, rpt. in *The New Historicism Reader,* ed. H. Aram Veeser (New York: Routledge, 1994), 88–115; Philip Corrigan and Derek Sayer, *The Great Arch: English State Formation as Cultural Revolution* (Oxford: Basil Blackwell, 1985), 43–71; David Cressy, *Bonfires and Bells: National Memory and the Protestant Calender in Elizabethan and Stuart England* (Berkeley: University of California Press, 1989), 1–129. For an introduction to the pageantry of royal entries and progresses and Lord Mayoral shows, see David Bergeron, *English Civic Pageantry 1558–1642* (Columbia, South Carolina: University of South Carolina Press, 1971); for a recent account that usefully emphasizes records of eye-witness impressions of royal spectacle rather than official printed accounts, see R. Malcolm Smuts, "Public ceremony and royal charisma: the Engish royal entry in London, 1485–1642," in *The First Modern Society: Essays in English History in Honour of Lawrence Stone,* ed. A. L. Beier, David Cannadine, and James M. Rosenheim (Cambridge: Cambridge University Press, 1989), 65–93.

content and sponsorship of the pageantry, which suggests that this collective urban social drama maintained a connection to the civic tradition of Corpus Christi processions and plays.[12] In choosing to memorialize the antecedent civic progress rather than the actual coronation rite, the new regime marked its preference for secular ceremony over sacred ritual as a medium of royal legitimation; and in the scope and quality of the Queen's own speech, action, and bearing toward the pageants' presenters and the populace at large, she heralded the new importance that her reign would give to the performativity of sovereignty.[13]

12. Miri Rubin points out that "in those towns where political power and wealth were exercised through craft gilds, like York, Coventry, Beverley, Norwich, dramatic cycles were supported and presented by the crafts, expressing both the processional-communal and the sectional elements in town life" (*Corpus Christi*, 275). In some significant respects, the dramatic traditions of late medieval London differed from those of such towns. Mervyn James maintains that in London, even in the late middle ages, "the celebration of Corpus Christi never acquired a public and civic status, and play cycles of the Corpus Christi type never developed. London had its great cycle plays; but the London cycle was performed by professional actors, and had no connection either with Corpus Christi or the city gilds" (*Society, Politics and Culture*, 41–42). Rubin appears to dispute this assertion, and presents a more complex picture of processional and dramatic elements in the capital's Corpus Christi festivities. She starts from the position that "once we discard a view which imputes a necessary development of the Corpus Christi drama into full-cycle form we are better able to appreciate the variety of dramatic forms which evolved for Corpus Christi, and the ubiquity of dramatic creation" (*Corpus Christi*, 275). She maintains that, although "London never developed a town-wide celebration for the feast, a project which is almost unthinkable in so large and varied a city," it nevertheless sustained "a series of processions related to parish churches, fraternities, crafts." The most comprehensive of these was the "grete play" organized by the Skinners' Company, presented over several days "in the form of *tableaux vivants*" (275–76).

13. Two related studies by Richard C. McCoy focus on a shift, in Elizabeth's coronation, from the traditional emphasis on sacred ritual to one on secular ceremony: See, "'The Wonderfull Spectacle': The Civic Progress of Elizabeth I and the Troublesome Coronation," in *Coronations: Medieval and Early Modern Monarchic Ritual*, ed. Janos M. Bak (Berkeley: University of California Press, 1990), 217–27; and, "'Thou Idol Ceremony': Elizabeth I, *The Henriad*, and the Rites of the English Monarchy," in *Urban Life in the Renaissance*, ed. Susan Zimmerman and Ronald F. E. Weissman (Newark, Delaware: University of Delaware Press, 1989), 240–66. Susan Frye, *Elizabeth I: The Competition for Representation* (New York: Oxford University Press, 1993), 22–55, has recently analyzed in detail the central

The custom of celebrating the Queen's Accession Day began to flourish following the suppression of the Catholic-led Northern Rising and the great York Corpus Christi play in 1569 and the promulgation of the Papal Bull excommunicating Queen Elizabeth on Corpus Christi Day 1570. As Mervyn James put it, "under Protestantism, the Corpus Christi becomes the Body of the Realm" (*Society, Politics and Culture*, 41). At the same time, the Queen's Privy Council and the court nourished the professional theatre—if only to the limited extent that it could be construed as serving their own interests. Such a position is evidenced by instructions from the Privy Council to the City in 1572,

> in favor of certein persones to have in there howses, yardes, or back sydes, being overt & open places, such playes, enterludes, commedies & tragedies as maye tende to represse vyce & extoll vertwe, for the recreacion of the people, & therby to drawe them from sundrye worser exercyses.[14]

By the mid 1570s, several professional acting companies were performing regularly in the vicinity of London and occasionally at court; these companies enjoyed the patronage of the monarch and her leading courtiers, including several members of the Privy Council. Thus, the secure establishment and royal licensing of a fully professional, secular, and commercial theatre in later Elizabethan London was contemporaneous with the effective suppression of the religious drama and the relative decline of local amateur acting traditions in the rest of England.[15] This was not merely a coincidence nor a natural evolution; rather, it was a logical conjunction in the process of state formation. London was the financial, mercantile, legal, and administrative center of this state and by far the most densely populated and

---

importance to Elizabeth's coronation entry of the economic relationship between the Crown and the City. For *The Quene's Majestie's passage through the citie of London to westminster the daye before her coronacion* (1559), I have used the text in *Elizabethan Backgrounds*, ed. Arthur F. Kinney (Hamden, Connecticut: Archon Books, 1975), 7–39; quotation from 16.

14. Minute of City Court of Aldermen, 20 May 1572; rpt. in Chambers, *Elizabethan Stage*, 4:269.

15. Of course, what I characterize as the fully professional, secular, and commercial later Elizabethan theatre was not confined to London. On the contrary, travelling professional companies—which included all of those liveried companies that played regularly in London—also worked some of the regional towns of England throughout the period.

complexly organized social space in Elizabethan England. A stable and successful professional theatre was a cultural and commercial manifestation of London's unique size, wealth, sophistication, and diversity.[16] Whether as a means of entertaining the court or diverting the people, the professional theatre seems to have been perceived by the Crown as potentially if indirectly useful, both as an instrument for the aggrandizement of the dynastic nation-state and for the supervision and governance of its subjects.

16. On the extraordinary growth and importance of London in the later sixteenth and early seventeenth centuries, see the essays collected in F. J. Fisher, *London and the English Economy, 1500–1700*, ed. P. J. Cornfield and N. B. Harte (London: Hambledon Press, 1990); and *London, 1500–1700: The Making of the Metropolis*, ed. A. L. Beier and R. Finlay (London: Longman, 1986).

☽
•

CHAPTER TWO

A THEATRE OF CHANGES

The goal of religious reformers during the sixteenth century was, as Keith Thomas has put it, "to eliminate theatricality from church ritual and decoration, and to depreciate the role of the priesthood."[17] Thomas points out that, "by the eve of the Reformation," the rituals that had accumulated around the sacraments "had become crucial 'rites of passage', designed to ease an individual's transition from one social state to another, to emphasize his new status and to secure divine blessing for it" (36). To most of the faithful, the essence of their religion was not an abstruse theological system but rather a collection of immediate and familiar ritual practices that endowed their material existence with greater coherence and value. Religion was "a limitless source of supernatural aid, applicable to most of the problems likely to arise in daily life."[18] By about 1580, the Elizabethan regime had suppressed most of the ritual practices and popular religious festivities of late medieval Catholic culture. The spectacles of royal and civic power that were put in their place may have had some success in gratifying the cravings of the populace for visual and auditory splendor. But, unlike so many of the rituals, ceremonies, dramas, and other cultural practices suppressed by the architects of religious reform and political centralization, these ceremonies of state did not

17. Keith Thomas, *Religion and the Decline of Magic* (New York: Charles Scribner's Sons, 1971), 76.

18. Thomas, *Religion and the Decline of Magic*, 77; also see the extensive analysis in Eamon Duffy, *The Stripping of the Altars: Traditional Religion in England c. 1400–c. 1580* (New Haven and London: Yale University Press, 1992), "Part I: The Structures of Traditional Religion."

address the quotidian experiences, needs, and desires of the various subordinate social groups—merchants and traders, artisans and farmers, apprentices and servants, day laborers and women—who constituted the overwhelming majority of the English nation.

What symbolic forms were designed or appropriated in order to address the problems that daily life posed to the subjects of Elizabethan power? In *Religion and the Decline of Magic*, Thomas presents massive evidence that sixteenth- and seventeenth-century English men and women sought a substitute for the metaphysical aid of the medieval church in a welter of occult practices. We may speculate that a visit to the theatre might have provided another alternative for some of those who inhabited or visited London and could afford the relatively modest price of admission.[19] Indeed, in his *Survay of London* (1598), John Stow recalls the guild-sponsored religious pageants of late medieval London and construes the professional and public theatre of his own time as an explicit replacement for them. In a section on "Sports and Pastimes of old Time used in this City," he writes of such defunct pastimes, that:

> These, or the like exercises, have been continued till our time, namely, in stage plays, whereof ye may read in anno 1391, a play by the parish clerks of London at the Skinner's Well besides Smithfield, which continued three days together, the king, queen, and nobles of the realm being present. And of another, in the year 1409, which lasted eight days, and was of matter from the creation of the world, whereat was present most part of the nobility and gentry of England. Of late time, in place of those stage plays, hath been used comedies, tragedies, interludes, and histories, both true and feigned; for the acting whereof certain public places, as the Theatre, the Curtain, &c., have been erected.[20]

The drama performed in the professional playhouses provided its audiences with a distinctive source of affective and intellectual stimu-

19. For information on the cost of a visit to the theatre relative to the cost of living in late Elizabethan London, see Ann Jennalie Cook, *The Privileged Playgoers of Shakespeare's London, 1576–1642* (Princeton: Princeton University Press, 1981), 168–271, passim.; also see Andrew Gurr, *Playgoing in Shakespeare's London* (Cambridge: Cambridge University Press, 1987), 26–27.

20. John Stow, *A Survay of London*, ed. Henry Morley (London: Routledge, 1890), 119.

lus and satisfaction, an experience that was collective and commercial, public and profane.[21] That this experience was not only compelling but also transient insured that audience demand would remain high. Andrew Gurr has recently calculated that, "on a conservative estimate the playhouses in their seventy-five years probably entertained their customers with close to fifty million visits" (*Playgoing in Shakespeare's London*, 59). The public theatre of late Elizabethan London was the hallmark of an emergent professional and entrepreneurial entertainment industry, the rapid success of which was incidentally abetted by the aggrandizing religious and political policies of the Elizabethan state.

In *As You Like It*, the melancholy Jaques sententiously observes that

> All the world's a stage,
> And all the men and women merely players;
> They have their exits and their entrances,
> And one man in his time plays many parts,
> His acts being seven ages.
>
> (*AYL*, 2.7.139–43)[22]

---

21. Michael O'Connell, "The Idolatrous Eye: Iconoclasm, Anti-Theatricalism, and the Image of the Elizabethan Theater," *ELH* 52 (1985), 279–310, argues that Reformist Elizabethan antipathy toward the late medieval Biblical drama was a consequence of "a two-fold alteration in religious sensibility. There is first the vigorous rejection of the idea that God, Christ, or the sacred events of biblical history should be physically represented. And secondly . . . there is a new literalism in the attitude toward scripture" (186). He draws upon an earlier published form of my argument in order to advance the thesis that, "though . . . formally secular," the drama of Shakespeare's theatre has strong affinities with an "incarnational religious aesthetic" (305). O'Connell's perspective on the relationship between the Elizabethan theatre and "the recently banished medieval stage" stresses "continuities, a mending of the rents in the social and religious fabric"; in closing, he hypothesizes "the Elizabethan and Jacobean stage . . . as a competing—idolatrous—religious structure" (307). I want to disassociate my own secularist perspective on sociocultural change from O'Connell's recuperation of the Shakespearean theatre for an aesthetic of late medieval Catholic spirituality.

22. Shakespeare's plays are cited by act, scene, and line. Unless otherwise noted, I have used the text in *The Complete Works of Shakespeare*, ed. David Bevington, 4th ed. (New York: HarperCollins, 1992).

Shakespeare's plays reveal many traces of the older drama's intimate connection to the annual agrarian and ecclesiastical cycles.[23] But perhaps more conspicuous and pervasive than these are the connections between Shakespearean comic and tragic forms and the Elizabethan life cycle—the sequence of acts performed in several ages by Jaques's social players. Typically, Shakespeare generates dramatic action by combining conflicts grounded in such fundamental cultural categories as ethnicity, lineage, generation, gender, political faction, and social rank. Interpersonal conflicts—and also intrapersonal ones—give human and dramatic embodiment to ideological contradictions. Shakespeare frequently focuses dramatic action precisely *between* the social acts, between the sequential ages, in the fictive lives of his characters. Many of the plays turn upon points of transition in the life cycle—birth, puberty, marriage, death (and, by extension, inheritance and succession)—where discontinuities arise and where adjustments are necessary to basic interrelationships in the family, the household, and the society at large.

These dramatic actions have a partial affinity with rites of passage, which give a social shape, order, and sanction to human existence. Such transition rites impose culture-specific thresholds upon the life cycle; and, by the same symbolic process, they conduct social actors safely from one stage of life to the next. In other words, transition rites mediate the discontinuities which they themselves have articulated.[24] The theatrical analogy to transition rites is not limited to the

23. For a detailed study of the professional drama of Shakespeare and his contemporaries in relationship to the Elizabethan calendar of religious and folk festivals, see François Laroque, *Shakespeare's festive world: Elizabethan seasonal entertainment and the professional stage*, trans. Janet Lloyd (Cambridge: Cambridge University Press, 1991). Also see R. Chris Hassel, *Renaisance Drama and the English Church Year* (Lincoln: University of Nebraska Press, 1979).

24. See Pierre Bourdieu, *Outline of a Theory of Practice*, trans. Richard Nice (Cambridge: Cambridge University Press, 1977), 127–28:

> The temporal distribution of tasks and rites, that is, the chronological structure of the agrarian year or the cycle of life, is the product at once of the *diacritical intent* (separation) which orders by opposing, and the *synthetic intent* (union) which creates *passages* between the contraries by means of *rites* (of passage).

The paradigm for transition rites—the triadic movement from separation through marginality to reincorporation—was formulated in Arnold Van Gennep's classic, *The Rites of Passage* (1909), trans. M. B. Vizedom and G. L. Caffee (Chicago: Uni-

fictional space-time within the play. The actual process of theatrical performance, marked off in both time and space from the normal flow and loci of social activity, offered to its audience—and, of course, to its performers—an imaginative experience that partially and temporarily removed them from their normal places, their ascribed subject positions. In this sense, for the Queen's common subjects, to go to the public playhouse to see a play was to undergo a marginal experience; it was to visit the interstices of the Elizabethan social and cognitive order.[25]

To some official as well as to some self-appointed guardians of

---

versity of Chicago Press, 1960). More recent key theoretical discussions in the anthropological literature include Victor Turner, *Dramas, Fields, and Metaphors* (Ithaca: Cornell University Press, 1974), and Edmund Leach, *Culture and Communication* (Cambridge: Cambridge University Press, 1976). See Catherine Bell, *Ritual Theory, Ritual Practice* (New York and Oxford: Oxford University Press, 1992), for an important analysis and critique of ritual as a category of both experience and theoretical discourse.

Van Gennep's paradigm underlies the two most influential theories of Shakespearean comedy to have been elaborated during the past half century: the opposed and complementary models of C. L. Barber and Northrop Frye. See C. L. Barber, *Shakespeare's Festive Comedy: A Study of Dramatic Form in Relation to Social Custom* (Princeton: Princeton University Press, 1959), and Northrop Frye, *A Natural Perspective: The Development of Shakespearean Comedy and Romance* (New York: Harcourt, Brace, 1965). To summarize the differences between Barber and Frye: the former emphasizes the cathartic element in festive misrule and the reaffirmation of social norms; the latter emphasizes the millenarian element in comic romance and the affirmation of social change. In other words, the difference of perspective between Barber and Frye adumbrates the containment/subversion debate recently raging in Shakespeare studies.

An early version of my argument in the present section appeared in "The Purpose of Playing: Reflections on a Shakespearean Anthropology," *Helios*, n. s., 7 (1980), 51–74. Relevant studies of ritual patterns in Shakespearean drama published since that time include Marjorie Garber, *Coming of Age in Shakespeare* (London: Methuen, 1981); Lynda E. Boose, "The Father and the Bride in Shakespeare," *PMLA* 97 (1982), 325–47; Edward Berry, *Shakespeare's Comic Rites* (Cambridge: Cambridge University Press, 1984); *True Rites and Maimed Rites: Ritual and Anti-Ritual in Shakespeare and His Age*, ed. Linda Woodbridge and Edward Berry (Urbana and Chicago: University of Illinois Press, 1992); Linda Woodbridge, *The Scythe of Saturn: Shakespeare and Magical Thinking* (Urbana and Chicago: University of Illinois Press, 1994).

25. Regarding the physical and symbolic locus of the public amphitheatres in "the liberties"—on the social, jurisdictional, and ideological margins—of Elizabe-

the Elizabethan social and cognitive order, the imaginative license of theatrical experience was an abomination. The popular theatre was a uniquely threatening phenomenon because it was the physical and ideological site of convergence for a panoply of perceived innovations and perversions. Echoing the rhetoric of the "Exhortacion concernyng Good Ordre and Obedience to Rulers and Magistrates," Stephen Gosson declared the potential consequence of theatrical performances by professional players to be no less than the utter corruption of the social body and the destruction of the state:

> In Stage Playes for a boy to put on the attyre, the gesture, the passions of a woman; for a meane person to take upon him the title

---

than London, see Steven Mullaney, *The Place of the Stage: License, Play, and Power in Renaissance England* (Chicago: University of Chicago Press, 1988), 1–59. He writes that,

> in traditional . . . cultures, the margins of the social structure were embodied in literal areas like the Liberties of London. When the margins of society are thus realized on the threshold of the community, shaped into arenas of representation and given over to public ritual and spectacle, part of what is manifested in them will be the vulnerability of the social structure itself. (38)

Mullaney's provocative and important study sometimes gives the impression that the city and its liberties formed a closed and autonomous dyadic system. In describing a ritual dialectic between an orderly urban center and the exotic anomalies lying at its edges, Mullaney seems to me to draw the spatial and cognitive boundary lines of late Elizabethan London at once too boldly and too narrowly. This is a consequence of downplaying the fluidity and dynamism of the material and ideological processes that knit early modern London to its liberties, and knit both to the Court, the home counties, and the regions of England. Similarly, in stressing the ideological estrangement of the theatre that was located in the liberties—"its displacement provided it with something approaching an exterior vantage point upon the culture it was both a part of, yet set apart from" (54)—Mullaney appears to discount the degree to which this professional and commercial theatre and its participants were integrated into the socioeconomic, political, and cultural fabric of their time and place. It should also be noted that the liberties of London varied not only in their location but also in the status and interests of their inhabitants. Thus, it was the opposition of the wealthy, gentle, and influential residents and property owners in the liberty of Blackfriars that, in 1596, prevented James Burbage from turning his newly acquired property there into an indoor theatre. Because of opposition from such eminent denizens of the liberties, the opening of the Blackfriars theatre to adult professional players was delayed for a dozen years. (See the "Petition by Inhabitants of Blackfriars to Privy Council," printed in Chambers, *Elizabethan Stage*, 4:319–20.)

of a Prince with counterfeit porte, and traine, is by outwarde signes
to shewe them selves otherwise then they are, and so within the
compasse of a lye. . . .

We are commanded by God to abide in the same calling
wherein we were called, which is our ordinary vocation in a com-
monweale. . . . If privat men be suffered to forsake theire calling
because they desire to walke gentlemen like in sattine & velvet,
with a buckler at theire heeles, proportion is so broken, unitie dissolved, harmony confounded, that the whole body must be dis-
membred and the prince or the heade cannot chuse but sicken.[26]

Playing was without a place among traditional callings, and the professional players' assumptions of various roles—their protean shifts
of social rank, age, and gender—seemed to some to be a willful confusion and subversion of the divinely ordained categories of difference that had brought order out of chaos at the foundation of the
world.[27] The discrimination of statuses was of pervasive concern to
the Elizabethan sociopolitical elite; those who did not know and

26. Stephen Gosson, *Plays confuted in five actions* (1582), facsimile ed. (New
York: Johnson Reprint Corp., 1972), C5r, G6v–G7v.

27. Although one among several interconnected kinds of category violation,
cross-dressing seems to have generated an unusually strong negative affect among
some antitheatrical polemicists. The recent burgeoning of feminist and gay perspectives in literary and historical studies has led to intense scholarly interest in
cross-dressing in Elizabethan plays and on the Elizabethan stage, and in the
implications of such representations and practices for the analysis of Elizabethan
ideologies of gender and sexuality. Among the numerous recent studies of cross-
dressing in Elizabethan theatre and society, see: J. W. Binns, "Women or Transvestites on the Elizabethan Stage? an Oxford Controversy," *Sixteenth-Century Journal*
5 (1974), 95–120; Lisa Jardine, *Still Harping on Daughters: Women and Drama in the
Age of Shakespeare* (1983; 2nd ed., New York: Columbia University Press, 1989),
9–36; Laura Levine, "Men in Women's Clothing: Anti-theatricality and Effemini-
zation from 1579 to 1642," *Criticism* 28 (1986), 121–43, now expanded into a book
by the same title (Cambridge: Cambridge University Press, 1994); Kathleen
McLuskie, "The Act, the Role, and the Actor: Boy Actresses on the Elizabethan
Stage," *New Theatre Quarterly* 3 (1987), 120–30; "Fiction and Friction," in Stephen
Greenblatt, *Shakespearean Negotiations: The Circulation of Social Energy in Renaissance
England* (Berkeley: University of California Press, 1988), 66–93; Jean E. Howard,
"Crossdressing, the Theatre, and Gender Struggle in Early Modern England,"
Shakespeare Quarterly 39 (1988), 418–40, rev. as "Power and Eros: Crossdressing in
dramatic representation and theatrical practice," in Jean E. Howard, *The Stage and
Social Struggle in Early Modern England* (London and New York: Routledge, 1994),
93–128; Stephen Orgel, "Nobody's Perfect: Or, Why Did the English Stage Take
Boys for Women?" *South Atlantic Quarterly* 88 (1989), 7–29.

keep their places might be punished. As antitheatrical tracts like Gosson's make explicit, the professional players were a stunning anomaly: They were men who made their living by pretending to be what they were not; their calling was to imitate the callings of others. The dramatic companies lavished money upon costumes, the readiest signs of social distinction in a stratified and deferential society. They bought the hand-me-downs of aristocrats and courtiers, in which to play at being aristocrats and courtiers. And when they were in costume, and in performance, they were exempt from the sumptuary laws that were so carefully designed to enforce a congruity between the appearance and the reality of status.[28]

In the third part of Shakespeare's *Henry VI*, Richard, Duke of Gloucester—the future Richard III—boastfully soliloquizes that he can "add colors to the chameleon, / Change shapes with Proteus for advantages, / And set the murderous Machiavel to school" (3.2.191–93). As Jonas Barish has pointed out, in the drama of Shakespeare and his contemporaries, the figures of Proteus and the chameleon are negatively associated with the dissimulations of "the ambitious actor-politician."[29] The dramatic incorporation and censure of such a figure would seem to be a means by which the public and professional theatre sought to project, and thereby pre-emptively to contain, the dangerously subversive potential that its own mimetic powers appeared to pose to those cultural and political authorities who were in a position to harass it. At the same time, however, the uncontainable supplement of dramatic energy and pleasure generated by the acting of

28. On sumptuary laws in early modern England, see Wilfred Hooper, "The Tudor Sumptuary Laws," *English Historical Review* 30 (1915), 433–49; N. B. Harte, "State Control of Dress and Social Change in Pre-Industrial England," in *Trade, Government and Economy in Pre-Industrial England: Essays presented to F. J. Fisher*, ed. D. C. Coleman and A. H. John (London: Weidenfeld and Nicolson, 1976), 132–65; Frank Whigham, *Ambition and Privilege: The Social Tropes of Elizabethan Courtesy Theory* (Berkeley: University of California Press, 1984), 155–69.

29. Jonas Barish, *The Antitheatrical Prejudice* (Berkeley: University of California Press, 1981), 101. Barish's book is a magisterial intellectual history of antitheatricality in the West. On 96–117, he discusses the association of the actors' mimickry with the figures of Proteus and the chameleon. He documents the ambivalent Renaissance symbology of Proteus and the chameleon: the dominant tradition associated them with guile, deceit, and inconstancy, while a more occult counter-tradition celebrated them as emblems of the human capacity for self-transformation and growth.

such a character as Richard III rendered that very theatrical power all the more palpable. By the third decade of the seventeenth century, it had become possible to invoke the god of metamorphoses in order to praise in print the most renowned professional players contemporaneous with Shakespeare. Edward Alleyn, who created the roles of Tamburlaine and Faustus, Marlowe's dangerously aspiring heroes, was admiringly remembered by Thomas Heywood as "Proteus for shapes."[30] Richard Burbage, the leading player of The Lord Chamberlain's Men—who first created the role of Richard III, as well as those of Hamlet, Othello, and Lear—was remembered by Richard Flecknoe as "a delightful Proteus, so wholly transforming himself into his Part and putting off himself with the Cloathes, as he never (not so much as in the Tyring-house) assum'd himself again until the Play was done."[31] This theatrical shape-shifting was, at least in theory, carefully licensed and circumscribed. Under such simultaneously constraining and privileged circumstances, the affective power of the players' protean art upon both Elizabethan audiences and upon the players themselves must have been quite extraordinary.

It is a gauge of the social value, and the market value, accruing to their protean skills that at least some of these player-entrepreneurs— notably, Alleyn, Burbage, and Shakespeare—managed within a remarkably short time to metamorphose themselves into relatively wealthy and respected citizens.[32] A Jacobean Character of "A Common Player" mocks the players' desire for upward social mobility:

> His chiefe essence is, *A daily Counterfeit:* He hath beene familiar so long with out-sides, that he professes himselfe (being unknowne) to be an apparant Gentleman. . . . Take him at the best, he is but

30. Thomas Heywood, prologue to Perkin's revival of *The Jew of Malta* (1633), cited in M. C. Bradbrook, *The Rise of the Common Player: A Study of Actor and Society in Shakespeare's England* (Cambridge, Massachusetts: Harvard University Press, 1962), 127.

31. Richard Flecknoe, *A Short Discourse of the English Stage* (1664), extract rpt. in Chambers, *Elizabethan Stage*, 4:368.

32. On the profession of player in Elizabethan England, and the socioeconomic fortunes of particular individuals, see Bradbrook, *The Rise of the Common Player;* Gurr, *The Shakespearean Stage 1574–1642*, 80–114; Gerald Eades Bentley, *The Profession of Player in Shakespeare's Time 1590–1642* (Princeton: Princeton University Press, 1984). It is important to note that the substantial estates built up by Alleyn, Burbage, and Shakespeare were not due to the profitability of acting *per se* but rather to entrepreneurial activities both within and beyond the stage business.

a shifting companion; for hee lives effectually by putting on, and putting off.[33]

In an apparent riposte, the Character "Of an Excellent Actor" (1615) observes, not with outrage but rather with admiration, that

> all men have beene of his occupation: and indeed, what hee doth fainedly that doe others essentially: this day one plaies a Monarch, the next a private person. Heere one Acts a Tyrant, on the morrow an Exile: A Parasite this man to night, to morow a Precisian, and so of divers others.[34]

In this sense, when they were laboring in their vocation, these particular members of the commonwealth were temporarily living a metasocial relationship to their fellow subjects and to their own society. In some significant respects, then, the protean player of the Elizabethan public theatre was the very personification of the changeful social realities denounced or suppressed in the homilies' scheme of things. He exemplified a human capacity "to change shapes . . . for advantages"; he was—by profession—out of place.

Within the discursive order of Elizabethan culture, drama was not classified as *rite* but rather as *play;* it was a socially marginal activity, an entertainment offered for sale to anyone who could pay the relatively modest price of admission. I am suggesting, however, that in a society in which the dominant social institutions and cultural practices were predicated upon an ideology of unchanging order and absolute obedience, an emergent commercial entertainment that was still imbued with the heritage of suppressed popular and religious traditions could address vital collective needs and interests that those dominant institutions and practices had sought to appropriate or to suppress, or had merely ignored. It is characteristic of Shakespeare's plays to subject their protagonists to vividly represented experiences of cognitive and ideological dissonance, to both comic and tragic disruptions and confusions of expectations and norms. These individually and collectively experienced anomalies, discontinuities, and contradictions vary considerably in tone and in their dramatic consequences, being shaped according to the distinct canons of comic and tragic form and mood. The fictions enacted in the Elizabethan theatres could make

33. J. Cocke, "A common Player" (1615), rpt. in Chambers, *Elizabethan Stage*, 4:255, 257.

34. Attributed to John Webster; rpt. in Chambers, *Elizabethan Stage*, 4:258.

no supernatural or ritually efficacious claim to effect safe passages in the changeful lives of their audiences. However, this theatre did articulate symbolic frameworks for the affirmation of both human resourcefulness and human endurance. By so doing, it may have helped some in its heterogeneous audience of social players not only to adjust to but also to manipulate to their own advantage the ambiguities and conflicts, the hardships and opportunities arising from the contradictory realities of change.

Elizabethan sources describe the drama in various and contrary ways: as an incitement to virtue or to vice; as an innocuous if pleasing diversion; as a lucrative and wicked business. We might add that, in particular instances and under particular circumstances, the effect of the Elizabethan drama-in-performance may have been to neutralize social discontent and to assuage personal anxieties or to provoke reflection upon the origins and ends of social institutions and personal existence. It would be all too easy to reduce these alternative effects of assuagement and provocation to merely another version of the containment/subversion opposition. The Elizabethan theatre's unstable articulation of sociopolitical domination and/or resistance is the focus of my concern in Part One of this book. In the heat of our current critical debates about the politics of the Elizabethan theatre, we should not, however, forget that, for its Elizabethan producers and consumers, this drama-in-performance was a cultural practice and a collective process with motivations and consequences that went far beyond an explicitly and narrowly political function. Perhaps we need to remind ourselves that the Elizabethan drama-in-performance also had the capacity to work as a cognitive and therapeutic instrument—that is, to function *ideologically*, in the most general and most enabling senses of that term. In other words, the symbolic actions performed in the theatre had the immediate, if frequently transitory, capacity to stimulate the intellect and to promote the emotional well-being of their actual and vicarious participants. Plays-in-performance might proffer aids to understanding and to endurance in the theatre of the world; they could be used (in Kenneth Burke's phrase) as equipment for living. They were commercial entertainments, pleasurably purveying information, counsel, and fantasy. This combination made them highly desirable cultural commodities; it was the innovative formula for the Elizabethan theatre's spectacular, if precarious, success.

CHAPTER THREE

ANATOMIES OF PLAYING

Throughout the course of Shakespeare's career in the theatre, the purpose of playing was much in dispute. In his *Treatise on Playe*, Sir John Harington defines the fundamental category of human activity called "playe" as "a spending of the tyme eyther in speeche or action, whose onely end ys a delyght of the mynd or the speryt."[35] Like such influential modern authors of treatises on play as Johan Huizinga and Roger Caillois, Harington stresses its nature as diversion or recreation, as a gratuitous and unproductive pastime, defined in antithesis to the practical realities of *negotium* that constitute everyday life.[36] However, Harington does not share the post-Kantian aesthetic perspective of his modern counterparts; he grounds his defense of gratuitous play in the values and prerogatives of the Renaissance courtier and gentleman. Nor will he celebrate all practices or practioners of play. "Stage-playes," along with "enterludes, tumblers, jesting fools, and scoffers, masking and dawncing," are included in the second of Harington's three "kyndes" of play—namely, that consisting "of unseemly pleasures, provoking to wantonesse" (157). His condemnation appears to be directed at popular and public entertainments that appeal to the debased wits and wayward wills of the vulgar many.

35. "A Treatise on Playe," which appears to have been written late in the reign of Queen Elizabeth, was first printed in John Harington, *Nugae Antiquae*, ed. Henry Harington, 3 vols. (1779; rpt. Hildesheim: Georg Olms, 1968), 2:154–208; quotation from 173. Subsequent page references are to volume two of this edition.
36. See Johan Huizinga, *Homo ludens*, trans. (Boston: Beacon Press, 1955); Roger Caillois, *Man, Play, and Games*, trans. Meyer Barash (New York: Free Press, 1961); and, for an important critique of the ideological presuppositions of Huizinga and Caillois, Jacques Ehrmann, "Homo ludens revisited," in *Game, Play, Literature*, ed. Ehrmann (*Yale French Studies* 41 [1968]), 31–57.

However, after having roundly condemned the drama in such conventionally antitheatrical terms, he adds that, in his own opinion, "in stage-playes may bee much good, in well penned comedies, and specially tragedies" (160). Those plays sufficiently learned and elevated to be able to "delyght . . . the mynd or the speryt" of courtly ladies and gentlemen are to be allowed. Harington's equivocation between the disapprobation and the defense of playing seems to be status-specific, whether the distinction be between base and gentle kinds of play or between the responses of vulgar and elite audiences to the same kinds of play. Harington's ambivalence is characteristic of courtly attitudes toward the drama.

Harington's conception of the purpose of playing may be usefully compared to the contemporaneous opinion of Shakespeare's Hamlet. As "the glass of fashion and the mold of form" (3.1.156), the paragon who fuses courtly grace and wit with university learning and introspection, Hamlet is Shakespeare's personification of the elite audience for his own plays. The learnedly antic prince invented by the public player-playwright is a connoisseur of plays, playing, and playgoers. For a taste of the first player's quality, he requests a speech that was "never acted, or if it was, not above once, for the play . . . pleased not the million; 'twas caviar to the general. But it was—as I received it, and others, whose judgments in such matters cried in the top of mine—an excellent play, well digested in the scenes, set down with as much modesty as cunning" (*Hamlet*, 2.2.435–40). Hamlet's description of this play implies that he knows it only as a text for readers—which is also the condition of our knowledge of *Hamlet*. Subsequently, he sees fit to instruct the players in their mystery: "Suit the action to the word, the word to the action, with this special observance, that you o'erstep not the modesty of nature. . . . Now, this overdone or come tardy off, though it makes the unskillful laugh, cannot but make the judicious grieve, the censure of the which one must in your allowance o'erweigh a whole theater of others" (3.2.17–19, 24–28); "And let those that play your clowns speak no more than is set down for them; for there be of them that will themselves laugh, to set on some quantity of barren spectators to laugh too, though in the meantime some necessary question of the play be then to be considered" (38–43). It is the elite perspective of the learned and courtly *reader* and *auditor*—rather than that of the popular *spectator*—that consistently characterizes Hamlet's tastes and his prejudices.

The Prince avers that "The purpose of playing . . . is, to hold as't were the mirror up to nature, to show virtue her feature, scorn her own image, and the very age and body of the time his form and pressure" (3.2.20–24). Because the stage play is both the product of a particular time and place and a circumscribed and reflexive space of representation, it may simultaneously exemplify and hold up to scrutiny the historically specific "nature" that it mirrors; it bears the pressure of the time's body but it may also clarify the form of the age. Hamlet implies that play can be serious and that jest can be earnest; that the seeming gratuitousness of play can mask its instrumentality. Through the persona of the Prince, the Elizabethan playwright voices the notion that theatrical fictions are forms of ethically and politically purposeful play. Plays that are well written and well performed imprint exemplary images of virtuous and vicious behavior upon the minds of their audiences, disposing them to emulate virtue and to repudiate vice. Thus, Hamlet defends the theatre upon the same high moral ground from which its enemies sought to destroy it.

However, Shakespeare's presentation of Hamlet's argument for drama's profound moral force is hardly unambiguous. By his reiterated disparagement of the vulgar majority of playgoers, the learned and courtly Hamlet implies that the theatre can work its ethical effect only upon those auditors with a prior disposition to attend to its "necessary question[s]" (3.2.42); those of "the groundlings, who . . . are capable of nothing but inexplicable dumb shows and noise" (10–12), those "barren spectators" to whom the extemporising clowns make their frivolous appeal, would appear to be impervious to the purpose of playing. Hamlet's vantage point on the theatre is not only limited but is surely intended to be so; it is not coterminous with that of the common player-playwright who has authored him, but is rather Shakespeare's characterization and dramatic internalization of the perspective of the elite segment within his own audience. Furthermore, the royal hero's own subsequent behavior and the actual outcome of the dramatist's play are far more equivocal—both ethically and politically—than the high theatrical principles espoused by Hamlet himself might lead us to expect. *Hamlet* incorporates Hamlet's desire for the drama to be ethically unequivocal in its purpose and force, and his wish that its actual performance proceed exactly as scripted, but *Hamlet* also continually and ironically undermines

Hamlet's wishes and expectations. The playwright's perspective on the purpose of playing is more capacious, popular, and equivocal than that of the Prince. Playing at the Globe, Shakespeare and the Lord Chamberlain's Men seem to have sought out a *via media* between the plebian theatre of Henslowe and the elitism characteristic of the boys' companies and the private theatres. As Anthony Scoloker put it in his *Epistle* to *Daiphantus, or the Passions of Love* (1604), "Faith it should please all, like Prince *Hamlet*." [37]

Like some Elizabethan apologists for poetry, and like Shakespeare's Hamlet, those few who defend the theatre in print do so by reversing the judgments of the theatre's detractors; nevertheless, their arguments remain constrained within the terms of the dominant antitheatrical discourse. In what is probably the most extended and informative of such defenses, *An Apology for Actors* (1612), Thomas Heywood argues that "playing is an ornament to the Citty"; that, thanks to playing and play-writing, "our *English* tongue ... is now ... continually refined"; and that "playes have made the ignorant more apprehensive, taught the unlearned the knowledge of many famous histories." Turning the oft-reiterated complaints of the civic magistrates inside out, Heywood proclaims that London's public and professional theatre is to be construed as a source of civic and national consciousness and pride, and as a most effective instrument for the inculcation of virtuous knowledge and the fashioning of obedient subjects. Enlarging upon the "true use" of plays based upon English chronicle histories—of which Shakespeare's form the largest and most celebrated corpus—Heywood maintains that these

> are writ with this ayme, and carryed with this methode, to teach the subjects obedience to their King, to shew the people the untimely ends of such as have moved tumults, commotions, and insurrections, to present them with the flourishing estate of such as live in obedience, exhorting them to allegeance, dehorting them from all trayterous and fellonious strategems. [38]

37. Excerpt printed in E. K. Chambers, *William Shakespeare: A Study of Facts and Problems*, 2 vols. (Oxford: Clarendon Press, 1930), 2:214–15. On the unusually broad appeal of the Globe repertoire, see Gurr, *The Shakespearean Stage*, 230, and *Playgoing in Shakespeare's London*, 151, where Scoloker is also cited.

38. Thomas Heywood, *An Apology for Actors* (1612) rpt. with I. G., *A Refutation of the Apology for Actors* (1615), facsimile ed. (New York: Garland, 1973), F3r-v.

Thus, according to Heywood, the intended effect of Elizabethan history plays was to exemplify in vivid word and action the moral lessons inscribed in the state homily "concernyng Good Ordre and Obedience to Rulers and Magistrates." Heywood embraces the terms dictated by the antitheatrical discourse and turns them to his own uses; he defends his profession by claiming that those "that are chaste, are by us extolled, and encouraged in their vertues. . . . The unchaste are by us shewed their errors" (*Apology,* G1v). Heywood's representation of the affective power of theatrical performance remains didactic and rigorously behavioristic. Although his defense is unequivocal, the terms in which it is framed do not fully comprehend the cultural practice that he is seeking to defend.

In order to find an Elizabethan perspective that gives full weight to the affective power of theatrical performance, to its pleasures and its dangers, and that does so in a rhetorically compelling fashion, we must—ironically—look to those divines, magistrates, and putatively regenerate former players who attacked the theatre as an immoral force. The extensive antitheatrical discourse of Elizabethan and Jacobean pamphlets, sermons, and official documents provides a negative testimonial to the popularity and effectiveness of professional playing in the public playhouses. To take this discourse seriously is to respect the intelligence and sincerity of contemporary opponents, and also to appreciate that the Elizabethan theatre may have exercised a considerable but unauthorized and therefore deeply suspect affective power upon those Elizabethan subjects who experienced it. For example, consider the rhetoric of a letter from Edmund Grindal, then bishop of London, to Sir William Cecil. Writing early in the Elizabethan reign, and a dozen years before the opening of the Theatre, Grindal offers advice about measures to be taken against a recent outbreak of plague:

> Ther is no one thinge off late is more lyke to have renewed this contagion, then the practise off an idel sorte off people, which have ben infamouse in all goode common weales: I meane these Histriones, common playours; who now daylye, butt speciallye on holydayes, sett up bylles, wherunto the youthe resorteth excessively, & ther taketh infection: besides that goddes worde by theyr impure mowthes is prophaned, and turned into scoffes; for remedie wheroff in my judgement ye shulde do verie well to be a meane, that a proclamation wer sette furthe to inhibitte all playes for one whole yeare (and iff itt wer for ever, it wer nott amisse) within the

Cittie, or 3. myles compasse, upon paynes aswell to the playours, as to the owners off the howses, wher they playe theyr lewde enterludes.[39]

One especially striking feature of the bishop's observation is the ambiguity in its epidemiology, the rhetorical force projected by its metaphorical identification of moral and medical discourses. The language of the letter suggests that the act of playgoing is itself the material source of the "contagion," that the youthful auditors quite literally take their "infection" from the "impure mouths" of the players. For Grindal, playing and plague are synonymous.

Hostility to plays, players, and playhouses varied enormously in source, motive, and intensity. There were some who did not oppose occasional dramatic performances by amateurs, and/or private dramatic performances by professionals that were intended exclusively for elite audiences in the royal court, noble households, inns of court, colleges, or guildhalls.[40] The Elizabethan antitheatrical prejudice was aimed most specifically and consistently at professional acting companies performing in public amphitheatres that charged for admission and whose audiences were largely although not exclusively

39. Letter of 23 February 1564; excerpt printed in Chambers, *Elizabethan Stage*, 4:266–67.

40. For example, the Act of Common Council of London of 6 December 1574, an unusually comprehensive attempt by the municipal authorities to regulate the texts and performances of plays, targeted those who owned venues suited to the performance of commercial entertainments:

No Inkeper Tavernkeper nor other person whatsoever within the liberties of thys Cittie shall openlye shewe or playe, nor cawse or suffer to be openlye shewed or played, within the hous, yarde or anie other place within the Liberties of this Cyttie anie playe, enterlude, Commodye, Tragidie, matter, or shewe, which shall not be firste perused and Allowed . . . by suche persons as by the Lorde Maior and Courte of Aldermen . . . shalbe appoynted.

Explicitly excluded from the terms of this act were

anie plaies, Enterludes, Comodies, Tragidies, or shewes to be played or shewed in the pryvate hous, dwellinge, or lodginge of anie nobleman, Citizen, or gentleman, which shall or will then have the same thear so played or shewed in his presence for the festyvitie of anie marriage, Assemblye of ffrendes, or otherlyke cawse withowte publique or Commen Collection of money of the Auditorie or beholders theareof. (Rpt. in Chambers, *Elizabethan Stage*, 4:273–76; quotations from 274, 276)

The Act made clear, however, that even plays performed for such private occasions were still to be held accountable for "the publishinge of unchaste, sedycious, and unmete matters."

composed of apprentices and servants, artisans and modest trades-people.[41] However, even if the players were not adult professionals performing in a public playhouse, the social implications of *commercial* entertainment might alone be sufficiently alarming to provoke extreme measures.

A telling example comes from a resolution in the Accounts of the Master of the Merchant Taylors Company for 16 March 1574:

> Whereas at our comon playes and suche lyke exercises whiche be comonly exposed to be seene for money, everye lewd persone thinketh himself (for his penny) worthye of the chiefe and most comodious place without respecte of any other either for age or estimacion in the comon weale, whiche bringeth the youthe to such an impudente famyliaritie with theire betters that often tymes greite contempte of maisters, parents, and magistrates foloweth thereof, as experience of late in this our comon hall hath sufficyently declared, where by reason of the tumultuous disordered persones repayringe hither to see suche playes as by our schollers were here lately played, the Maisters of this Worshipful Companie and their deare ffrends could not have entertaynmente and convenyente place as they ought to have had, by no provision beinge made, nothwithstandinge the spoyle of this howse, the charges of this Mystery, and theire juste authoritie which did reasonably require the contrary. Therefore . . . yt is ordeyned . . . that henceforthe theire shall be no more plays suffered to be played in

---

41. The classic work on the audiences of the Elizabethan theatres is Alfred Harbage, *Shakespeare's Audience* (New York: Columbia University Press, 1941). Harbage stresses the social heterogeneity and predominant commonality of the audiences in the public theatres. His conclusions are sharply challenged in Ann Jennalie Cook, *The Privileged Playgoers of Shakespeare's London, 1576–1642* (Princeton: Princeton University Press, 1981), who argues that even the public theatres of the period were predominantly the playground of the privileged few. In reaction against Harbage's fundamentally democratic Shakespeare, Cook produces an emphatically elitist Shakespeare that flies in the face of much statistical and anecdotal evidence. For critiques of Cook, and judicious reconsiderations of the whole question of the social composition of theatre audiences, see Martin Butler, *Theatre and Crisis 1632–1642* (Cambridge: Cambridge University Press, 1984), appendix 2, "Shakespeare's unprivileged playgoers," 293–306; and Gurr, *Playgoing in Shakespeare's London*, esp. 3–5, 49–79. Gurr's picture is more complex than those of Harbage and Cook, and takes into account variations among particular theatres and shifts over several decades. He suggests "that despite the infrequent reference to their presence citizens were the staple, at least of amphitheatre audiences, throughout the period. . . . Citizens . . . and their lesser neighbours the prosperous artisan class [were] a kind of silent majority in the playhouses" (64).

this our Comon Hall, any use or custome heretofore to the contrary
in anywise notwithstandinge. (Quoted in Chambers, *Elizabethan
Stage*, 2:75)

Here the occasion is a dramatic performance by the boys of the London Merchant Taylors School, founded in 1561 by Richard Mulcaster;
and the venue is the Common Hall of the company itself. According
to this account, the masters of the company were prepared to take
the drastic step of forbidding the continuation of their own custom,
not because of anything explicitly objectionable in the content of the
boys' play or in the nature of their performance, but because of the
composition and conduct of the audience that had been drawn to
the event. Making payment of a penny the only criterion of admission had had the unintended consequence of levelling the hierarchical distinctions of honor and authority, the protocols of precedence
and deference, upon which "this Worshipful Companie" and the social order at large were structured. If "everye lewd persone thinketh
himself (for his penny) worthye of the chiefe and most comodious
place without respecte of any other either for age or estimacion in
the comon weale," then by the same token such persons might think
their own judgments and opinions to be equally worthy of authority
in the commonweal. Exchange value had subverted the principles of
degree, priority, and place, leading inexorably from impudent famil-
iarity to contempt, and from contempt to tumultuous disorder. The
Masters of the Worshipful Company of the Merchant Taylors were
appalled at the dire implications of the commodification of culture.
At that very moment, however, other members of London's middling
ranks were on the verge of institutionalizing such a culture industry
in the public and professional amphitheatres sited in the liberties
of London.

The public playhouses were attacked as the breeding ground of
plague and vice, traffic congestion and mob violence, inefficient
workers and dangerous ideas. In 1597, the Lord Mayor and aldermen
of London petitioned the Privy Council to suppress stage plays,
which they accused of causing numerous "inconveniences"; their petition is a compendium of the complaints that had been lodged
against the performance of plays in the public theatres during the
previous two decades. For example, they assert, with palpable alarm,
that the plays performed in the commercial theatres

are a speciall cause of corrupting . . . Youth, conteninge nothinge
but unchaste matters . . . being so as that they impresse the very
qualities & corruptions of manners which they represent. . . .
Whearby such as frequent them, beinge of the base & refuze sort
of people or such young gentlemen as have small regard of credit
or conscience, drawe the same into imitacion and not to the
avoidinge the like vices which they represent.[42]

These authoritative opponents represent plays, players, and playhouses as powerful agencies within Elizabethan society, and construe
their power to be both utterly corrupt and utterly corrupting. The
actors are believed to impress vicious images upon the minds of the
most susceptible and dangerous groups in the general population,
the lowly and the youthful. These impressions are here conceived of
as material and absolute, and also as wholly malign: Unlike Thomas
Heywood, the city fathers claim that theatrical images of vice always
compel imitation, never aversion.[43] Those who attacked the theatre
and those who defended it were agreed upon its compelling affective
powers. Theatrical performance was thought to have the capacity to
effect moral changes in its audience—whether for better or for worse.
Plays might inspire, instruct, reform, delight, terrify, sadden, entrap,

42. The Lord Mayor and Aldermen to the Privy Council, 28 July 1597; rpt. in
Chambers, *Elizabethan Stage*, 4:322. Many of the complaints contained herein—
and even some of the phrasing—are reproduced from a letter from the Lord
Mayor to Lord Burghley, dated 3 November 1594, requesting support for the suppression of a planned new playhouse as well as "all other places, if possibly it may
bee, whear the sayed playes ar shewed & frequented" (Chambers, *Elizabethan
Stage*, 4:316–17).

43. The 1597 petition of the Lord Mayor and Aldermen to the Privy Council
reiterates not only the petition of 3 November 1594 but also that of 13 September
1595 (Chambers, *Elizabethan Stage*, 4: 317–18). The latter appeal against "the common exercise of Stage Plaies" charges that they contain

   nothing but profane fables, Lascivious matters, cozonning devizes, & other
   unseemly & scurrilous behaviours, which ar so sett forthe, as that they
   move wholy to imitacion & not to the avoyding of those vyces which they
   represent, which wee verely think to bee the cheef cause aswell of many
   other disorders & lewd demeanors which appeer of late in young people
   of all degrees. (318)

The wording of this indictment seems to suggest that it is not merely the scurrilous content of the plays but the compelling manner of their performance ("which
are so sett forthe") that endows them with the almost satanic power to "move
wholy to imitacion."

corrupt, infect, or incite—in any case, they might do far more than pass the time.

The 1597 petition continues by indicting the public playhouses as

the ordinary places for vagrant persons, Maisterles men, thieves ... contrivers of treason, and other idele and daungerous persons to meet together. . . .

They maintaine idlenes in such persons as have no vocation & draw apprentices and other servauntes from theire ordinary workes and all sortes of people from the resort unto sermons and other Christian exercises, to the great hinderance of traides & prophanation of religion established by her highnes within this Realm.

To the extent that the Elizabethan church was a state institution through which the regime sought to shape and channel the spiritual lives of its subjects, the perceived threat to reformed religion posed by the theatres could also be construed as a political threat to the authority of the state. Thus, in their petition, London's city fathers appeal to the vital interests of the Queen with the charge that the theatres "draw ... people from the resort unto sermons ... to the ... prophanation of religion *established by her highnes within this Realm*" (emphasis added). And in 1615, the author of *A Refutation of the Apology for Actors* gravely avers that "God onely gave authority of publique instruction and correction but to two sorts of men: to his Ecclesiasticall Ministers, and temporal Magistrates: hee never instituted a third authority of Players. . . . Playes were ordained by, & dedicated to the Divell, which is enemy to God and al goodnes."[44] The important point to be extracted from this polemic is that the theatre was perceived to have constituted itself as an alternative site of authority within contemporary society, an authority radically different in its sources, appeal, and potential effects from that which sanctioned the dominant institutions of church and state.

The apocalyptic tone in which the godly were apt to preach or write against the theatre might upon occasion modulate into something entirely more pragmatic. Consider, for example, a letter to the Queen's secretary, Sir Francis Walsingham, dated 25 January 1587, in which an anonymous correspondent bemoans "the daylie abuse of Stage Playes":

---

44. I. G., *A Refutation of the Apology for Actors* (1615), facsimile ed., 57, 58.

Woe is me! the play howses are pestered, when churches are naked; at the one is not possible to gett a place, at the other voyde
seates are plentie. ... Yt is a wofull sight to see two hundred
proude players jett in their silkes, wheare five hundred pore
people sterve in the streets. But yf needes this mischief must be
tollerated ... yet for God's sake (Sir) lett every Stage in London
pay a weekly pention to the pore, that *ex hoc malo proveniat aliquod
bonum.* (Quoted in Chambers, *Elizabethan Stage,* 4:303–4)

The writer combines a charitable concern for the material welfare of
the poor with a realistic assessment of the difficulty of suppressing
so popular and profitable a vice as playing, and this leads him to his
proposal that a part of those wicked profits might be put to virtuous
use by the commonwealth.[45]

Such tacit recognition and acknowledgment of the degree to
which the theatre was integrated into the urban socioeconomic fabric
could also take less compromising forms. In 1603, Henry Crosse
railed thus against the players: "These copper-lace gentlemen growe
rich, purchase land by adulterous Playes, & not a fewe of them usu-
rers and extortioners, which they exhaust out of the purses of their
haunters."[46] The theatre and its personnel are here identified with
the disruptive innovations of the marketplace. The players were not
only attacked because theatre was thought to be intrinsically immoral but also because the lowly and frequently disreputable practice
of playing had suddenly become a means to relative affluence and
upward social mobility—at least for those professionals who were
sharers in licensed and liveried companies and had profits sufficient
to acquire real estate and to engage in moneylending and other forms
of financial speculation. Those who inveighed against the public and
professional stage usually did so on the grounds that it was an affront
to godliness and a threat to the established social order. Depending
upon specific circumstances and shifting contexts, however, they
also seem to have been capable of viewing it as a potential source
of municipal revenue or as a direct competitor for the leisure
time of London's populace—and, perhaps, for their disposable

45. In this regard, see Ingram, *The Business of Playing,* 121–49, for extended
discussion of the 6 December 1574 Act of the Common Council of London, and
an argument that the chief intent of London's city fathers in asserting their regulatory authority was to find a new source of revenues to maintain the city's hospitals.

46. Henry Crosse, *Vertues Common-wealth: Or the High-way to Honour* (1603), excerpt printed in Chambers, *Elizabethan Stage,* 4:247.

income.[47] The purposes of antitheatricalism were no less diverse and divided than were the purposes of playing.

47. That the players were not only luring audiences away from the preachers but were also stealing paying customers away from other kinds of commercial entertainments is suggested in the revealing comments of Thomas Nashe (1592) and Henry Chettle (1592), rpt. in Chambers, *Elizabethan Stage,* 4:239, 243. The economic basis of hostility to the Elizabethan stage is stressed in Russell Fraser, *The War against Poetry* (Princeton: Princeton University Press, 1970); and Alfred Harbage, "Copper into Gold," in *English Renaissance Drama,* ed. Standish Henning, Robert Kimbrough, and Richard Knowles (Carbondale: Southern Illinois University Press, 1976), 1–14.

◡
•

Chapter Four

The Theatre, the City, and the Crown

In 1574, James Burbage and four of his partners in the Earl of Leicester's company were licensed by the Queen to perform "Commedies, Tragedies, Enterludes, stage playes, and such other like . . . aswell for the recreacion of oure loving subjectes, as for oure solace and pleasure when we shall thincke good to see them."[48] In principle, the only companies of players who were authorized to play in the public theatres that opened for business in 1576 were those who were the liveried retainers of great lords and could be employed occasionally for the solace of their masters and their masters' mistress. The building of those theatres, and the leasing of the land on which they were built, were financed by the capital and credit of prosperous London merchants and tradesmen, like Burbage's brother-in-law John Brayne, a freeman of the city Company of Gro-

---

48. Patent of 10 May 1574, rpt. in Chambers, *Elizabethan Stage*, 2:87–88. The terms of this patent seem to have been uniquely broad, for Leicester's Men were licensed thereby to perform "aswell within oure Citie of London and liberties of the same, as also within the liberties and fredomes of anye oure Cities, townes, Bouroughes &c whatsoever as without the same, thoroughte oure Realme of England." The only limiting conditions were that plays should be seen and allowed by the Master of the Revels—a court officer—and that there should be no performances during times of common prayer or plague in London. (See the discussion in Chambers, *Elizabethan Stage*, 1:281–83.) It would seem that, by the terms of this license, the Crown abrogated the authority of the City Corporation to control playing within its jurisdictions—an authority originally affirmed in the royal proclamation of 16 May 1559, prohibiting unlicensed interludes and plays, especially on matters of religion or policy. Thus, the patent represents an important instance of jurisdictional and ideological conflict between the Court and the City.

cers.[49] Thus, the foundation and continued viability of the public, professional theatres, their players, and their plays, depended upon a strategic alliance of aristocratic patronage and entrepreneurial investment. This conjunction defines the conditions of emergence of the public and professional theatre at an historically transitional moment. The Elizabethan theatre was sustained by a frequently advantageous but inherently unstable mixture of two theoretically distinct modes of cultural production: one, hierarchical and deferential, based upon traditional relations of patronage and clientage; the other, fluid and competitive, based upon market relations.

The Queen's license promoted the pleasures of her loving subjects and also protected the players from the terms of the recent "Acte for the punishement of Vacabondes and for the Releif of the Poore & Impotent" (1572). This act was one of the key legal instruments employed by the Elizabethan state in its parallel attempts to enhance its disciplinary and its pastoral powers, to enlarge its capacity to control its subjects, and minister to their welfare. According to the terms of this Act,

> All and everye persone and persones beynge whole and mightye in Body and able to labour, havinge not Land or Maister, nor using any lawfull Marchaundize Crafte or Mysterye whereby hee or shee might get his or her Lyvinge; & all Fencers Bearewardes Comon Players in Enterludes & Minstrels, not belonging to any Baron of this Realme or towardes any other honorable Personage of greater Degree . . . [and who] shall wander abroade and have not Lycense of two Justices of the Peace at the leaste . . . shalbee taken adjudged and deemed Roges Vacaboundes and Sturdy Beggers.[50]

49. For a reading of the fragmentary documentary evidence concerning Brayne, his relationship with Burbage, and his role in the financing of London's earliest theatres, see Ingram, *The Business of Playing*, 92–113, 182–218.

50. *An Acte for the punishement of Vacabondes and for Releif of the Poore & Impotent* (14 *Eliz.* c. 5), extract printed in Chambers, *Elizabethan Stage*, 4:269–71. The punishment prescribed was to be "grevouslye whipped, and burnte through the gristle of the right Eare with a hot Yron of the compasse of an Ynche about." The act was amended and continued in 1576 and 1584–85. For an excellent study of this central issue in Elizabethan-Jacobean social policy, see A. L. Beier, *Masterless Men: The Vagrancy Problem in England 1560–1640* (London: Methuen, 1985); on itinerant entertainers, see 96–99.

Chambers, *Elizabethan Stage*, 2:86, prints the text of a letter to the Earl of

In the case of itinerant, protean players, unstable locality was threateningly conjoined with unstable identity; vagabondage was conjoined with roguery. The distinction of liveried actors from rogues, vagabonds, and sturdy beggars was an attempt to accommodate the professional players to the status categories and social controls of a traditional, hierarchical, and deferential society. At the same time, however, it also implied an emergent understanding of the peculiar conditions of professional playing. The licensing of players depended upon a tacit recognition that their impersonations were not fraudulent deceptions but were rather a circumscribed and fictive mode of role-playing, and that professional playing was not mere idleness but a paradoxical form of labor—a recognition that playing could actually be a "Crafte or Mysterye." Of course, at the same time that it afforded a means of protection to professional players, the Queen's restriction of license to players who "belonged" to trusted members of the aristocracy and were approved by the justices of the peace was also an attempt to assert royal authority, an authority both to allow and to limit the scope of her subjects' will to play. Such assertions were made in the context of unceasing maneuvers and negotiations between the Crown and the various components of the political nation. In this chapter, I emphasize the role of the players, plays, and playhouses in articulating the relationship between the Crown and the civic oligarchy; in the following chapter, I focus upon an attempt to employ them in a confrontation between the nobility and the Crown.

In 1584, "the Queenes Majesties poore Players" petitioned the Privy Council to send "favorable letters unto the L. Mayor of London," that they might be allowed to play publicly within the city, "wheras the tyme of our service draweth verie neere, so that of necessitie wee must needes have exercise to enable us the better for the same, and also for our better helpe and relief in our poore lyvinge, the season of the yere beynge past to playe att anye houses without

---

Leicester, signed by Burbage and five other players, requesting that he retain them as his "houshold Servaunts and daylie wayters" and provide them with a license certifying the same, "for avoydinge all inconvenients that maye growe" by reason of "a certayne Proclamation out for the revivinge of a Statute touchinge retayners."

the Cittye." Concisely conjoining the motives of royal service and financial necessity, the players' petition justifies public playing not merely as a means of practicing for court performance but also as a legitimate means of livelihood in its own right. As we have seen from the terms of her 1574 license to the Earl of Leicester's Men, the Queen had already made it quite clear that she was agreeable to such arrangements. However, the recorder for the Corporation of the City of London presumed to differ. To the players' petition, he responded that "it is not convenient that they present before her majestie such playes as have ben before commonly played in open stages before all the basest assemblies in London." Their prior public performance having contaminated them with commonness, openness, and baseness, such plays were deemed by the Queen's subject to be wholly inappropriate for her viewing. The real source of the Corporation's concerns, however, was not the royal command performance but rather the prior public performance that it rationalized and legitimated. The Corporation appears to have been deeply disturbed by the implications of the professionalization of playing:

> It hath not ben used nor thought meete hertofore that players shold make their lyving on the art of playing, but men for their lyvings using other honest and lawfull artes, or retteyned in honest service, have by companies learned some enterludes for some encreasce to their profit by other mens pleasures in vacant time of recreation.[51]

The notion that someone might earn his living by *playing* rather than by *working* was anathema to the conservative oligarchy of great merchants who ruled London and who profited most directly and immediately from the industry and order of its inhabitants.

The ideological as well as the physical and jurisdictional locus of the theatre was at the intersection of royal and civic interests; in certain situations, the theatre could and did become a site where the differences between those interests might be articulated and engaged.[52] An especially suggestive documentation of the City's atti-

---

51. Petition of the Queen's Players to the Privy Council, ca. November 1584, and Answer of the Corporation of London, enclosing the Act of Common Council of 6 December 1574; rpt. in Chambers, *Elizabethan Stage*, 4:298–302; quotations from 299, 300.

52. On "the struggle of Court and City," see Chambers, *Elizabethan Stage*, 1:269–307. The shifting history of the relationships among the Elizabethan state,

tude toward the players and toward their royal patronage is extant in a 1592 petition by the Lord Mayor to the Archbishop of Canterbury:

> By the daily and disorderlie exercise of a number of players & playeng houses erected within this Citie, the youth thearof is greatly corrupted & their manners infected with many evill & ungodly qualities. . . . In consideration whearof, wee most humbly beeseach your Grace . . . to voutchsafe us your good favour & help for the refourming & banishing of so great evill out of this Citie, which our selves of loong time though to small pourpose have so earnestly desired and endeavoured by all means that possibly wee could. And bycause wee understand that the Q. Majestie is & must be served at certen times by this sort of people, for which pourpose shee hath graunted hir lettres Patents to Mr. Tilney Master of hir Revells, by virtue whearof hee beeing authorized to refourm exercise or suppresse all manner of players, playes, & playeng houses whatsoever, did first licence the sayed playeng houses within this Citie for hir Majesties sayed service, which beefore that time lay open to all the statutes for the punishing of these & such lyke disorders. Wee . . . beeseach your Grace to call unto you the sayed Master of hir Majesties Revells . . . and to treat with him, if by any means it may bee devised that hir Majestie may bee served with these recreations as hath ben accoustomed (which in our opinions may easily bee don by the privat exercise of hir Majesties own players in convenient place) & the Citie freed from these continuall disorders.[53]

The Lord Mayor's letter to Archbishop Whitgift suggests that the Crown was usurping and vitiating the moral and legal authority over

---

the Corporation of London, and the Elizabethan commercial theatre is perhaps most readily traced in the collection of "Documents of Control," in Chambers, *Elizabethan Stage* 4:259–345. Like all who have written on these issues in recent decades, I have found Chambers's compilation to be an invaluable resource.

For a social historian's perspective on the relationship between the Crown and the City in the 1590s, see Ian W. Archer, *The Pursuit of Stability: social relations in Elizabethan London* (Cambridge: Cambridge University Press, 1991), 32–39. Also see Frank Freeman Foster, *The Politics of Stability: A Portrait of the Rulers in Elizabethan London* (London: Royal Historical Society, 1977), 133–51. Both of these studies emphasize the cooperative, mutually beneficial nature of the relationship between the city fathers and the Crown. That Archer's book barely mentions the theatres should temper the tendency of literary and dramatic historians and critics to make exorbitant claims about the social and/or political significance of the Elizabethan drama in its time.

53. The Lord Mayor to John Whitgift, Archbishop of Canterbury, 25 February 1591/2; printed in Chambers, *Elizabethan Stage* 4:307–08.

players that previously had been enjoyed and exercised by the City and that the instrument of this growing corruption and disorder was the Revels Office itself.[54] According to the Lord Mayor, the Master of the Revels was charged to reform or suppress playing but instead he actually countenanced it. (Mr. Tilney, after all, gathered the fruits of office by licensing plays, not by suppressing them.) Thus, from the perspective of London's city fathers, the Master of the Revels— an officer of the royal Court—had now become the City's unappointed Lord of Misrule; the licentiousness of the players was now licensed by authority of the Queen. The traditional task of the Office of the Revels had been "to select, organize, and supervise all entertainment of the sovereign, wherever the court might be."[55] The expansion of the role of this court office to include the supervision of *public* as well as courtly dramatic performances indicates that the Elizabethan regime was attempting to subject the symbolic and interpretive activities of its subjects to increasing scrutiny and regulation, at the same time that it was inventing new sources of revenue for itself and its clients.

The Lord Mayor made his appeal to the Archbishop and his indirect criticism of the court upon what he regarded as the common ground of religious and civic responsibilities, spiritual and temporal convictions. During the later sixteenth century, the religious opposition to players and to the newly established public playhouses included not only radical Puritan preachers but also orthodox Protestant clerics, who viewed the theatre as sharing the vanity and worldliness of the Roman Church and as replicating its spectacular and heathenish rites. The two institutions were frequently identified with each other and were made rhetorically interchangeable in Prot-

---

54. I assume that the Lord Mayor's reference to the City's assertion, and subsequent loss, of control over the licensing of commercial playing alludes to the Act of the Common Council of 6 December 1574, which was soon blunted by the licensing of the new public theatres. (See n. 40, above.)

55. Gerald Eades Bentley, *The Profession of Dramatist in Shakespeare's Time 1590–1642* (1971; rpt., Princeton: Princeton University Press, 1986), 147. On the Revels Office, also see Chambers, *Elizabethan Stage*, 1:71–105; Janet Clare, *"Art made tongue-tied by authority": Elizabethan and Jacobean Dramatic Censorship* (Manchester: Manchester University Press, 1990); Richard Dutton, *Mastering the Revels: The Regulation and Censorship of English Renaissance Drama* (Iowa City: University of Iowa Press, 1991).

estant polemics. Thus, for example, at the beginning of Elizabeth's reign, Bishop John Jewel ridiculed the papacy for bringing "the sacraments of Christ to be used now as a stage play . . . to the end that men's eyes should be fed with nothing else but with mad gazings and foolish gauds." The Bishop sought to discredit Catholic ritual by associating it with the sinister spectacle of the theatre, with its promotion of "mad gazings." In 1577—within a year of the opening of the Theatre—John Northbrooke was writing that people habituated to playgoing were now unashamed to avow "that playes are as good as sermons, and that they learne as much or more at a playe, than they do at God's worde preached." The analogy between playing and preaching, between viewing a theatrical performance and listening to a sermon, was obviously abhorrent to Northbrooke because, like Bishop Jewel, he construed the former activities as replications of the errors and sins of Catholic worship. More generally, the popular appeal of the public and professional stage must have posed a direct threat to the very notion of civic reformation, for it reintroduced, in a virulent new form, the benighted ceremonial and spectacular modality of collective experience that had been purged and replaced by the preaching and hearing of God's Word. In a sermon preached in London in 1607, William Crashaw attacked "the ungodly Playes and Enterludes so rife in the nation: what are they but a bastard of Babylon, a daughter of error and confusion, a hellish device (the divels owne recreation to mock at holy things) by him delivered to the Heathen, from them to the Papists, and from them to us?"[56] Crashaw understood theatricality as nothing less than an inheritance from Satan, a cultural pestilence transmitted down through human history. In the context of such vehemently maintained convictions, linking theatre and spectacle with papistical and satanic practices, the predilection of the Queen, her court, and many in the Elizabethan nobility for dramatic and spectacular entertainments must have

56. See: John Jewel, *An Apology of the Church of England* (1564), ed. J. E. Booty (Ithaca: Cornell University Press, 1963), 36; John Northbrooke, *A Treatise wherein Dicing, Dauncing, Vaine playes, or Enterluds, with other idle pastimes, &c., commonly used on the Sabboth day, are reproved by the Authoritie of the word of God and auntient writers* (1577), excerpts rpt. in Chambers, *Elizabethan Stage*, 4:198; William Crashaw, *The Sermons preached at the Crosse, Feb. xiiii, 1607* (1608), excerpts rpt. in Chambers, *Elizabethan Stage*, 4:249. On the hostility to the stage as a persistent feature of Western religious thought and polemic, see Barish, *The Antitheatrical Prejudice*.

posed moral and political difficulties for some of the most righteous
and articulate of the Queen's subjects.

In a letter written from Venice in 1606, Sir Henry Wotton openly
remarked upon the politics of spectacle as they were enacted in an
alien state:

> Yesterday was the Feast of Corpus Christi, celebrated by express
> commandment of the State (which goeth farther than devotion),
> with the most sumptuous procession that ever had been seen
> here. . . . The reasons of this extraordinary solemnity were two, as
> I conceive it. First, to contain the people still in good order with
> superstition, the foolish band of obedience. Secondly, to let the
> Pope know (who wanteth not intelligencers) that notwithstanding
> his interdict, they had friars enough and other clergymen to furnish
> out the day.[57]

The English king's ambassador confidently deciphered the political
purpose of this magnificent religious and civic ceremony: namely,
to advance the interests of the ruling oligarchy of the Most Serene
Republic against the unruliness of the Venetian populace, on the one
hand, and against the authority of the Pope, on the other. Wotton,
who had been a member of the Essex circle in the 1590s, was a well-
schooled observer of the mysteries of state. Doubtless, he now found
it both prudent and congenial to demystify the political appropriation
of the Feast of Corpus Christi in a context that was Italian, Catholic,
and civic, rather than English, Protestant, and monarchical. Venice
provided him with an exemplary, and comfortably alienated, demonstration of the politics of spectacle.

Among extant Elizabethan observations of the relationship between spectacle and power, one of the most cynical is to be found in
the notorious "note Containing the opinion of on Christopher Marly"
(1593), prepared for the Privy Council by Richard Baines shortly before Marlowe's death. Taking as his primary example the Machiavellian subtleties employed by Moses to maintain his power over the
Hebrews, Baines's Marlowe asserts "That the first beginning of Re-

---

57. Letter to the Earl of Salisbury, Venice, 26 May 1606; rpt. in *The Life and
Letters of Sir Henry Wotton*, ed. Logan Pearsall Smith, 2 vols. (Oxford: Clarendon
Press, 1907), 1:350. Compare the observation, recorded in his commonplace book,
that "The Spanish ambassador needed no spectacles in Venice, for sure States
represent most things far bigger than their truths" (*Life and Letters of Sir Henry
Wotton*, 2:497).

ligioun was only to keep men in awe." The originary function of religion was, by mystification, to facilitate the power of the few over the many. From this Marlovian premise, it follows "That if there be any god or good Religion, then it is in the papistes because the service of god is performed with more Cerimonies, as Elevation of the mass, organs, singing men, Shaven Crownes & cta. That all protestantes are Hypocriticall asses."[58] Baines's Marlowe gives his ironic approval to precisely those elements of Catholicism which the Protestant Bishop Jewel had excoriated as "a stage play" that feeds men's eyes "with nothing else but with mad gazings and foolish gauds"—precisely those elements that ambassador Wotton, with a politic detachment, observed in operation in Venice.

As must have been evident to Marlowe and to some of his fellow subjects, including Wotton, the Elizabethan regime made a concerted effort to implement its own ceremonies of mystification, and it did so precisely by appropriating and elaborating, in a largely secular context, the ritual and iconic aspects of Catholic worship. Yet by the very process of appropriating the spectacular theatre of medieval religion, the Elizabethan state contaminated its own strategies of legitimation. By the logic of radical Reformation thought, courtly culture was vulnerable to association with papist culture on the basis of their mutual association with theatricality and spectacle, and from this same perspective, courtly culture could be perceived as tainted by worldliness, moral corruption, and deceptive illusion. Thus, at the same time that the iconic, verbal, and performative arts played a central role in entertaining the sovereign and aggrandizing the state, they were also a potential liability to the very reverence and assent they were designed to procure. The tone of the Lord Mayor's 1592 petition to the Archbishop of Canterbury suggests a discomfort with, and even an oblique disapprobation of, the royal taste for theatrical entertainments. The troubled tone of this late Elizabethan municipal petition adumbrates tensions between Court and City, between aristo-

---

58. Richard Baines, "A note Containing the opinion of on Christopher Marly Concerning his damnable [opini] Judgement of Religion, and scorn of God's word" (BL Harleian 6848), printed in C. F. Tucker Brooke, *The Life of Marlowe* (London: Methuen, 1930), 98–100. Machiavelli's commentary on Livy's account of Roman religion, *Discorsi*, 1.11–14, is a *locus classicus* for Renaissance perspectives on religion as political mystification.

cratic and bourgeois cultures, between Anglican and Puritan modes of spirituality, that were to become increasingly explicit ideological oppositions during the Jacobean and Caroline reigns.[59] The Lord Mayor's remarks also point toward a representational and ideological tension within Elizabethan royal policy: On the one hand, such policy sought to control and direct the iconoclastic energies of popular Protestantism through the institutions of a reformed Elizabethan church, of which the devout Queen was the head; on the other hand, it sought to employ the representational resources of the arts to legitimate, to glorify, and to amuse a resplendent Renaissance court, of which the magnificent Prince was the center.

Despite the persistent antitheatricalism of London's civic elite, the Elizabethan royal government had demonstrated from the opening of the public commercial theatres that it was capable of viewing them in a moral light that was at least *relatively* positive. It will be remembered that, as early as 1572, the Privy Council had indicated to the City Court of Aldermen that it approved of "such playes, enterludes, commedies & tragedies as maye tende to represse vyce & extoll vertwe, for the recreacion of the people, & therby to drawe them from sundrye worser exercyses." In rebuttal, the aldermen "agreed that Master Townclark shall devyse a letter for answer of thother, to be sent unto my Lord Burleighe, signifiing to his honour, that it is thought very perillous ... to have such conventicles of people by such meanes called together, wherof the greatest number are of the meanest sorte."[60] The city fathers and the Privy Council were still arguing the same issue back and forth in the same terms more than two decades later. In a letter of 3 November 1594, the Lord Mayor of London wrote to Lord Burghley to sue for his support in the city's latest effort to suppress the public theatres. In the course of his plea, the Lord Mayor rebutted once more the argument in favor

59. On the politics of Stuart court culture, see Stephen Orgel, *The Illusion of Power: Political Theater in the English Renaissance* (Berkeley: University of California Press, 1975); P. W. Thomas, "Two Cultures? Court and Country under Charles I," in *The Origins of the English Civil War,* ed. Conrad Russell (London: Macmillan, 1973), 168–93; R. Malcolm Smuts, *Court Culture and the Origins of a Royalist Tradition in Early Stuart England* (Philadelphia: University of Pennsylvania Press, 1987).

60. Minute of City Court of Aldermen, 20 May 1572; rpt. in Chambers, *Elizabethan Stage,* 4:269.

of playing that had already been endorsed by Burghley and the Privy Council so many years earlier:

> I am not ignorant (my very good L.) what is alleadged by soom for defence of these playes, that the people must have soom kynd of recreation, & that policie requireth to divert idle heads & other ill disposed from other woorse practize by this kynd of exercize. Whearto may bee answeared . . . that as honest recreation is a thing very meet for all sorts of men, so no kynd of exercise, beeing of itself corrupt & prophane, can well stand with the good policie of a Christian Common Wealth. . . . The sayed playes (as they are handled) ar of that sort, and woork that effect in such as ar present and frequent the same. (Rpt. in Chambers, *Elizabethan Stage*, 4:316–17)

The City and the state maintained diametrically opposed positions concerning the very nature of the public theatre: The former held it to be in essence corrupt and inimical to the welfare of the common-wealth, whereas the latter held it to be frequently benign and poten-tially beneficial to the maintenance of public order and control, either through the inculcation of doctrine or through the displacement and release of social pressures.

In the year 1600—at a time of great socioeconomic uncertainty and political ferment, when London's professional and commercial theatres were enjoying unprecedented popularity and success—the Privy Council sought strictly to limit the number and location of play-houses, the frequency and times of performances, and the number of companies that would be allowed to play. In setting forth these or-ders, the Privy Council summarized the complex attitude of the state toward the theatre at the end of the century and the close of the reign:

> Forasmuch as yt is manifestlie knowne and graunted that the mul-titude of the said houses and the misgovernment of them hath bin made and is dailie occasion of the idle riotous and dissolute livinge of great numbers of people, that leavinge all such honest and painefull Course of life, as they should followe, doe meete and assemble there, and of maine particuler abuses and disorders that doe there uppon ensue. And yet neverthelesse yt is Considered that the use and exercise of such plaies, not beinge evill in yt self, may with a good order and moderacion be suffered in a well gov-erned estate, and that, hir Majestie beinge pleased at some times to take delighte and recreacion in the sight and hearinge of them, some order is fitt to bee taken for the allowance and mainteinance

of suche persons, as are thoughte meetest in that kinde to yeald hir Majestie recreacion and delight, & consequentlie of the howses that must serve for publique playenge to keepe them in exercise. To the end therefore, that bothe the greatest abuses of the plaies and plaienge houses maye be redressed, and the use and moderacon of them retained, The Lordes and the rest of hir Majesties privie Councell, withe one and full Consent, have ordered in manner and forme as followeth.[61]

The Privy Council's order reiterates the familiar and convenient fiction that the professional players' public performances kept them in readiness to perform at court. However, the order's justification for the allowance of public playing goes well beyond consideration of the ruler's personal pleasures: It also justifies the allowance of a carefully limited and controlled public theatre upon the ground that such a theatre has its own legitimate place in a secure and flourishing commonwealth. The Privy Council's order fully acknowledges all of the massive social problems that were perennially blamed upon the theatres; nevertheless, it is unequivocal in its approach to correction in terms of more precise controls rather than total suppression. The official understanding made explicit here is that, although the performance of plays in the public theatre might sometimes, *in practice*, be subject to abuses, the theatre was not inherently corrupt or corrupting—that, indeed, with careful regulation, it could be made to serve the interests of the commonweal and the state by inculcating "good order and moderacion" in its audiences.

61. "An order sett downe by the lordes and others of hir Majesties privye Councell the 22 of June 1600 to restrain the excessive number of Plaie howses & the imoderate use of Stage plaies in & about the Cittye"; rpt. in Chambers, *Elizabethan Stage*, 4:329–31; quotation from 330. Also see the discussion in Wickham, *Early English Stages*, 2:2:9–29. Wickham construes the document in the context of a crisis between 1597 and 1603 concerning the fate of the public theatres. The resolution by the Crown in support of the theatres prepared the way for the more authoritarian control of the stage during the Jacobean reign; furthermore, by aligning itself unmistakably with the theatre, "the monarchy . . . prompted all those who were [the theatre's] enemies to align themselves against the monarchy" (26). Although obviously attractive to literary critics and theatre historians, this argument may grant the theatre unwarranted political importance as a precipitating cause of the English Civil War. If we were to continue arguing in a cause-and-effect mode, we might maintain with equal validity that, by aligning itself with the monarchy, the theatre prompted enemies of the crown to align themselves against the stage. However, my own impulse would be to seek a more dialectical mode of interpretation.

The Privy Council directed its attention to specific playhouses, in which particular companies under the patronage of individual Privy Councilors performed. In its effort "to restrain the excessive number of Plaie howses and the imoderate use of Stage plaies in & about the Cittye," the Elizabethan government went so far as to limit public dramatic performances to just two theatres: "There shall bee about the Cittie two howses and noe more allowed to serve for the use of the Common Stage plaies." One of these was to be the Globe, the exclusive venue of "the Servantes of the L. Chamberlen" (Chambers, *Elizabethan Stage,* 4:330, 331). Thus, under the terms of the Privy Council's order, the members of Shakespeare's company were to be among the few commoners left in London who were officially permitted to play. The perspective of the council was situational, focusing upon particular dramatic repertoires and the immediate circumstances of their performance and reception. Thus, the further implication of the council's orders is that, although public dramatic performance might indeed have considerable representational power, the actual ethical and political intent and consequences of such power could only be determined in local instances. The terms of the Privy Council's order of 1600 evidence a well-considered, systematic, and comprehensive policy for state limitation and regulation of London's popular playhouses. There is no evidence, however, that the order was actually implemented or enforced. The theoretical rigor of control was repeatedly undermined by its practical lapses. And in the shifting gaps between the theory and practice of state regulation, the players and playwrights of the Elizabethan theatre discovered a conceptual space for the exercise of their own authority.

◡

CHAPTER FIVE

FROM THE STAGE TO THE STATE

Such an understanding as that implied in the Privy Council's order of 1600 seems to me to be conformable with what we know of the part played by Shakespeare's company in the notorious Essex rebellion of 1601, and of the royal response to that performance. This singular conjunction of drama and sedition has been made a basis for much generalizing about the political valence of the Elizabethan theatre; for this reason, it demands at least a brief reconsideration here.[62]

62. The topical connections were first fully set out in Evelyn May Albright, "Shakespeare's *Richard II* and the Essex Conspiracy," *PMLA* 42 (1927), 686–720; were contested in Ray Heffner, "Shakespeare, Hayward and Essex," *PMLA* 45 (1930), 754–80; and were defended and elaborated in Albright, "Shakespeare's *Richard II*, Hayward's *History of Henry IV*, and the Essex Conspiracy," *PMLA* 46 (1931), 694–719.

A number of recent critics (myself included) have cited the special performance of *Richard II* to exemplify the involvement of the Elizabethan theatre in Elizabethan politics: See, for example, Louis Montrose, "Celebration and Insinuation: Sir Philip Sidney and the Motives of Elizabethan Courtship," *Renaissance Drama*, n.s., 8 (1977), 3–35, rpt. in *Renaissance Drama as Cultural History: Essays from* Renaissance Drama *1977–1987*, ed. Mary Beth Rose (Evanston: Northwestern University Press and The Newberry Library Center for Renaissance Studies, 1990), 367–99; Stephen Greenblatt, "Introduction," in *The Forms of Power and the Power of Forms in the Renaissance*, ed. Stephen Greenblatt (*Genre* Special Topics: 7 [1982]), 3–5; Stephen Orgel, "Making Greatness Familiar," ibid., 45; Jonathan Dollimore, "Introduction: Shakespeare, Cultural Materialism and the New Historicism," in *Political Shakespeare*, ed. Dollimore and Sinfield, 8–9; Leonard Tennenhouse, *Power on Display: The Politics of Shakespeare's Genres* (New York: Methuen, 1986), 88.

For a valuable analysis of many of the relevant historical materials, and a critique of some recent anecdotal uses of the Essex episode in Shakespeare studies, see Leeds Barroll, "A New History for Shakespeare and His Time," *Shakespeare Quarterly* 39 (1988), 441–64. For an illuminating interpretation of the conspiracy

On the afternoon of Saturday, 7 February 1601, Shakespeare's company performed at the Globe a "play of the deposyng and kyllyng of Kyng Rychard the second" that was presumably—although not incontrovertibly—Shakespeare's *Tragedie of King Richard the second.*[63] The first quarto of Shakespeare's play—"As it hath beene publikely acted by the right Honourable the Lorde Chamberlaine his Servants"—had been printed in 1597; two more quarto printings followed in 1598. Presumably, the book of the play had been allowed by the Master of the Revels when it began its life on the stage, in about 1595. The revival performed on Saturday, 7 February 1601, had been commissioned a day or two earlier by several of the conspirators; eleven of them—but not the Earl himself—actually attended the performance. On the morning following, the Earl of Essex and his friends staged their own ill-conceived performance at Essex House and in the open streets of London. They failed to win over the populace; the conspiracy began to unravel almost immediately, and the attempted coup was crushed before the following day. Subsequently, in the course of investigating the conspiracy, the Privy Council questioned one of the Lord Chamberlain's players, Augustine Phillips, and took testimony from some of the conspirators regarding the Globe performance. As a consequence of the investigation, several of those who had arranged and attended that Globe performance as a prelude to their rebellion were tried and executed for treason. In at least one case, that of Sir Gelly Meyricke, steward to the Earl of Essex, procurement of the performance at the Globe was among the acts that were used in evidence.

As I have already indicated, the Privy Council's order of 1600 had stipulated that "there shall bee about the Cittie two howses and noe more allowed to serve for the use of the Common Stage plaies" and that one of these should be the Globe as occupied by "the Servantes

---

in the context of the late Elizabethan politics of honor, see "At the crossroads of the political culture: the Essex revolt, 1601," in James, *Society, Politics and Culture*, 416–65. Also see Richard C. McCoy, *The Rites of Knighthood: The Literature and Politics of Elizabethan Chivalry* (Berkeley: University of California Press, 1989), 79–102.

63. The play performed on 7 February 1601 is so identified in the deposition by Augustine Phillips (18 February 1601), Shakespeare's fellow sharer in the Lord Chamberlain's company. The text of the deposition is printed in Chambers, *William Shakespeare*, 2:325. In the following discussion, I assume that the play in question was Shakespeare's *Tragedie of King Richard the second.*

of the L. Chamberlen" (Chambers, *Elizabethan Stage,* 4:330, 331). Given so recent and powerful a demonstration of the state's trust and favor, it may be thought that the implication of Shakespeare's company in the events of the Essex revolt would have proven professionally disastrous. But the players' reputation and livelihood emerged from the crisis apparently unscathed. Indeed, the Lord Chamberlain's Men performed at court before the Queen just a few days later, on the night of Shrove Tuesday, 24 February. On the morning following the players' presentation, the Earl of Essex gave his own final command performance. Upon a scaffold in the Tower, before an exclusive audience of lords, gentlemen, and divines, the Earl prayed that he be forgiven and that the Queen be blessed, affirmed both his own good intentions toward the Queen and the justice of his condemnation, and at the last put his head upon the block.[64] This conjunction of courtly entertainment and state execution may have been merely fortuitous, but it is tempting to see it as an intended royal response to the conjunction of tragic actions that had been devised by the conspirators a little more than a fortnight earlier. From this perspective, the extension of an invitation to the professional players of Shakespeare's company to perform again at court affirmed the continuity of royal favor toward the Lord Chamberlain's Men, and simultaneously confirmed the continuity of royal authority over the public theatre; it was a symbolic assertion that the state was secure and that its subjects were loyal.

What was the motive of the Essex party in requesting and subsidizing that particular performance of *Richard II?* Like the Elizabethan Privy Council, many modern scholars and critics tend to assume that the performance was intended to incite the playgoing public of London to insurrection—or, at least, to predispose them to sympathize with the Earl's claim that he had been victimized by the upstart caterpillars of the commonwealth who now controlled the sovereign and that he was justified in rising to his own defense. There is a basis for this hypothesis in the events surrounding the publication and suppression of John Hayward's prose narrative, *The First Part of the Life and raigne of king Henrie the IIII* (1599). One of the reasons why Hayward's history of Henry IV was of interest to the Essex faction

64. See, for example, the "Account of the execution of the Earl of Essex" in *Calendar of State Papers Domestic,* 1598–1601, vol. 278, art. 112, pp. 592–94.

and of concern to the Privy Council was that it abandoned providentialist historiography for one that was indebted to the perspectives of Tacitus and Machiavelli. Hayward's book embraced an understanding of history and politics as processes shaped by the interaction of strumpet Fortune with the will and intellect of the individual human agent. There is considerable evidence to suggest that the identification of Essex with Bolingbroke was current and had perhaps been surreptitiously encouraged by the Earl himself.[65] The hypothesis that the conspirators expected and desired the other spectators to identify Essex with Bolingbroke seems to assume that the Globe audience would have approved Bolingbroke unhesitatingly as the hero of the play. Such an assumption begs complex questions of interpretation in both performance and reception—issues about which the extant evidence allows little scope for speculation. The related but distinct

65. For a critical edition of the text and a detailed account of the controversy surrounding its printing and suppression, see *The First and Second Parts of John Hayward's The Life and Raigne of King Henrie IIII*, ed. John J. Manning, Camden Fourth Series, vol. 42 (London: Royal Historical Society, 1992). Quotations are from this edition. Also see Margaret Dowling, "Sir John Hayward's Troubles Over His *Life of Henry IV*," *The Library*, 4th series, 11 (1931), 212–24, which prints excerpts from the Attorney General's notes on his interrogations of Hayward. Hayward's text was first printed with a Latin dedicatory epistle to the Earl of Essex, followed by a preface, "A. P. to the Reader," extolling histories for setting forth "not onely precepts, but lively patterns, both for private directions and for affayres of state" (62). Within a few days of publication, the Earl of Essex complained to the Archbishop of Canterbury, who ordered that the Epistle be removed; an attempted second edition, with a new Epistle Apologetical by Hayward, was confiscated and burned on the Archbishop's orders. It was rumored that the Earl delayed his complaint until after the book had been widely circulated. This was also part of the official story, as incorporated into the government's "Directions for the preachers," intended for dissemination from the pulpit in the wake of the Earl's subsequent revolt:

> Two years since, a history of Henry IV. was printed and published, wherein all the complaints and slanders which have been given out by seditious traitors against the Government, both in England and Ireland, are set down, and falsely attributed to those times, thereby cunningly insinuating that the same abuses being now in this realm that were in the days of Richard II, the like course might be taken for redress. This book was no sooner published but that the Earl, knowing hundreds of them to be dispersed, would needs seem the first that disliked it, whereas he had confessed that he had the written copy with him to peruse 14 days, plotting how he might become another Henry IV (*Calendar of State Papers Domestic*, 1598–1601, vol. 278, art. 63, p. 567).

hypothesis, that the commissioned performance of *Richard II* was intended to catalyze a popular uprising, must rely upon an assumption that the eleven conspirators who attended the performance in question did not have the capacious Globe to themselves; that they must have shared the dramatic experience with a reasonable number of ordinary playgoers, upon whom the play might have worked the desired seditious effect.[66]

There certainly existed at least an appearance of complicity by the Lord Chamberlain's men in a seditious action that was of the gravest possible national significance; and the whole experience was doubtless chastening to the players. Nevertheless, the perpetually suspicious and vigilant Privy Council quickly exonerated them. It has been reasonably suggested, "because they played the whole affair by the book—only performing an 'allowed' text and in their assigned playing-place—that, unlike Hayward, [the Chamberlain's Men] did not suffer severely for their indiscretion, wilful or otherwise" (Dutton, *Mastering the Revels*, 124). But this benign official response to the players may also have been due in part to the refusal of the inhabitants of London to give active support to the Earl on the morning following the play's performance. To the Elizabethan government, the spectacular failure of Essex in his attempt to arouse the Queen's subjects in the streets of London may not have signified that the theatre was politically ineffectual but rather that the players' performance of their playwright's play was innocent of seditious intent. Indeed, the Privy Council may have judged the players' intention by means of the audience's response. Such an assumption would have implied, by negation, a fundamental conviction that the theatre was powerful indeed.

Unlike the players and the populace, however, the conspirators shaped the import of the play to their own dangerous fantasies. Such is the implication of certain comments in the records of the revolt.

---

66. Filled to capacity, the Globe would likely have held about three thousand customers (see Gurr, *Playgoing in Shakespeare's London*, 18–22). Its audience for a successful play on a topical and controversial subject, performed on a Saturday afternoon, is likely to have numbered more than eleven. Of course, it is possible, although highly unlikely, that the conspirators really did have the Globe almost to themselves, and that they were content to have it so. In that case, however, we might then want to ask why they had not rather requested a private performance at Essex House.

There is, for example, the report of the trial of Sir Gelly Meyricke, at which Sir Edward Coke, the attorney general, cited Meyricke's insistence to the players, during arrangements for the performance, that "they must needs have the play of *Henry IV*," in which there was "set forth the killing of the King upon a stage." (By identifying the play in question with Henry IV rather than with Richard II, the report strengthens its association with Hayward's notorious history.) Francis Bacon provides a vivid parallel description of Meyricke's theatrical enthusiasms: "So earnest hee was to satisfie his eyes with the sight of that tragedie which hee thought soone after his lord should bring from the stage to the state."[67] In conjunction, these comments strongly suggest that one of the conspirators' primary motives in commissioning the performance was to rouse *themselves* to action. They wished to witness a vividly dramatic re-enactment of that historical event which they hoped to emulate in deed almost immediately following the performance. It seems, in other words, that the Essex conspirators subscribed to the belief that drama has the capacity to imitate action and, by example, to impel its audience to action—an understanding that they shared with the theatre's most vocal defenders and detractors. *Richard II*, as compellingly performed by the Lord Chamberlain's Men at the Globe, might well be thought to have stirred the conspirators to emulate Bolingbroke's successful precedent, to have emboldened and resolved them to execute their dangerous and doubtful designs. Such an effect is clearly what at least one of the conspirators sought in the performance and what, in principle, both critics and defenders of the theatre thought it capable of effecting. However, the subsequent exoneration of the players from any charge of complicity implies that neither in their play nor in their performance of it were they deemed by the authorities to be responsible for the constructions applied by the conspirators.

67. The relevant excerpts from the report of the trial and from Francis Bacon's *Declaration of the Practises and Treasons . . . by Robert late Earle of Essex* (both 1601), are reprinted in Chambers, *William Shakespeare*, 2:325–26. In his own examination, Meyricke attempted to portray himself as merely a casual spectator: "He can not tell who procured that play to be played at that tyme except yt were Sr Charles Percye, but as he thyncketh yt was Sr Charles Percye. Thenne he was at the same play and Cam in somwhat after yt was begon, and the play was of Kyng Harry the iiijth, and of the kyllyng of Kyng Richard the second played by the L. Chamberlen's players" (ibid., 324).

There is evidence that the Earl himself took a Hamlet-like interest in representations of aristocratic sedition and regicide, both written and acted. Consider the following charge, made sometime after
Essex had violated his royal commission as commander of the English expeditionary force in Ireland and had returned to the court
without the Queen's permission:

> His underhand permitting of that most treasonous booke of Henry
> the fourth to be printed and published, being plainly deciphered
> not onely by the matter, and by the Epistle itself, for what ende
> and for whose behoof it was made, but also the Erle himself being
> so often present at the playing thereof, and with great applause
> giving countenance and lyking to the same.[68]

The official report appears to conflate Hayward's printed politic history with a dramatic entertainment on the same subject. This com-
ment becomes particularly intriguing in conjunction with the famous
and puzzling remark attributed to Queen Elizabeth, following the
1601 revolt, that "this tragedy was played 40tie times in open streets
and houses" (Chambers, *William Shakespeare*, 2:327). There is no
available evidence to confirm that the dramatic performances mentioned in either of these accounts were of Shakespeare's *Richard II*.
Nevertheless, the two anecdotes constitute evidence suggesting that
any public representation in late Elizabethan London of the de-
thronement and murder of King Richard II would have been politically volatile and would have stirred strong topical interest.

Shakespeare and his company were engaging a delicate topic
when they originally produced *The Tragedy of King Richard II* in the
mid 1590s. Surely, they were knowingly treading upon dangerous
ground when they agreed to a special public performance for the Essex faction in 1601. What, then, may have motivated them to agree
to such a performance? Let us consider the text of the sworn statement taken from Shakespeare's fellow sharer, Augustine Phillips, on
18 February 1601:

> He sayeth that . . . Sr Charles Percy Sr Josclyne Percy and the L.
> Montegle with some thre more spak to some of the players in the
> presans of thys examinate to have the play of the deposyng and

68. "An Abstract of the Erl of Essex his Treasons" (24 July 1600), printed in
Chambers, *William Shakespeare*, 2:323.

kyllyng of Kyng Richard the second to be played the Saterday next
promysyng to gete them xl*s*. more then their ordynary to play yt.
Wher thys Examinate and hys fellowes were determyned to have
played some other play, holding that play of Kyng Richard to be
so old & so long out of use as that they should have small or no
Company at yt. But at their request this Examinate and his fellowes were Content to play yt the Saterday and had their xl*s*. more
then their ordynary for yt and so played yt accordyngly. (Quoted
in Chambers, *William Shakespeare*, 2:325)

The conspirators came to the players with a request for a special performance of a play on a controversial and potentially dangerous subject. Understandably, the players hesitated to comply. Nevertheless,
the lords and gentlemen were insistent, and the players finally de-
ferred to the wishes of their betters. After all, not only were the members of the delegation men of honor and substance in their own right,
they were also the intimate friends and followers of the preeminent
earls of Essex and Southampton, both of whom were generous benefactors of scholars and poets. Thus, one subtext of Phillips's deposition is the vulnerability of inferiors and clients to the pressures ex-
erted by their superiors and patrons.

But there is also another subtext that is ideologically at variance
with the first—one based not upon codes of social deference or political allegiance but upon market calculations and professional judgments. According to Phillips's testimony, the conspirators presented
their request to the players wholly in terms of financial gain, "promysyng to gete them xl*s*. more then their ordynary to play yt"; the players resisted on a mixture of commercial and professional grounds,
"holding that play of Kyng Richard to be so old & so long out of use
as that they should have small or no Company at yt." The players
were finally persuaded by the conspirators, and their performance
was rewarded according to the financially advantageous terms agreed
upon: they "had their xl*s*. more then their ordynary for yt and so
played yt accordyngly." The players were to receive from the conspirators more than their usual take from a public performance, and that
profit would have been over and above whatever they took in from
the ordinary paying customers who may also have attended. Although
the topic was potentially inflammatory, it was also the case that *Richard II* had already been allowed for public performance and for subsequent printing by the licensing authorities—although not, perhaps,

without prior censorship.[69] As I have already noted, the title page of
the first quarto (1597) claims to present the play "As it hath been
publikely acted by the right Honourable the Lorde Chamberlaine his
Servants." The printing of a second and then a third quarto in the
next year, 1598, was unprecedented for a Shakespearean play at this
date, and suggests an unusually strong reader interest.[70] This demand
presumably came from the same politic readership that, a few months
later, would be so eager to obtain copies of Hayward's *Life and Raigne
of King Henrie IIII*.[71] Thus, we may have reason to suspect that Phillips was being somewhat disingenuous when he claimed, in 1601,

69. Some 160 lines of the so-called "deposition scene" of *Richard II* (4.1) appear for the first time in print in the 1608 Quarto, which on the title page adver-
tises the additional material and the play's recent staging: "With new additions of
the Parliament Sceane, and the deposing of King Richard. As it hath been lately
acted by the Kinges Majesties Servantes, at the Globe." It is usually assumed that
the additions in the 1608 text were part of the original version and were performed
during the reign of Elizabeth but that the scene was censored in the Elizabethan
printed editions. For a justifiably skeptical view of these assumptions, see Barroll,
"A New History for Shakespeare and His Time," 448–49. For a recent critical
review of the issues, see Clare, *"Art made tongue-tied by authority,"* 47–51; Dutton,
Mastering the Revels, 124–27.

70. Whatever the bases of reader demand—whether entertainment, edifica-
tion, or conspiracy—the primary motive of the Lord Chamberlain's Men in
allowing their precious playscript to be printed was presumably financial. This
was a critical juncture in the company's history and fortunes: The Burbages' lease
on the Theatre property ran out in April 1597 and could not be renewed; at the
same time, the company was being prevented from performing in the Blackfriars
property that James Burbage had purchased and refurbished for their use. As
Andrew Gurr has pointed out, "the players shared the problem of their financier's
lack of cash. The release of several Shakespeare playbooks, *Richard III*, *Richard
II*, *1 Henry IV* and *Love's Labour's Lost*, amongst the most popular plays in their
repertoire, to the publisher Andrew Wise in 1597 and 1598 was a cash-raising device they had never used before and never used again. The shortage of cash and
the lack of a playhouse were the crisis out of which the Globe was born" ("Money
or Audiences: The Impact of Shakespeare's Globe," 7).

The convergence of artistic, commercial, and political forces that is evident in
the printing of *Richard II* aptly illustrates that, within the society of Elizabethan
England, the status of the theatres and their plays, as well as the status of the
players and their dramatists, was at once powerfully determined and radically contingent.

71. Evidence for a strong reader demand derives from the testimony of John
Wolfe, the printer of Hayward's history, when he was examined by Attorney Gen-

that the play was "so old & so long out of use as that they should have small or no Company at yt." The motivations of the players do not seem to have been *political*—if we construe that term narrowly, to mean actively promoting the agenda of a particular faction. The players' motives were, nevertheless, shaped by considerations of a distinctly *ideological* character. More precisely, in agreeing to perform the play in their public playhouse, the Lord Chamberlain's Men seem to have been motivated by a combination of social deference and commercial gain. The players' acceptance of the conspirators' commission exemplifies the unstable conjunction of patronage-based and market-based modes of cultural production that was characteristic of the public and professional theatre; it aptly manifests the ambiguous status of the Shakespearean stage within the shifting socioeconomic and cognitive frameworks of late Elizabethan England.

---

eral Coke on 13 July 1600. Wolfe testified that "500 or 600 copies were sold before" the Bishop's order was received, "as no book ever sold better. After receiving such order, cut out the epistle and the residue, being 500 or 600, sold shortly after." A few weeks later, a second, revised edition of 1500 copies, prefaced by an "epistle apologetical," was readied for sale, "the people calling for it exceedingly," but it was confiscated and burned by the authorities. See *Calendar of State Papers Domestic*, 1598–1601, vol. 278, art. 28, pp. 450–51.

CHAPTER SIX

◗
•

THE POWER OF PERSONATION

I

In his *Chronicles of England, Scotland, and Ireland* (1587), Holinshed
reports that, in her response to a parliamentary petition for the execution of Mary, Queen of Scots, Queen Elizabeth told the joint delegation of lords and commons, "we princes . . . are set on stages, in the
sight and view of all the world dulie observed; the eies of manie behold our actions; a spot is soone spied in our garments; a blemish
quicklie noted in our dooings."[72] The putative royal phrase, "we
princes . . . are set on stages, in the sight and view of all the world,"
has sometimes been invoked to epitomize what Stephen Greenblatt
has called "the whole theatrical apparatus of royal power" and to
make the point that "Elizabethan power . . . depends upon its privileged visibility."[73] Indeed, Greenblatt goes so far as to suggest that,
because "a poetics of Elizabethan power" is synonymous with "a
poetics of the theater," the drama produced in the Elizabethan public theatres is always already co-opted by the state: "It is precisely
because of the English form of absolutist theatricality that Shakespeare's drama, written for a theater subject to state censorship, can

72. "A Report of Hir Majesties most gratious answer, delivered by hir selfe
verballie . . . in hir chamber of presence at Richmond, the twelfe daie of November 1586," in *Holinshed's Chronicles of England, Scotland, and Ireland*, 6 vols. (1808;
rpt., New York: AMS Press, 1965), 4:934.
73. For the first quotation, see Stephen Greenblatt, *Renaissance Self-Fashioning*
(Chicago: University of Chicago Press, 1980), 167; for the second, Greenblatt,
Shakespearean Negotiations, 64. The Queen's speech is invoked in each instance.
The latter citation occurs near the end of a chapter focused on the second tetralogy of Shakespeare's English histories ("Invisible Bullets," *Shakespearean Negotiations*, 21–65).

be so relentlessly subversive: the form itself, as a primary expression of Renaissance power, helps to contain the radical doubts it continually provokes" (*Shakespearean Negotiations*, 64, 65).

Richard Helgerson has recently rewritten the extreme form of the new historicist containment argument, disassociating it from the Elizabethan theatre in general, only in order to attach it more firmly and censoriously to Shakespeare specifically. Helgerson poses Shakespeare as the exemplar of an emergent, elitist "author's theater" that betrayed its popular roots and sought socioeconomic advancement by pandering to the pleasures and prejudices of the court and the monarch.[74] The focus of his analysis is upon Shakespeare's English histories, which, he charges, "subjected commoners to a steady stream of abuse, turned radical protest to ridicule, undermined the sympathetic union of high and low, associated carnival with rebellion and clowns with criminal misrule, mocked or ignored the values of ballad history, and all the while celebrated (even as they questioned) the power and mystery of state" (241). That parenthetical qualification should give us pause. Earlier in his argument, Helgerson has taken Shakespeare to task because

> the central problematic of Shakespeare's history plays concerns the consolidation of monarchic rule. Legitimacy and efficacy are the main points at issue. . . .
> But while achieving his obsessive and compelling focus on the ruler, Shakespeare excluded another object of concern, the ruled. Identifying himself, his plays, his company, and his audience with the problematics of early modern kingship, he left out of consideration the no less pressing problematics of subjecthood. (238–39)

One might, of course, question the censure of Shakespeare for what he didn't write about, but what I would question is the basic claim that Shakespeare is unconcerned with the "problematics of subjecthood." When Helgerson writes that "Shakespeare's history plays are concerned above all with the consolidation and maintenance of royal power" (234), he implies that to be so concerned is *ipso facto* to support and celebrate such power. It seems to me that his argument gives insufficient weight to the fact that Shakespeare, his company, and his audience were all subjects of the early modern monarchical

---

74. See Richard Helgerson, *Forms of Nationhood: The Elizabethan Writing of England* (Chicago: University of Chicago Press, 1992), 195–245.

state; that such subjects collaborated in producing, by and for themselves, acute theatrical anatomies of the political processes to which they were subjected; and that by doing so, they were demonstrating a serious and sophisticated concern with the "problematics" of their own "subjecthood."[75]

In this chapter and throughout this book, I wish to resist arguments that bind the practices of the professional Elizabethan theatre to the practices of the Elizabethan state and that bind Shakespearean theatricality to political absolutism.[76] Being without the benefit of recent arguments for the containment of subversion, Queen Eliza-

75. Part of the problem with Helgerson's argument is that, like many other recent discussions of the Elizabethan theatre, it is grounded in reductive binary oppositions—in this case, between a players' theatre and an authors' theatre, between popular and elite cultures. Helgerson's extreme claim that, in the society of Shakespeare's England, "between the extremes of high and low, noble and base, there was only semiotic vacancy, a noplace without meaning" (206), wholly effaces the vast "middling sort" whose culture, values, and interests were by no means semiotically unrepresented. For a sense of the various, contradictory, and relatively nuanced terms in which contemporaries represented the early modern social fabric, see David Cressy, "Describing the Social Order of Elizabethan and Stuart England," *Literature and History* 3 (1976), 29–44; Keith Wrightson, "The Social Order of Early Modern England: Three Approaches," in *The World We Have Gained: Histories of Population and Social Structure*, ed. Lloyd Bonfield, Richard M. Smith, and Keith Wrightson (Oxford: Basil Blackwell, 1986), 177–202; Keith Wrightson, "Estates, degrees, and sorts: changing perceptions of society in Tudor and Stuart England," in *Language, History and Class*, ed. Penelope J. Corfield (Oxford: Basil Blackwell, 1991), 30–52; also see Theodore Leinwand, "Shakespeare and the Middling Sort," *Shakespeare Quarterly* 44 (1993), 284–303. Helgerson seems to acknowledge that the ideological positioning of the theatre and of Shakespeare within it may have been rather more complex, when he remarks in passing that "the commercialism of the public theater, may in the long run have been more radically disruptive than any popular revolt" (230).

76. Stephen Orgel, *The Illusion of Power: Political Theater in the English Renaissance*, is a seminal study of the politics of Renaissance theatricality that is focused upon the spectacular theatre of the Stuart court. Orgel's work had a formative influence on much of the criticism, usually labelled "New Historicist," that was produced in the United States beginning in the late 1970s—including my own. However, his insights into the workings of absolutist court theatricality were sometimes inappropriately extended by others into the political dynamics of the popular theatre.

The view that an absolutist Elizabethan-Jacobean state allows or produces subversion so as to further its own hegemony is derived from a particular reading

beth failed to appreciate that the drama was safely in hand. Consider, for example, the celebrated remark, "I am Richard II. know ye not that?" This pointed observation may suggest that she shared with the members of the Essex circle a habit of reading histories that found analogies and parallels between the shape of the past and the shape of the present. However, as the rest of the Queen's putative conversation with William Lambarde makes emphatically clear, she found the ideological implications of Tacitism to be not only seditious but sacrilegious:

---

of Foucault and is most closely associated with Greenblatt's work, and in particular, with the essay, "Invisible Bullets" (1985), rpt. in Greenblatt, *Shakespearean Negotiations*, 21–65; see, in particular, 64–65, from which I quote at the beginning of this section. For a similar perspective, see Tennenhouse, *Power on Display*, esp. 15; Christopher Pye, *The Regal Phantasm: Shakespeare and the Politics of Spectacle* (London: Routledge, 1990), esp. 43–44.

Writing in response to those like Greenblatt who suggested that the Elizabethan-Jacobean theatre was an instrument of the absolutist state, some critics have argued for the other side of the binary opposition, for a fundamentally contestatory or subversive relationship of the theatre and its drama to the absolutist state and to the providentialist ideology underpinning it. The contrary argument for a subversive theatre is made in stimulating if schematic fashion in Jonathan Dollimore, *Radical Tragedy: Religion, Ideology and Power in the Drama of Shakespeare and his Contemporaries* (Chicago: University of Chicago Press, 1984); and in a provocative essay by Franco Moretti, "'A Huge Eclipse': Tragic Form and the Deconsecration of Sovereignty," in *The Forms of Power and the Power of Forms in the Renaissance*, 7–40. Both of these studies focus upon the ideological implications of a particular dramatic genre and the content of particular plays, rather than upon the ideological implications of such cultural practices as playwriting, playing, playgoing, and play-hating.

For an especially astute and flexible analysis of the relationship of Elizabethan tragedy to religious and political orthodoxy, see "Tragedy, God, and Writing: *Hamlet, Faustus, Tamburlaine*," in Alan Sinfield, *Faultlines: Cultural Materialism and the Politics of Dissident Reading* (Berkeley: University of California Press, 1992), 214–51. Sinfield stresses that "state intervention in writing was actually intermittent," that "writers, as a category, might well find themselves situated at a point of conflicting affiliation and hence relative autonomy," and that "the boundaries of expression were differently set for different groups and at different political conjunctures" (247–48). My own perspective on the ideological location of the Elizabethan theatre coincides with Sinfield's. In the Prologue to this book, I have provided a more extended discussion and critique of the *subversion/containment* opposition and the relationship between Foucauldian and New Historicist perspectives.

W. L.   'Such a wicked imagination was determined and
           attempted by a most unkind Gent. the most adorned
           creature that ever your Majestie made.'
Her   'He that will forget God, will also forget his benefactors;
Majestie. this tragedy was played 40tie times in open streets and
           houses.'[77]

As David Kastan has pointed out, Lambarde's use of the term "imagination" has a legal force, since the Tudor law of treason defined it in
part as the "imagining and compassing of the death of a king."[78] Like
the power of the imagination in Lambarde's usage, the power of the
theatre in Queen Elizabeth's usage may take on an instrumental
force. The Queen's reference to "this tragedy . . . played 40tie times
in open streets and houses" has often been taken literally by literary
historians, as referring to multiple performances of a tragic drama on
the subject of Richard II, despite the implausible implications of
such a reading. The attributed royal remark seems to me to make
better sense when taken metaphorically, as an application of the *theatrum mundi* trope to the recurrent enactment of treason in a theatre-
state in which "princes . . . are set on stages, in the sight and view of
all the world." In this sense, the remark attributed to the Queen is
cognate with Bacon's description of Sir Gelly Meyricke's "wicked
imagination": "so earnest hee was to satisfie his eyes with the sight
of that tragedie which hee thought soone after his lord should bring
from the stage to the state."

Let me return to my initial quotation from Queen Elizabeth's reputed speech of 1586, which strongly suggests that the "privileged
visibility" of royal power also entails potential liabilities, that visibility implies vulnerability. The ironic tenor of the Queen's observation
is that her privileged position exposes her to "the sight and view of

77. "That which passed from the Excellent Majestie of Queen Elizabeth, in
her Privie Chamber at East Greenwich, 4 Augusti 1601, 43 Reg. sui, towards William Lambarde," printed in Chambers, *William Shakespeare*, 2:326–27.

78. See David Scott Kastan, "Proud Majesty Made a Subject: Shakespeare
and the Spectacle of Rule," *Shakespeare Quarterly* 37 (1986), 459–75; quotation
from 473. Also see John Bellamy, *The Tudor Law of Treason* (London: Routledge &
Kegan Paul, 1979), 9–82. As Kastan remarks, "Certainly both Essex and Elizabeth
understood the playing of *Richard II* on the eve of the rebellion as part of the
treasonous imagining, as an invitation to the populace to participate—either in
the fiction or in fact—in the deposition of an anointed king" (472).

all the world . . . the eies of manie": It subjects her to the scrutiny of her own subjects and solicits the approbation of her inferiors. As Queen Elizabeth herself seems ruefully to have understood, to set princes on public stages meant in practice that the state could not fully control the charismatic royal image. Thus, there was good reason why the state was hostile to explicit personations of the reigning monarch upon the public stage and sought to regulate strictly all iconic and verbal representations of the Queen. Greatness could be, and routinely was, appropriated for representation within an affective and commercial transaction between the players and their common audiences. A significant segment of the audiences for whom princes were set on stages was made up of what Sir Thomas Smith classified as "the fourth sort or classe amongest us." According to Smith, this sort included "marchantes or retailers which have no free lande, copiholders, and all artificers. . . . These have no voice nor authoritie in our common wealth, and no account is made of them but onelie to be ruled, not rule other."[79] Other significant segments of the popular theatre audiences whom its players and playwrights sought to please—namely, women, servants, and apprentices—did not even rate a mention from Smith. Nevertheless, despite the exclusion of all these groups from what constituted the Elizabethan political nation, payment of a penny might entitle some of them to observe and to judge the player-kings who were allowed their "little scene, / To monarchize" (*Richard II*, 3.2.164–65) upon the public stages.[80] When

79. Thomas Smith, *De Republica Anglorum* (1583), ed. L. Alston (1906; rpt., Shannon: Irish University Press, 1972), 46.

80. For a recent, judicious, and comprehensive discussion of the social composition, personal comportment, and dramatic tastes of the Elizabethan playgoing public, see Gurr, *Playgoing in Shakespeare's London*. In his discussion of women playgoers (55–63), Gurr notes that they formed a "high proportion" of the audiences, and that "women from every section of society went to plays" (55, 57). On the presence of women in large numbers in the paying audiences of the public theatres, and its possible ideological and material consequences for the players and their repertories, see Jean E. Howard, "Scripts and/versus Playhouses: Ideological Production and the Renaissance Public Stage," *Renaissance Drama*, n. s., 20 (1989), 31–49; rpt. in *The Matter of Difference: Materialist Feminist Criticism of Shakespeare*, ed. Valerie Wayne (Ithaca: Cornell University Press, 1991), 221–36; and now republished in revised form in Howard, *The Stage and Social Struggle in Early Modern England*, 73–92. Also see Richard Levin, "Women in the Renaissance Theatre Audience," *Shakespeare Quarterly* 40 (1989), 165–74.

the Earl of Essex complained to Queen Elizabeth, during his con-
finement in 1600, that "shortly they will play me in what forms they
list upon the stage," he addressed one who fully understood the nature of his concern.[81] In the case of Essex or Elizabeth (as in the
metatheatrical case of Shakespeare's defeated Cleopatra), the performativity of power is a mystery of state, and the prospect of losing
control over one's self-presentation arouses palpable alarm.

In the contemptuous words of Shakespeare's Henry V, the effect
of such public theatrical transactions was to make "greatness, subject
to the breath / Of every fool" (*Henry V,* 4.1.232–33). The immediate
object of Henry's private scorn is a soldier whom he has encountered
while walking, incognito, through the English camp on the night before the battle of Agincourt. Michael Williams—a common subject,
but one whom Shakespeare by no means represents as a fool—is
drawn into a conversation with "Henry le Roy," during the course of
which he presumes to question the honor of King Henry. Alone now,
on the night before the battle, the King voices his disdain for the
subjects whom he will exhort as his "brothers" (4.3.60) on the following morning. Of course, the king is, in actuality, not alone; as the
metatheatricality of the Choruses in *Henry V* so insistently reminds
us, the King is also subject to the breath of the mere player who
personates him and to the imaginative capacities of the paying auditors to whom he is played: "For 'tis your thoughts that now must
deck our kings" (Prologue, 28). The Prologue to *Henry V* makes perhaps the most explicit Shakespearean appeal to the contractual relationship between playwright, players, and audience in the production
of theatrical illusion and to the imaginative authority of the common
subject in constituting the political authority of the sovereign. Shakespeare's popular play *The Life of King Henry the Fifth* is (at least, in its
folio version) by turns a trenchant anatomy and an enthusiastic display of performative kingship. And in the scene under discussion,
soliloquy is so deployed as to require its sovereign personage to make
his own resentful acknowledgment of his subjection to representation.[82]

81. A letter of 12 May 1600, printed in *Calender of State Papers, Domestic,* vol.
274, item 138; quoted in Chambers, *Elizabethan Stage,* 1:324–25.

82. These observations are not meant to deny that the play's representation
of King Henry is heroic. However, the heroic royal image is only clear, consistent,
and unequivocal when the play is subjected to selective editing. In fact, we cannot

King Henry's soliloquy emphasizes the heavy burdens of kingship:

> We must bear all. O hard condition,
> Twin-born with greatness, subject to the breath
> Of every fool, whose sense no more can feel
> But his own wringing! What infinite heartsease
> Must kings neglect that private men enjoy!
> And what have kings that privates have not too,
> Save ceremony, save general ceremony?
> And what art thou, thou idol ceremony?

---

be sure when or if Elizabethan audiences actually heard the king's private remark:
The play's first quarto (1600), which appears to be the memorial reconstruction of
a substantially abridged performing version, cuts in its entirety the soliloquy in
question, as well as the Prologue and the other Choruses. Also cut from the quarto
are three full scenes (1.1, 3.1, 4.2), and parts of several other scenes. All of these
appear in the folio text—which, textual scholars generally agree, is derived from
the playwright's draft. For a summary of the textual problems, see Gary Taylor's
Introduction to his edition of *Henry V* in The Oxford Shakespeare (Oxford: Oxford
University Press, 1982), 12–26.

See Annabel Patterson, *Shakespeare and the Popular Voice* (Cambridge, Massachusetts and Oxford: Basil Blackwell, 1989), 71–92, for an interesting discussion
of the implications of the differences between the quarto and folio versions. Patterson's analysis focuses upon the celebratory allusion to the Earl of Essex in the
Chorus to Act Five, in the context of the Hayward controversy and the subsequent
insurrection. The quarto text significantly reduces—although it certainly does not
wholly expunge—the elements in the folio text that are dissonant with the
martial-heroic theme. The quarto title runs: "The Cronicle History of Henry the
fift, With his battell fought at *Agin Court* in *France*. Togither with *Auntient Pistoll*.
*As it hath sundry times been played by the Right honorable the Lord Chamberlaine his ser-
vants*." As is suggested by the title's highlighting of a famous battle victory and a
memorable comic role from the *Henry IV* plays, the emphasis of the quarto text is
patriotic, martial, and comic—a sure-fire formula for a popular success. Thus, as I
have suggested in discussing the performance of *Richard II* on the eve of the Essex
revolt, the artistic decisions of the Lord Chamberlain's Men and their playwright
were at least as likely to be directed by commercial as by explicitly political considerations—which is not to suggest that such commercial considerations were
without ideological implications.

For the Q1 and F texts of *Henry V*, I have used, respectively: *Shakespeare's Plays
in Quarto: A Facsimile Edition of Copies Primarily from the Henry E. Huntington Library*, ed. Michael J. B. Allen and Kenneth Muir (Berkeley: University of California Press, 1981); and *The First Folio of Shakespeare: The Norton Facsimile*, prep.
Charlton Hinman (New York: W. W. Norton, 1968).

> . . .
> What is thy soul of adoration?
> Art thou aught else but place, degree, and form,
> Creating awe and fear in other men?
>
> (*Henry V,* 4.1.231–38, 243–45)

The King's ambivalent apostrophe to "thou idol ceremony"—with its subsequent invocation of

> the balm, the scepter, and the ball,
> The sword, the mace, the crown imperial,
> The intertissued robe of gold and pearl,
> The farcèd title running 'fore the king
>
> (258–61)

—evokes both the polemical religious discourse against images, vestments, and plays, and the politic Machiavellian discourse on the utility of state spectacles. Indeed, Henry's judgment that the essence of royal ceremony is to create "awe and fear in other men" accords with the opinion that Richard Baines attributed to Christopher Marlowe: "That the first beginning of Religioun was only to keep men in awe." It is one thing for the drama of the public theatres to imitate the practice of ceremonial mystification by monarchs, and something quite different for it to combine that miming with an anatomy of the practice being mimed, an anatomy that is placed in the mouth of the monarch himself. By allowing his common audience in the public theatre to listen to the King's soliloquy, the playwright is making them privy to the secrets of state.

Sir Henry Wotton appreciated the dangers of demystification that attended the setting of princes on stages. The context is a letter in which he relates the accidental destruction of the Globe by fire during a performance of Shakespeare's *Henry VIII:*

> The Kings's players had a new play, called *All is true,* representing some principal pieces of the reign of Henry VIII, which was set forth with many extraordinary circumstances of pomp and majesty, even to the matting of the stage; the Knights of the order with their Georges and garters, the Guards with their embroidered coats, and the like: sufficient in truth within a while to make greatness very familiar, if not ridiculous.[83]

83. Letter to Sir Edmund Bacon, 2 July 1613, in Logan Pearsall Smith, *The Life and Letters of Sir Henry Wotton,* 2:32–33. Also see Orgel, "Making Greatness

It is not without interest that Wotton's observation is provoked by the performance of a play on the subject of English dynastic history, one that concludes by celebrating the birth of the reigning King's immediate predecessor, Elizabeth Tudor. Nevertheless, the possibly subversive political content of this or any other particular play is not at issue here. Wotton remarks upon a potential challenge to the authority of the great that is specifically stylistic and formal. Whereas Wotton observes the process of mystification at work in the Venetian Corpus Christi pageantry, he observes the process of *de*mystification at work at the Globe. The difference would seem to lie in whether the medium of representation and the means of cultural production are in the hands of the state or in those of its subjects. His concern is focused upon the inherent capacity of dramatic representation in the public theatre—even when ostensibly celebratory in its text and entrusted to "the King's players" for its performance—to appropriate and to demystify what Greenblatt calls the "absolutist theatricality" of the monarchy, and to do so by the very process of staging it.

Thus, if "kingship always involves fictions, theatricalism, and the mystification of power" (Greenblatt, *Renaissance Self-Fashioning,* 167), then fiction and theatricalism may also be the very media through which royal power is demystified. The "poetics of the theater" is founded upon an opposition and dialogical interplay of characters, interests, and ideologies. Through various formal means, the drama enacted in the Elizabethan playhouses creates a multiplicity of perspectives. Yet within the context of an absolutist ideology, such multiplicity signified an inherent capacity to produce heterodoxy. A practical consequence of theatrical illusion was that it could provide some measure of protection against the censorship, suppression, and punishment that otherwise threatened a cultural practice that was *formally disposed* to put into question absolutist and univocal claims. Thus, I would propose that any "poetics of Elizabethan power" must be founded upon a recognition that such power does not inhere fully and exclusively in the theatricality of the state and that "the English form of absolutist theatricality" that characterizes the ideology of Elizabethan-Jacobean monarchy is less likely to be reinforced than it

---

Familiar," in *The Forms of Power and the Power of Forms in the Renaissance;* and Kastan, "Proud Majesty Made a Subject: Shakespeare and the Spectacle of Rule."

is to be destabilized when it is represented in the Shakespearean theatre.

II

Writing in reaction against the now dominant critical tendency to politicize Renaissance drama—whether as an instrument of contestation or of containment, Paul Yachnin has recently claimed that the Elizabethan-Jacobean theatre was fundamentally irrelevant to issues of power and that it cultivated its own irrelevance. Thus, he asserts that,

> as a result of both the vigor of Elizabethan government censorship and the compliance of the players with that censorship, the theater of the late Elizabethan and early Stuart period came to be viewed as powerless, unable to influence its audience in any purposeful or determinate way. The dramatic companies won from the government precisely what the government was most willing to give: a privileged, profitable, and powerless marginality.[84]

Such a conclusion goes against the massive evidence—briefly surveyed in chapters 3 and 4 above—that many guardians of Elizabethan religious, social, and political orthodoxy thought that the theatre was very powerful indeed and that it was powerful in the worst possible way. Furthermore, the persistent concern of the state to regulate the drama, even while tolerating or supporting it, does not argue for the perception that it was a trivial and impotent cultural practice.

Yachnin argues further that

> the acquisition of their own theaters had the peculiar effect . . . of liberating the players from their dependence upon aristocratic sponsors and so freeing them to address a variety of topics in an objective spirit, and, at the same time, of diminishing the power of the theater to influence the political issues about which it was now free to speak. (60)

It is an overstatement to characterize the players as suddenly liberated from dependence upon aristocratic patronage by their acquisi-

---

84. Paul Yachnin, "The Powerless Theater," *English Literary Renaissance* 21 (1991), 49–74; quotation from 50. This essay is both thoughtful and provocative, and I have benefitted from finding so much in it with which to disagree.

tion of playhouses.[85] After all, there is considerable and familiar evidence to affirm that the commercial theatre—and Shakespeare's company, in particular—continued to maintain an important relationship to aristocratic and royal patronage, both financial and legal, throughout the Elizabethan-Jacobean period. It is undoubtedly true that the formal and thematic horizons of the drama were enlarged by the increasing socioeconomic heterogeneity of its audience. However, the consequence of such a change must surely have been to *complicate* the ideological positioning of the professional theatre and its repertoire, not to *neutralize* it. The commercial theatrical companies of Elizabethan London were attempting to articulate and to satisfy the collective desires of an increasingly large and diverse potential market. The venture undertaken by the Elizabethan entertainment industry was hardly disinterested; it had not left all ideology behind but was rather in the vanguard of an emergent ideology, that of entrepreneurial capitalism.[86] When Yachnin associates the commodification of Elizabethan drama with the achievement of objectivity and freedom, he is writing from a position within a later phase of that same ideology.

It has sometimes been claimed that the salient point about the role of the theatre in the Essex conspiracy is that, in failing to catalyze a rebellion, it proved itself to be merely ineffectual and irrelevant. Thus, as an example of the players' paradoxical liberation into powerlessness, Yachnin cites Shakespeare's *Richard II*, and its performance on the eve of the Essex revolt: "*Richard II* is able to represent politi-

85. If by "the acquisition of their own theatres" is meant outright ownership of the actual playing structures, then the number of players involved is extremely small—perhaps half of the total being the half dozen "housekeepers" in the Lord Chamberlain's/King's Men. See G. E. Bentley, *The Profession of Player in Shakespeare's Time*, 5–6.

86. For stimulating explorations of the relationship between the Elizabethan-Jacobean theatre and the emergence of merchant capitalism, see Don E. Wayne, "Drama and Society in the Age of Jonson: Shifting Grounds of Authority and Judgment in Three Major Comedies," *Renaissance Drama* 13 (1982), rpt. in *Renaissance Drama as Cultural History: Essays from* Renaissance Drama *1977–1987*, ed. Mary Beth Rose, 3–29; Jean-Christophe Agnew, *Worlds Apart: The Market and the Theater in Anglo-American Thought, 1550–1750* (Cambridge: Cambridge University Press, 1986); Douglas Bruster, *Drama and the Market in the Age of Shakespeare* (Cambridge: Cambridge University Press, 1992).

cal issues openly by producing a political message which is depoliticized (that is, incapable of exerting determinate political influence) by virtue of being bifurcated, or two-faced" (66). Here Yachnin makes clear that what he intends by the sweeping and provocative claim that the theatre was powerless is the hardly controversial point that it could not effectively shape and control the specific political opinions and behaviors of all those in its audience. To frame the issues in terms of drastic antinomies—between "determinate political influence" and "powerlessness" or between political "power" and the "freedom" of artistic disinterestedness—is to foreclose upon an analysis of the more mediated and subtle ways in which the Elizabethan theatre appropriated, shaped, questioned, and publicly disseminated socially significant meanings, values, and beliefs.

According to Yachnin, "the overall meaning or point of view" of *Richard II* "is designed to be indeterminate, open to a range of interpretations arrayed along an axis between orthodoxy, providentialism, and hierarchy at one pole and subversion, Realpolitik, and revolution at the other" (66). It is a critical commonplace that this play takes a multiple perspective upon the historical events which it represents.[87] But this critical commonplace must, itself, be historicized. The multiplicity of perspective characteristic of Shakespeare's plays has been construed, according to the canons of modern literary criticism, as a hallmark of Shakespeare's ambivalence and complexity; it has been celebrated as the achievement of negative capability, universal humanity, aesthetic disinterestedness, intellectual inquisitiveness, and/ or the transcendence of ideology. In an Elizabethan context, however, such characteristics may have had a more precise and consequential ideological valence. The providentialist doctrine that pro-

---

87. For a classic statement, stressing a "dialectic" of "one-eyed" oversimplifications of perspective in the history plays, an "ambivalence" that is ultimately resolved in the Shakespearean plenitude, see A. P. Rossiter, *Angel with Horns* (1951; rpt., London: Longmans, Green, 1961), 40–64. The "morality" of Shakespeare's "political agnosticism," is argued in Wilbur Sanders's stimulating study, *The Dramatist and the Received Idea: Studies in the Plays of Marlowe and Shakespeare* (Cambridge: Cambridge University Press, 1968), 143–93. For a recent discussion, stressing the contradictions among the ideologies available to Shakespeare, see the chapter on "Ideological Conflict, Alternative Plots, and the Problem of Historical Causation," in Phyllis Rackin, *Stages of History: Shakespeare's English Chronicles* (Ithaca: Cornell University Press, 1990), 40–85.

vided the interpretive framework for a central strain of Tudor historiography was also the basis for both the political discourse that legitimated the Elizabethan state and the personality-cult that exalted the Queen. As is made abundantly clear by so basic and widely disseminated a text as the official "Exhortacion concernyng Good Ordre and Obedience to Rulers and Magistrates," the principles of "orthodoxy, providentialism, and hierarchy"—which formed the core of this dominant discourse on Elizabethan state power—made no allowance whatsoever for alternatives or for indeterminacy: "Where there is no right ordre, there reigneth all abuse, carnell libertie, enormitie, syn and babilonicall confusion" (*Certain Sermons or Homilies,* 161). Those who advocated, or appeared to advocate, "subversion, Realpolitik, and revolution"—whether in print or in action—were guilty of sedition and were frequently deemed to be satanic agents or to be merely depraved; they were subject to whatever modes of control and punishment the regime could muster.

The tacitly antiprovidentialist *realpolitik* that was of immediate relevance to Shakespeare's *Richard II* and to the scholars and courtiers in the Essex circle was based upon the *politique* reading and contemporary application of Tacitus's Roman history.[88] Mervyn James characterizes Renaissance Tacitism as

88. A foundational text was provided by Sir Henry Savile's 1591 translation of Tacitus's *Agricola* and the first four books of the *Historiae,* with a commentary, an original essay on the Roman art of war, and a prefatory narrative history, "The Ende of Nero and Beginning of Galba," meant to account for events between the end of Tacitus's *Annales* and the beginning of his *Historiae.* It was in his original narrative of the revolt against Nero that Savile formulated a heterodox position on resistance to monarchs. See the important article by David Womersley, "Sir Henry Savile's Translation of Tacitus and the Political Interpretation of Elizabethan Texts," *Review of English Studies,* n. s., 42 (1991), 313–42. Womersley writes that Savile

> seeks to rescue the act of resistance to a monarch from the status of a hideous irruption of chaos, and instead to present it, in the manner of the Huguenot political thinkers, as a political and legal act like any other which does not necessarily involve any rending of the fabric of national political life. It would be difficult to overstate the vigour and abruptness with which this challenges the prevailing political orthodoxies of late sixteenth-century England. (329)

Savile, the Warden of Merton College, Oxford, had connections to Essex's secretary, Henry Cuffe, whom the Earl subsequently accused of leading him into sedition, and also with Essex himself, who had extended his patronage and (according to Ben Jonson in his *Conversations*) had authored the prefatory "A. B. to the

the "politic" art by means of which the historical actor, his will powered by passion and interest, attained his objectives, which were understood in terms of the pursuit and preservation of dominance. . . . History simply became a field for the play of the heroic energy of the autonomous political will, seeking to dominate events by its command of the politic arts. It was an approach which, by comparison with that of the providentialist historian, could be thought of as "atheist"; for the historical actors it presented were seen as released from the sanctions and controls imposed by morality and law, and underwritten by religion. (*Society, Politics and Culture*, 421)

Hayward's Tacitean perspective on the downfall of Richard II was fundamentally secular, pragmatic, and relativist. In the formulation of F. J. Levy, "Hayward's book was the first realization in England of a history in which the causes of events were seen in terms of the interrelationship of politics and character rather than in terms of the working out of God's providence."[89] The Elizabethan government might have regarded such a perspective as dangerously heterodox under any circumstances; it was certain to regard it as seditious when the context was English rather than Roman history; when the pivotal event was the deposition of an anointed king; and when the consequence of usurpation was the establishment of the Lancastrian dynasty, through which the Tudors traced their own tenuous hereditary claim to the throne. Shakespeare's *Richard II* does not explicitly *advocate* a Tacitean understanding of history and government, any more than it advocates the acts of "subversion, Realpolitik, and revolution" that it also represents. Instead, the play incorporates both providentialist and *politique* paradigms as opposing structures of meaning, through which particular characters apprehend the shape of history; it mobilizes these paradigms as the conflicting terms in which characters enact and interpret the events in which they are enmeshed.

Reader" for Savile's edition of Tacitus. Following the Earl's revolt, Savile was put under restraint by order of the Privy Council.

89. See F. J. Levy, "Hayward, Daniel, and the Beginnings of Politic History in England," *Huntington Library Quarterly* 50 (1987), 1–34; quotation from 2. I am also indebted to David Womersley, "Sir John Hayward's Tacitism," *Renaissance Studies* 6 (1992), 46–59. On the habits of reading in the Essex circle, which applied classical histories to current political conditions, also see Lisa Jardine and Anthony Grafton, "'Studied for Action': How Gabriel Harvey Read His Livy," *Past & Present* 129 (November 1990), 30–78.

There is a rhetorical basis for the dialectical nature of Elizabethan dramatic form in the intellectual interplay of debating positions that was cultivated in the humanist academic curriculum of the time.[90] The plays of the professional theatre motivate such positions in terms of conflicts existing among, and within, human characters; and they incarnate these characters-in-conflict in professional players who interact upon a stage. Andrew Gurr has pointed out that, partly as a consequence of the professionalization of playing, the art of characterization seems to have undergone a dramatic change of its own by the end of the sixteenth century, a change that may be apprehended in a significant terminological shift:

> In the sixteenth century the term "acting" was originally used to describe the "action" of the orator, his art of gesture. What the common stages offered was "playing." . . . What the players were presenting on stage by the beginning of the [seventeenth] century was distinctive enough to require a whole new term to describe it. This term, the noun "personation," is suggestive of a relatively new art of individual characterisation, an art distinct from the orator's display of passions or the academic actor's portrayal of the character-types. . . . The first use of the term "personation" is recorded . . . in 1599–1600, at the end of the great decade in which Alleyn and Burbage made their reputations. It is probably not stretching plausibility too far to suggest that the term was called into being by the same developments—in the kinds of parts given the actors to play and their own skill in their parts—that made two great tragedians succeed the extemporising clowns on the pinnacle of theatrical fame. By 1600 characterisation was the chief requisite of the successful player. (*Shakespearean Stage*, 99–100)

A significant formal and stylistic component of this emergent mode of characterization was the development of the soliloquy into an effective theatrical convention for the expression of interior conflict, dialogue, or meditation. Raymond Williams has observed that, in the later Elizabethan drama, the soliloquy instantiates "new and subtle modes and relationships" in characterization and in the dynamic between actors and audience; and that these "were in themselves developments in social practice, and are fundamentally connected with

90. On the homology between Elizabethan dramatic structure and rhetorical traditions of inquiry in humanist education, see Joel Altman, *The Tudor Play of Mind: Rhetorical Inquiry and the Development of Elizabethan Drama* (Berkeley: University of California Press, 1978).

the discovery, *in dramatic form*, of new and altered social relationships, perceptions of self and others, complex alternatives of private and public thought."[91] Williams resists the assumption that formal developments merely reflect social and ideological changes, insisting instead upon a dialectical mode of analysis: "The formal innovation is a true and integral element of the changes themselves: an articulation, by technical discovery, of changes in consciousness which are themselves forms of consciousness of change" (*Culture*, 142). Williams's conception of the reciprocal relationship between formal innovation and changes in consciousness is relevant not only to the device of the soliloquy but to the whole phenomenon of personation as it emerged in the drama of the late Elizabethan and Jacobean public and professional theatres.

In the culture of early modern England, the development of a professional and commercial theatre and the conceptual and practical establishment of dramatic personation were consonant with other material and ideological developments—capital accumulation, market calculation, contractual relations, and "possessive individualism"—that manifested the emergence of what we now characterize as merchant capitalism and bourgeois subjectivity.[92] More immediately and particularly, these theatrical developments coincided with the keen interest of the late Elizabethan sociopolitical and intellectual elites in the employment of Tacitean/Machiavellian paradigms in order to speculate upon the acquisition of power and the legitimation of authority, upon the relationship between agency and history, subjects and the state. Such an interest represented a conceptual challenge and a perceived political threat to the absolutist preten-

91. Raymond Williams, *Culture* (London: Fontana, 1981), 139–43; quotation from 142. Also see "On Dramatic Dialogue and Monologue (particularly in Shakespeare)," in Raymond Williams, *Writing in Society* (London: Verso, n.d.), 31–64.

92. On the ideological changes, focused upon the understanding of human nature, that heralded the emergence of capitalism and modernity in England, see C. B. Macpherson, *The Political Theory of Possessive Individualism, Hobbes to Locke* (Oxford: Oxford University Press, 1964); and Albert O. Hirschman, *The Passions and the Interests: Political Arguments for Capitalism before Its Triumph* (Princeton: Princeton University Press, 1978). On the complex relationship between these developments and the Renaissance theatre, see the important discussions in Wayne, "Drama and Society in the Age of Jonson"; and Agnew, *Worlds Apart*, 101–48.

sions of the sovereign. In comparison with the medieval civic religious drama, the professional drama of the Elizabethan commercial theatres marked a decisive shift in the coordination of playing dimensions: a reorientation of the dramaturgical axis from the vertical plane, which related earthly events to a divinely ordained master narrative, to the horizontal plane, upon which human characters interact within an imagined social space. This shift of emphasis from a metaphysical to a social dialectic implied that the temporal and mutable human realm of second causes had become the locus of dramatic action. And the increasing concern of players and dramatists with individual characterization in the motivation of dramatic action suggests that this mode of drama was especially congenial to Tacitean/Machiavellian views of historical process.

Like Mervyn James's use of the term "historical actor," F. J. Levy's use of the term "character" in his description of Hayward's Tacitism suggests that, in English history plays and tragedies of state—genres that were central to the late Elizabethan theatrical repertoire—the creation and motivation of characters was a cultural development of considerable philosophical and political import. The resonance is particularly suggestive in light of Levy's observation that Hayward's historical writing was both generally indebted to dramatic form and specifically influenced by the characterization of the royal actors in Shakespeare's history plays.[93] Whether or not Queen Elizabeth actually said that "we princes . . . are set on stages, in the sight and view of all the world dulie observed," the player-playwright who was her subject was likely to have read in Holinshed that she had. In any case, when he came to write his second tetralogy of English history plays, Shakespeare dramatized the theatricality of power as a recurrent contest among historical actors to control the *personation* of the King.[94]

93. On the possible debt of Hayward's printed history of Henry IV to Shakespeare's *Richard II*, see Levy, "Hayward, Daniel, and the Beginnings of Politic History in England," 16, 19; and, on the possible debt of his unfinished and unpublished continuation of the history to the later plays of Shakespeare's second tetralogy, see Levy, 20 and n. 57. The continuation is printed from manuscript in the recent edition by John J. Manning.

94. See James L. Calderwood, *Metadrama in Shakespeare's Henriad:* Richard II *to* Henry V (Berkeley: University of California Press, 1979), for a pioneering study of the metatheatrical dimension of Shakespeare's second tetralogy. As Calderwood

III

Shakespeare incorporates a dramatistic paradigm for the understanding of political action within *The Tragedy of King Richard the Second*. Indeed, he puts the *theatrum mundi* trope at the center of the Duke of York's description of the civic royal entry that epitomizes the revolution of the times. Bolingbroke rides in triumph through the open streets of London, skillfully eliciting the assent of his popular audience:

> You would have thought the very windows spake,
> So many greedy looks of young and old
> Through casements darted their desiring eyes
> Upon his visage. . . .

Duch. Alack, poor Richard, where rode he the whilst?

York. As in a theater the eyes of men,
> After a well-graced actor leaves the stage,
> Are idly bent on him that enters next,

---

declares, his approach is "devoted to the self-reflexive aspects of the plays. . . . Instead of regarding language as a means toward political ends, I would find Shakespeare solving problems of language by means of politics. Political affairs, in other words, become metaphors for art" (4). In part, I was reacting against the aesthetic impetus of Calderwood's frequently acute and suggestive work when I first advanced an historicized account of the metatheatricality of the Elizabethan drama and the protean powers of the Elizabethan players in "The Purpose of Playing: Reflections on a Shakespearean Anthropology" (1980).

The perspective adumbrated in my earlier work has since been developed, in regard to Shakespeare's English histories, in two valuable essays by David Kastan: "Proud Majesty Made a Subject: Shakespeare and the Spectacle of Rule"; and "'The King Hath Many Marching in His Coats', or What Did You Do during the War, Daddy?" in *Shakespeare Left and Right*, ed. Ivo Kamps (New York and London: Routledge, 1991), 241–58. Also according with my perspective is that in the chapter on "Kings and Pretenders: Monarchical Theatricality in the Shakespearean History Play," in Jean E. Howard, *The Stage and Social Struggle in Early Modern England*, 129–53. The central argument of this fine study, which was published after my own had reached final form, is that

> there is a considerable difference between how theatricality is represented as a threat to identity and social stability in the three plays dealing with the reign of Henry VI and in the plays dealing primarily with Bolingbroke and his son. The difference . . . has centrally to do with whether or not theatrical practice is represented as an external threat *to* monarchy or as constitutive *of* monarchy. . . . It is the plays dealing with Bolingbroke and his son . . . that most insistently mark their modernity by demonstrating the inseparability of theatricality from social being. (130)

Thinking his prattle to be tedious,
Even so, or with much more contempt, men's eyes
Did scowl on gentle Richard.
. . .
But heaven hath a hand in these events,
To whose high will we bound our calm contents.
To Bolinbroke are we sworn subjects now,
Whose state and honor I for aye allow.

(5.2.12–15, 22–28, 37–40)

York's theatrical metaphor is apposite, because Bolingbroke has found out his way to the throne by demonstrating a mode of performativity far more flexible and forceful than that of his cousin-king. Shakespeare locates the decisive confrontation between these modes at Flint Castle, where the anointed king capitulates to the royal rebel (3.3). In Shakespeare's fiction of history, even old hereditary nobles like the Duke of York must have recourse to politic tropes of theatricality when they attempt to apprehend events that cannot be comfortably accommodated within the terms of a providentialist framework. Immediately before the fatal confrontation at Flint Castle, York had cautioned his nephew Bolingbroke, "Take not, good cousin, further than you should, / Lest you mistake the heavens are over our heads" (3.3.16–17). When York returns to such terms at the conclusion of the quoted speech from Act Five, scene two, it is clear that providentialism has now been accommodated to *realpolitik*. As Sir John Harington quipped, in a letter to Prince Henry (1609), "Treason dothe never prosper, What's the reason? / Why, if it prosper, none dare call it Treason" (*Nugae Antiquae*, 2:144). He who seeks to control the personation of the king will also seek to control the writing of history. Thus, at the end of *The First Part of King Henry the Fourth*, having defeated the Percies, who had earlier helped him to the crown, Bolingbroke—now King Henry IV—is bold to assert, "Thus ever did rebellion find rebuke" (*1 Henry IV*, 5.5.1).

When Hotspur remarks wryly during the final battle that "the King hath many marching in his coats" (*1 Henry IV*, 5.3.25), he refers to the ploy of dressing King Henry's retinue like the King himself in order to confuse the rebels. Confronting King Henry after having mistakenly killed two others in his stead, Douglas demands, "What art thou / That counterfeit'st the person of a king?" In response to

Henry's assertion that he is "The King himself," Douglas remains doubtful: "I fear thou art another counterfeit; / And yet, in faith, thou bearest thee like a king" (5.4.27–28, 29, 35–36). This brief episode most suggestively stages the clash between essentialist and performative notions of legitimacy that pervades the comic as well as the heroic scenes of Shakespeare's second tetralogy of English histories. Earlier in the same play, Hal and Falstaff perform a "play extempore" (2.4.281) before a base and familiar audience in a London tavern—a common enough venue for the itinerant players before the advent of the amphitheatres. "Do thou stand for my father and examine me upon the particulars of my life" (376–77), suggests Hal; and Falstaff embraces his part with such relish that Mistress Quickly is provoked to exclaim, "O Jesu, he doth it as like one of these harlotry players as ever I see!" (395–96). When the players exchange parts, the mock morality play becomes a mock deposition scene:

> *Prince.* Dost thou speak like a king? Do thou stand for me, and I'll play my father.
> *Falstaff.* Depose me? If thou dost it half so gravely, so majestically, both in word and matter, hang me up by the heels for a rabbit-sucker or a poulter's hare.
>
> (432–36)

This comically impudent metatheatrical example suggests why the Elizabethan regime refused to countenance personations of the prince. Through its foregrounding of the volatile representational resources and effects of the theatrical impulse, the Elizabethan drama demonstrated a potentially dangerous capacity to subject the ruler to ridicule and to demean the royal office.

When, at the end of their "play extempore," Hal in the adoptive voice of kingship banishes Falstaff (481), he is rehearsing the scene of banishment that he will perform in earnest at the end of *The Second Part of King Henry the Fourth* (*2 Henry IV,* 5.5.47–70). This later royal performance takes place in the open streets of London, as the new king comes forth from his coronation. The prodigal Prince Hal's transformation into the judicious King Henry the Fifth is here publicly staged; Henry ceremoniously and definitively repudiates the carnal body of Falstaff and confirms his own identification with the mystical body of kingship. However, in the very first scene in which Hal appears (*1 Henry IV,* 1.2), Shakespeare has taken pains to make his audience aware that the ostensibly prodigal prince has already plotted his own trajectory to the crown:

> So when this loose behavior I throw off
> And pay the debt I never promisèd,
> By how much better than my word I am,
> By so much shall I falsify men's hopes;
> And like bright metal on a sullen ground,
> My reformation, glittering o'er my fault,
> Shall show more goodly and attract more eyes
> Than that which hath no foil to set it off.
>
> (*1 Henry IV*, 1.2.202–09)[95]

The foil that sets off Shakespeare's Lancastrian plays is the earlier, crudely effective and apparently successful *Famous Victories of Henry the Fifth*.[96] There are many striking stylistic and structural differences between the plays' treatments of Hal's trajectory. But the decisive difference that concerns me here is that, in the earlier play, both the initial profligacy and the eventual conversion of "the yoong Prince" are represented as being genuine and unequivocal. These two representations—one of apparently sincere and the other of strategically fabricated conversion—operate in fundamentally different modes of theatricality: The former reproduces the mystifications of charismatic kingship, while the latter imaginatively represents the active production of such mystifications; the former performs a parable, while the latter performs the performance of a parable. The legitimacy of King Henry IV—and of his "heir apparent," as Falstaff tauntingly calls Hal—is tainted by deposition and regicide. Under these dangerously unstable circumstances, the action of the two parts of *Henry IV* is vir-

---

95. For an analogous moment, see Hal's speech to his father, King Henry IV, at their first staged meeting (3.2.132–56). Here Hal lays out the process through which, at the expense of Hotspur, he will prove himself the true inheritor in the play's final scenes, on the field at Shrewsbury.

96. Anonymous but frequently attributed to Richard Tarlton or Samuel Rowley, *The Famous Victories of Henry the Fifth* was entered in the Stationers' Register in 1594 but the earliest extant copy was printed in 1598. We learn from *Tarlton's Jests* that Tarlton played the clown's part of Dericke; thus, the play was presumably composed before 1588, the year of Tarlton's death. I have used the text in *Chief Pre-Shakespearean Dramas*, ed. Joseph Quincy Adams (Cambridge, Massachusetts: Houghton Mifflin, 1924).

tually defined by the contest to control the personation of the King, and its counterpointing Falstaffian parody. Indeed, it could be argued that Shakespeare was drawn to Henry's reign in part because it gave unusual scope for an imaginative exploration of the interplay between theatricality and political legitimation.

The performance of plays in the Elizabethan public theatre put into action a dialectic among characters within the playworld; a dialectic between the fictional world of the characters and the experiential world of the audience; and a dialectic between the professional players and those who paid to see them play. Through this multidimensional theatrical dialectic of identification and estrangement, the Elizabethan drama produces that "objectivity" which modern criticism has come to see as its formal and conceptual hallmark. However, to historicize this objectivity effect is to clarify that the "objectivity" required to represent the dominant as merely one among a range of possible positions is itself a perspective with profound political implications. Within the specific constraints of the dominant Elizabethan ideology, freedom of interpretation and indeterminacy of meaning were inherently dangerous and potentially subversive notions.[97] It is precisely by appropriating the authoritative Elizabethan principles of "orthodoxy, providentialism, and hierarchy," and then (in Yachnin's phrase) arraying them indeterminately along an axis of interpretive positions, that Shakespeare's history plays *decenter* those principles and demystify their claim to the status of divine and immutable truth.

97. For an overview of the legal and institutional aspects of Elizabethan censorship, see D. M. Loades, "The Theory and Practice of Censorship in Sixteenth-Century England," *Transactions of the Royal Historical Society*, 5th ser., 24 (1974), 141–57; on the interacting practices of censorship and interpretation in Elizabethan literary culture, see Annabel Patterson, *Censorship and Interpretation: The Conditions of Writing and Reading in Early Modern England* (1984; rpt., with a new Introduction, Madison: University of Wisconsin Press, 1990). On dramatic censorship, see Bentley, *The Profession of Dramatist in Shakespeare's Time*, 145–96; Clare, '*Art made tongue-tied by authority*'; Dutton, *Mastering the Revels*.

CHAPTER SEVEN

☽

THE CROSS-PURPOSES
OF PLAYING

In its various manifestations—including the regulation of the drama—the concern taken by the Queen and her council "for the recreation of oure loving subjectes" exemplifies the process of state formation through concerted efforts to expand and to systematize ideological state apparatuses.[98] The Privy Council attempted to restrict the number of professional acting companies and the number and location of playhouses, and all plays for public playing were made subject to censorship, licensing, and the payment of fees to the Master of the Revels. By such means as these, the royal government at once enjoyed and protected but also sought to limit, control, and profit from the professional theatre. Perhaps the general point to be made here concerning the attitude of the Elizabethan state toward the Elizabethan theatre is that it was complex and equivocal; that it was not constant but was subject to numerous shifts, variations, and inconsistencies; and that some of these were consequences of fundamental anomalies and contradictions, while others resulted from merely local or temporary exigencies. And what of the attitude of the Elizabethan theatre toward the Elizabethan state? The extant

98. For a general reading of Elizabethan policy from such a perspective, see Corrigan and Sayer, *The Great Arch*, 55–71. For the concept of "ideological state apparatuses" (which is not used by Corrigan and Sayer), see Louis Althusser, *Lenin and Philosophy and Other Essays*, 127–86. In *Drama of a Nation: Public Theater in Renaissance England and Spain* (Ithaca: Cornell University Press, 1985), Walter Cohen, working within Marxian categories, "pursues a single and simple hypothesis: that the absolutist state, by its inherent dynamism and contradictions, first fostered and then undermined the public theater" (19–20). Cohen views the drama of the Elizabethan public theatre as exemplifying a transient moment of patriotic and populist national unity.

evidence concerning the ideological positioning of the professional playhouses and their plays, both from the plays themselves and from other sources, is—unsurprisingly—ambiguous, diverse, contradictory. This suggests, on the one hand, that, in practice, the Elizabethan theatre must have proved a rather unreliable ideological apparatus in the service of the Elizabethan state. On the other hand, as the circumstances of the Essex revolt suggest, it was at least equally difficult to enlist the professional Elizabethan theatre as a vehicle for concerted seditious action.

The Lord Chamberlain's Men gave a metatheatrical demonstration of the equivocal place of the stage, the cross-purposes of playing, when they performed *Hamlet* at the Globe. Within Shakespeare's play, "the tragedians of the city" have come "to offer . . . service" to the Prince. Although "their residence, both in reputation and profit, was better both ways," they are now compelled to leave their public playhouse, temporarily reverting to itinerant status and seeking royal patronage because keen competition in the city's entertainment industry has hurt their profits (*Hamlet*, 2.2.316–62).[99] The melancholy Hamlet is excited by the prospect of the players' visit; and in this unwonted enthusiasm, the King seeks occasion to mollify his "chiefest courtier . . . and [his] son" (1.2117), and to divert him from his malcontented brooding:

99. The textual status of *Hamlet* is, of course, notoriously vexed. Despite the impressive credentials on its title page—"As it hath beene diverse times acted by his Highnesse servants in the Cittie of London: as also in the two Universities of Cambridge and Oxford, and else-where"—the first quarto (1603) appears to be an abridgement, and probably a memorial reconstruction, for the popular theatre. A more appropriate candidate for performance in academic venues would have been the second quarto (1604), "Newly imprinted and enlarged to almost as much againe as it was, according to the true and perfect Coppie." In comparison with this second ("good") quarto, the text of the first folio (1623) registers some significant omissions and additions. Among the latter is the elaborate passage on then-current theatrical conditions in London, which I have cited in my text; this passage, on the growing taste for boys' companies and private theatres, has a precedent in Q1 but none in Q2. What relationship *any* of these printed, readerly texts bears to contemporaneous performances of *Hamlet* is unknown and probably unknowable. For purposes of my discussion, I have used a modern edition that takes Q2 as its copy-text and incorporates readings from F. Where a difference between texts is important for my argument, I have noted it.

It doth much content me
To hear him so inclined.
Good gentlemen, give him a further edge
And drive his purpose into these delights.

(3.1.24–27)

Claudius hopes that Hamlet's purpose will be vitiated in playing. However, he unwisely entrusts the office of Master of the Revels, and its censoring authority, to Hamlet himself:

King.   Have you heard the argument? Is there no offense in't?
Ham.   No, no, they do but jest, poison in jest. No offense i'the world.

(3.2.230–33).

The antically disposed Prince mocks the King's conviction that the drama is an innocuous pastime; he has a rather different notion of what it would mean to "drive his purpose into these delights." Hamlet's sententious speech on "the purpose of playing" (3.2.1–45) is spoken in the context of his own particular purposes: "The play's the thing / Wherein I'll catch the conscience of the king" (2.2.604–05).[100] The princely patron of the city's professional players will employ a courtly command performance as an ethical instrument for the determination of political action; Hamlet will place a dramatic performance at the center of his design to de-legitimate the monarch.

Immediately upon the arrival of the players, Hamlet requests that the company's leading player recite "a passionate speech" (2.2.431–32) describing the murder of Priam, and then, that these "tragedians of the city" (2.2.329) "play something like the murder of [his] father / Before [his] uncle" (2.2.596–97). Shakespeare's Hamlet subscribes to a belief in the doubly mimetic capacity of drama—its status as a representation of, and provocation to, action. By employing the theatre's powerful capacity to move its audience by a mixture of language and gesture, he seeks to confirm the King's occulted guilt and, simultaneously, to galvanize his own revenge, to rouse himself to regicide:

---

100. In *An Apology for Actors*, Heywood recounts some sensational case histories (G1v–G2v), in which guilty creatures sitting at a play were so moved by the feigned action that they spontaneously confessed their hidden crimes.

I'll observe his looks;
I'll tent him to the quick. If 'a do blench,
I know my course.

(2.2.597–99)

In the very process of catching the king in his metatheatrical
mousetrap, however, Hamlet himself becomes so affected by the
power of theatrical mimesis that he exposes his own suspicions and
intentions to the king. Serving as Chorus to the play-within-the-play
as well as Master of the Revels, Hamlet identifies the regicide as a
lively image not only of his uncle's consummated crime but of his
own prospective revenge: "This is one Lucianus, nephew to the
King. . . . Begin, murderer. . . . Come, the croaking raven doth bellow
for revenge" (*Hamlet*, 3.2.242, 250–52). As repeatedly happens in
Hamlet, the playwright's ironic designs defeat the characters' purposes and puzzle their wills. Or, as the player King puts it, in *The
Murder of Gonzago*,

Our wills and fates do so contrary run
That our devices still are overthrown;
Our thoughts are ours, their ends none of our own.

(3.2.209–11)

The strategies of Claudius and Hamlet enact opposed and complementary courtly attitudes toward the theatre: At the same time that
the monarch construes it as a means of diversion, his chiefest courtier
construes it as a means of subversion.[101] Regardless of the opposed

---

101. William Keeling, Captain of *The Dragon*, an East India Company vessel
bound for the East Indies via the Cape of Good Hope, made the following entry
in his journal for 31 March 1608: "I envited Captain Hawkins to a ffishe dinner,
and had Hamlet acted abord me: which I permitt to keepe my people from idlenes
and unlawful games, or sleepe." Himself the instrument of merchant venturers,
the captain uses the drama of the public theatres to control the subjects of his
petty commonwealth. He stages a performance of *Hamlet* so as to keep his men
from precisely the kinds of behavior that the antitheatricalists accused the theatre
of promoting. He seems to have shared the opinion of the Privy Council—and
Claudius—that the theatre was a means, not of subversion but of diversion.
Earlier in the voyage, on 30 September 1607, he records that "Captain Hawkins
dined with me, wher my companions acted Kinge Richard the Second." These
entries are printed in Chambers, *William Shakespeare*, 2:334–35.

intentions and expectations of the Prince and the King, however, Hamlet's "mousetrap" has an ambiguous and unpredictable effectivity within the world of Shakespeare's play. The play's accumulation of "purposes mistook / Fall'n on th'inventors' heads" (5.2.386–87) ironically chronicles the failure of a Tacitean will to action.

As for the travelling company of professional players, their materially self-interested motives are evidently to maintain their livelihood and to insure the continuance of princely patronage. They are hardly in a position to refuse either Hamlet's choice of repertory—"Dost thou hear me, old friend? Can you play *The Murder of Gonzago?*"—or his request that they include in their performance, "a speech of some dozen or sixteen lines which [he] would set down and insert in't" (2.2.537–38, 541–42). The Lord Chamberlain's Men probably first performed *Hamlet* at the Globe not long before their infamous performance of *Richard II*. Some editors have suggested that the text of the second quarto (1604) obliquely alludes to the tumultuous events of 1601, in which the company had played a minor role. When Hamlet asks, concerning the players, "How chances it that they travel? Their residence, both in reputation and profit, was better both ways," the only answer that he gets in Q2 is brief, tentative, and cryptic: "I think their inhibition comes by the means of the late innovation" (2.2.330–33). The notion of a prohibition on public playing precipitated by an insurrection was a construction readily available to Shakespeare's readers, for whom the recent Essex revolt would have been the obvious topical referent.[102] In *Hamlet* (or, at least, in the readerly text of Q2), Shakespeare appears to have been acutely sensitive to the power and danger entailed by his play's theatrical mimesis of affairs of state. *Hamlet* is a metatheatrical tragedy of state; it internalizes the relationship of the public, professional, and commercial theatre to the court, thereby foregrounding the cultural politics of that relationship. Thus, it gives imaginative form to some of the same ideas and interests that came into play when the Earl of Essex's friends propositioned the players. In its demonstration of a complex and contingent

102. For a lengthy and detailed argument in favor of this interpretation, see the *Arden Shakespeare* edition of *Hamlet*, ed. Harold Jenkins (London and New York: Methuen, 1982), 470–72. Jenkins notes that a rival interpretation maintains that the allusion is to the Privy Council's order of 1600.

interaction of diverse interests, the metaproduction of *The Murder of Gonzago* is emblematic of the real but limited, diffuse, and unstable power of the professional theatre within late Elizabethan society.

The inconclusive conclusions on offer here cannot rival, for sheer excitement, the bold assertions that have become commonplace in the critical literature on the Elizabethan theatre. However, from my perspective, any general characterization of the relationship between the Elizabethan theatre and the Elizabethan state in terms of an either/or choice between *subversion* and *containment*, between *resistance* and *complicity*, or between *power* and *freedom*, appears to be hopelessly reductive. A conceptual origin for the recently fashionable critical notion of "contained subversion" may be located in the ambiguity of the Elizabethan term, *license*, which implied that heterodoxy might be effectively controlled precisely by allowing it a conspicuously authorized expression. Although some recent discussions suggest that such a strategy was uniformly and unequivocally effective, the licensing of the Elizabethan drama by the Elizabethan state was merely an attempt at containment. In practice, this attempt was inconsistent and haphazard and was never uniformly and unequivocally effective. I suggest, furthermore, that it was wholly beyond the capacity of the Elizabethan state to achieve the uniform and absolute containment of alternative and oppositional discourses. Indeed, it could be argued that such total control is (as yet) beyond the power of any state.[103]

In my view, the professional, public, and commercial theatre of Elizabethan London did have a subtle and diffuse power of its own, but the direction and effectivity of that power were uncertain and intermittent. This theatrical power lay precisely in the combination of representational resources that enabled it to enact and to epitomize the *theatrum mundi* metaphor—resources that gave to it its specificity as a cultural institution, form, and practice. My point is that the source of this theatre's power was in its very *theatricality*, and in the implications of theatricality for the construction and manipulation of social rules and interpersonal relations—implications touching fundamental epistemological and sociopolitical issues of causality and legitimacy, identity and agency. Even if, in the texts and scenar-

---

103. I discuss the bases for this argument in the Prologue to this book, and at greater length in "New Historicisms."

ios of particular plays, such implications were not foregrounded—indeed, even if they were contained or suppressed—this power might nevertheless make itself felt in the process of performance, in which both the players and their audience participated actively in the making of meaning.[104] The theatrical power that I am seeking to describe did not lie in the explicit advocacy of specific political positions but rather in the implicit but pervasive suggestion—inhering in the basic modalities of theatrical representation and dramatic conflict—that all such positions are relationally located and circumstantially shaped and that they are motivated by the passions and interests of their advocates. In this precise and limited sense, Shakespearean drama as enacted in the Elizabethan theatre *formally* contested the dominant ideological assertions of the Elizabethan state.

104. Robert Weimann has brilliantly explored the importance of staging, performance, and actor-audience interaction to the collective creation of meaning in Elizabethan drama. See *Shakespeare and the Popular Tradition in the Theater,* esp. 208–60; and, among several subsequent studies: "History and the Issue of Authority in Representation: The Elizabethan Theater and the Reformation," *New Literary History* 17 (1985–86), 449–76, and "Bifold Authority in Shakespeare's Theatre," *Shakespeare Quarterly* 39 (1988), 401–17. Weimann writes that, "in appropriating the author's function and self-authorized performative in the world of the Elizabethan theater, the common actors (articulating and gesticulating the representing language) might utterly and on every level contradict the matter political and ideological which was represented" ("History and the Issue of Authority in Representation," 474). Also see Walter Cohen, *Drama of a Nation,* 183.

PART TWO

THE SHAPING FANTASIES OF *A MIDSUMMER NIGHT'S DREAM*

CHAPTER EIGHT

THE DISCORD OF THIS CONCORD

Like the professional theatre of which it is so conspicuously re-flexive an instance, *A Midsummer Night's Dream* is not an inert *product* of a hypostatic Elizabethan culture but rather a new *production* of a dynamic and unstable Elizabethan culture—a production that en-larges the dimensions of the cultural field and alters the lines of force within it. I shall appropriate the phrase "shaping fantasies"—which the playwright gives, perhaps ironically, to Theseus—in order to suggest the dialectical character of such cultural representations: The cultural fantasies by which *A Midsummer Night's Dream* has been shaped are also those to which it gives shape. The Elizabethan and Shakespearean cultural representations with which I shall be particu-larly concerned are those of gender and sexuality. Such representa-tions constitute ideological appropriations of human anatomy and physiology, sociohistorical constructions of sexual identity and differ-ence, and deployments of discourses of gender and sexuality to artic-ulate relationships of power. In discussing Elizabethan constructions of gender and sexuality, I construe them as distinct discourses that are nevertheless reciprocally related, in multiple and shifting ways, both to each other and to other modes of cultural, political, and socio-economic organization and experience.[1]

1. In the introduction to an earlier version of this study—"Shaping Fantasies: Figurations of Gender and Power in Elizabethan Culture" (1983)—I invoked "the Elizabethan sex/gender system." Here I was following the work of Gayle Rubin, "The Traffic in Women: Notes on the 'Political Economy' of Sex," in *Toward an Anthropology of Women,* ed. Rayna R. Reiter (New York: Monthly Review Press, 1975), 157–210. In a subsequent polemical essay, "Thinking Sex: Notes for a Rad-ical Theory of the Politics of Sexuality," in *Pleasure and Danger: Exploring Female Sexuality,* ed. Carole S. Vance (London: Routledge & Kegan Paul, 1984), 267–319,

In his introduction to the Arden edition of *A Midsummer Night's Dream*, Harold Brooks summarizes the consensus of modern criticism that "love and marriage is the [play's] central theme: love aspiring to and consummated in marriage, or to a harmonious partnership within it."[2] Such romantically inclined idealizations of married love tend to downplay the authoritarian and misogynistic aspects of *A Midsummer Night's Dream* that have proven an embarrassment to enlightened modern sensibilities. The play's dominant—although by no means uncontested—perspective on wedded bliss is in harmony with prevailing Elizabethan doctrines regarding marriage and the domestic economy: The household is a hierarchically organized social institution, analogous to the body politic, and based upon the reciprocal obligations of husbands and wives, parents and children, masters and servants; harmonious marital partnership is predicated upon the wife's obedience to her husband, as divinely authorized through such

---

Rubin reconsidered her earlier conflation, now arguing instead for the importance of maintaining an analytical distinction: "Gender affects the operation of the sexual system, and the sexual system has had gender-specific manifestations. But although sex and gender are related, they are not the same thing, and they form the basis of two distinct arenas of social practice" (308). In her recent book, *Desire and Anxiety: Circulations of Sexuality in Shakespearean Drama* (London and New York: Routledge, 1992), Valerie Traub takes Rubin's revised position as a point of departure for a lucid and provocative study of the dramatic construction of subjectivity and agency through the modalities of erotic desire and anxiety specific to early modern culture. Also see the essays collected in *Erotic Politics: Desire on the Renaissance Stage*, ed. Susan Zimmerman (New York and London: Routledge, 1992).

My emphasis in the present study is upon Elizabethan discourses of gender, not upon discourses of erotic desire. I share the perspective articulated in Joan Wallach Scott, *Gender and the Politics of History* (New York: Columbia University Press, 1988), that "gender is a constitutive element of social relationships based upon perceived difference between the sexes, and gender is a primary way of signifying relationships of power" (42). Throughout, my interest is in the intersection of gender with other culturally constituted discourses, including the sexual, in *A Midsummer Night's Dream* and in other Elizabethan texts. In certain instances, where the discourses of gender and sexuality coincide—and, specifically, in matters of physiology and reproduction—I continue to use the term, "sex/gender system."

2. *A Midsummer Night's Dream*, ed. Harold F. Brooks, *The Arden Shakespeare* (London: Methuen, 1979), cxxx. Quotations from *A Midsummer Night's Dream* (*MND*) follow this edition and are cited in my text by act, scene, and line.

scriptural texts as the Pauline epistles.[3] A tone and perspective very different from Brooks's is taken by Paul A. Olson in his article on "*A Midsummer Night's Dream* and the Meaning of Court Marriage," published in 1957 and influential on the play's critics for a generation.[4] Olson is not concerned with the social realities of Elizabethan marriage, courtly or otherwise, but with prescriptive theological and philosophical traditions regarding marriage and gender—traditions toward which his own discourse appears sympathetic. According to Olson, *A Midsummer Night's Dream* begins with a "movement toward an orderly subordination of the female and her passions to the more reasonable male," as epitomized in "the prospective marriage of Theseus and Hippolita." There follows "a Fall which brings the domination of unbridled passion" (101). Finally, the play "returns to a realization of the charity and cohesive community morality in which it began," when "Oberon regains his sovereignty over the fairy queen" and spiritual and physical love "are matched as they should be in any true marriage" (101, 115). By means of Olson's neo-patristic commentary, *A Midsummer Night's Dream* becomes a paean to "order"; it is an allegory that both exemplifies and justifies a homology among hierarchies of gender, social rank, intellect, and moral virtue. The sociopolitical perspective dominant in Shakespeare studies today inclines contemporary critics to decry precisely those patriarchal elements in the play with which Olson seems to have identified.[5] We are now likely to stress that the ultimately harmonious marital unions

3. On Elizabethan prescriptions concerning marriage and domestic relations, see Chilton Latham Powell, *English Domestic Relations, 1487–1653* (1917; rpt., New York: Russell & Russell, 1972); Kathleen M. Davies, "Continuity and Change in Literary Advice on Marriage," in *Marriage and Society: Studies in the Social History of Marriage*, ed. R. B. Outhwaite (London: Europa, 1981), 58–80; Suzanne W. Hull, *Chaste Silent & Obedient: English Books for Women 1475–1640* (San Marino, California: Huntington Library, 1982), esp. 31–70.

4. Paul A. Olson, "*A Midsummer Night's Dream* and the Meaning of Court Marriage," *ELH* 24 (1957), 95–119.

5. For an early feminist reading of the play, see Shirley Nelson Garner, "*A Midsummer Night's Dream*: 'Jack shall have Jill;/Nought shall go ill'," *Women's Studies*, 9 (1981), 47–63. Although Garner concurs with Olson in reading the play as an affirmation of "patriarchal order and hierarchy," she explicitly condemns that which Olson's rhetoric implicitly reaffirms. Unlike much of recent feminist Shakespeare criticism, Garner's analysis is relatively indifferent to historical issues.

of *A Midsummer Night's Dream* are achieved or imposed only at the end of an agonistic dramatic process, in which masculine authority over the unruly woman is reasserted by means of degradation and coercion. At the same time, our increasing awareness of the complicated textual and historical workings of ideology should make us wary of attributing any stable and unified ideological position to the play and/or to the playwright, a position that we may then proceed either to celebrate or to condemn.[6]

The contrasting perspectives of Brooks and Olson exemplify a tension between companionate and hierarchical perspectives in the critical interpretation of *A Midsummer Night's Dream*. This tension within the critical discourse reflects a tension already existing within Shakespeare's representations of gender and marriage; and the play shares this tension with other Elizabethan discourses and practices. Through his selection of exemplary texts, Olson constructs a version of "16th century marriage doctrines" (96) that is doctrinal in the narrow sense of the term, one that gives no sense of the range and flexibility of the discourses and practices of marriage and gender that circulated through Shakespeare's culture and through his plays. One of the salutary effects of the new historicist influence in Renaissance literary studies has been to encourage a rearticulation of literary and dramatic texts with other genres of written discourse, and with the textual and iconic traces of Elizabethan social practices that have

---

6. Stability and unity are terms congenial to the vision of the play presented in David Young, *Something of Great Constancy: The Art of "A Midsummer Night's Dream"* (New Haven: Yale University Press, 1966). Citing Olson's essay as an authority, Young asserts that "it is appropriate that Theseus, as representative of daylight and right reason should have subdued his bride-to-be to the rule of his masculine will. That is the natural order of things. It is equally appropriate that Oberon, as king of darkness and fantasy, should have lost control of his wife, and that the corresponding natural disorder described by Titania should ensue" (99–100). Young sees in *MND*, a "synthesis" of "divergent" courtly and popular "tendencies in the theater," for which the "marriage" of Titania and Bottom serves as an emblem: "Instead of the expected incongruity there was consistency, even a sense of inevitability" (58–59). His extended study of the play's style and structure (64–106) discovers "how closely they are related, how much a part of a single, overarching artistic purpose" (106). He interprets the play as a (meta)dramatic defense of the imagination, and of "the values of art, the consistent and coherent shape it may give to imaginative experience" (140). This important and influential monograph shaped my own earliest thinking about the play.

since become part of the historian's domain. In this chapter, I want
to consider briefly, in conjunction with *A Midsummer Night's Dream,*
two contrasting discourses in which Elizabethan notions of gender
and marriage were constructed: Protestant marriage manuals and the
popular, rowdy, and censorious expressions of community values generally known as *charivari.* My purpose is to destabilize the notion
of "16th century marriage doctrines" that is sometimes employed to
elucidate, in an unproblematized fashion, the gender ideology of *A
Midsummer Night's Dream* and other Shakespearean plays.

Our recognition that Shakespeare's dramatic discourse is traversed
by multiple and potentially contradictory ideological positions may
also helpfully complicate our response to the homiletic discourse of
Elizabethan-Jacobean marriage manuals. Recent work by social historians strongly suggests that sixteenth- and early seventeenth-
century Protestant texts on domestic relations were neither as original nor as representative as had been claimed by an earlier generation
of scholars, some of whom were unabashed apologists for the puritan
art of love.[7] Kathleen Davies, for example, maintains that the prescriptive familial discourse of the printed manuals effaces the "diversity of structure and behaviour" ("Continuity and Change in Literary
Advice on Marriage," 59) in the actual practices of Protestant families. I believe, however, that careful analysis of such texts can in fact
reveal the textual traces of diversity and division even here.

Let me briefly consider one such text, the massive tract entitled

7. Thus, Kathleen Davies writes that,
     in recent years social historians have questioned the use of such sources as
     direct evidence of attitudes and behaviour, and have mounted a sustained
     attack on the theory that their contents can be taken at face value. Demo-
     graphic studies show that literary sources have only a limited use in social
     history, since the patterns of behaviour which they describe may be highly
     unrepresentative.... Even among Puritan families there seems to have
     been a greater diversity of structure and behaviour than the texts sug-
     gest....
          As far as printed, and therefore popularly available, works on marriage
     and family life are concerned, I would question whether the stress on do-
     mesticity is in fact so very new or so peculiar to Protestants. ("Continuity
     and Change in Literary Advice on Marriage," 59, 60)
See Margaret Ezell, *The Patriarch's Wife: Literary Evidence and the History of the Family* (Chapel Hill: University of North Carolina Press, 1987), for an important argument regarding the practical influence and authority of mothers in arranging the
marriages of children in propertied families, regardless of patriarchalist doctrines.

Of Domesticall Duties, by the popular Jacobean Puritan preacher, William Gouge. In his Dedicatory Epistle to his Blackfriars parishioners, Gouge reveals that "When these Domestical Duties were first uttered out of the pulpit, much exception was taken against the application of a wives subjection to the restraining of her from disposing of the common goods of the family without, or against, her husband's consent." The specific issue regarding proprietary rights that is in contention between Gouge and some of his parishioners is one with profound ramifications for the status of married women, and for the very concept of their personhood. In her recent study, *Women and Property in Early Modern England*, Amy Louise Erickson has demonstrated in detail that "under common law a woman's legal identity during marriage was eclipsed—literally covered—by her husband. As a 'feme covert' she could not contract, neither could she sue nor be sued independently of her husband."[8] Gouge's position gains great authority from its scriptural basis and from its access to the pulpit and to print. However, he makes it quite clear that his own benignly but resolutely patriarchal perspective is far from enjoying universal acceptance, even among his own parishioners. What literary scholars have sometimes represented as *the* Elizabethan-Jacobean view of marriage is rather the printed heritage of the dominant position in what appears to have been a lively and ongoing debate. This debate was apparently serious enough to compel Gouge to present an *apologia:* "I so set down an husband's duties, as if he be wise and conscionable in observing them, his wife can have no just cause to complain of her subjection. . . . This just Apology I have been forced to make, that I might not ever be judged (as some have censured me) *an hater of women*."[9] From our perspective, Gouge's position may appear to be unequivocally antifeminist; nevertheless, it is important

---

8. Amy Louise Erickson, *Women and Property in Early Modern England* (London and New York: Routledge, 1993), 24. Furthermore, she points out that this state of affairs was one of the peculiarities of the English: "English men's use of coverture to control women economically was unique. Seventeenth-century legal theorists justified the system by the practical needs of household debt and credit management, but this explanation pales in view of the failure of the rest of Europe to employ the fiction of the unity of husband and wife" (233). On wives and property, see 99–151.

9. William Gouge, *Of Domesticall Duties* (London, 1622), facsimile ed. (Amsterdam: Theatrum Orbis Terrarum, 1976); Epistle Dedicatory, 3v–4r.

to note that Gouge himself, as his rhetorical emphasis clearly indicates, is most concerned that the women and men among whom he lives should not think him a misogynist. Gouge's text testifies that his pronouncements from the pulpit had already met with significant and articulate resistance and that he regarded such resistance as sufficiently credible that he should take pains to clarify and defend his position in print.

The controversy regarding the disposition of common property to which Gouge alludes points to an underlying tension or contradiction within orthodox Protestant marriage doctrines. This contradiction—one with potentially significant political implications—has been succinctly put by Susan Amussen:

> Other models of authority—parental and royal—downplayed the elements of partnership and gave clear dominance to the parent/ king. Most of the writers of household manuals knew that something was different between husband and wife. There was a further problem: the household manual was by and large a "Puritan" genre, and for Puritans the only absolute authority was God: before God all men—and women—were equal. Within the household they were trying to define an unequal partnership between spiritual equals: in all relationships, one had to be superior.[10]

Such ideological difficulties are evident in Gouge's exposition of Ephesians 5.22: "Wives submit your selves unto your owne husbands, as unto the Lord." Gouge offers no less than five responses to the question, "Why among other inferiours are wives first brought unto the schoole of Christ to learne their duty?"

> First, of all other inferiours in a family, wives are farre the most excellent, and therefore to be placed in the first ranke.
> Secondly, wives were the first to whom subjection was injoyned; before there was childe or servant in the world, it was said to her, *thy desire shall be subject to thine husband.*
> Thirdly, wives are the fountain from whence all other degrees spring: and therefore ought first to be cleansed.

10. Susan Dwyer Amussen, *An Ordered Society: Gender and Class in Early Modern England* (Oxford: Basil Blackwell, 1988), 46. On this contradiction, also see Keith Wrightson, *English Society 1580–1680* (London: Hutchinson, 1982), 90–104; and, for an important discussion from the perspective of literary and dramatic studies, Mary Beth Rose, *The Expense of Spirit: Love and Sexuality in English Renaissance Drama* (Ithaca: Cornell University Press, 1988), 116–31.

Fourthly, this subjection is a good patterne unto children and servants: and a great means to move them to be subject.

Fiftly, I may further adde as a truth, which is too manifest by experience in all places, that among all other parties of whom the Holy Ghost requireth subjection, wives for the most part are most backward in yeelding subjection to their husbands. (25–26)

The first response epitomizes the paradoxical position of the wife: She is the superior inferior. The second response shifts the basis for wifely precedence from the essential virtue and dignity of her estate to the historical primacy of her subjection; she is not only "the most excellent" of inferiors but also the very prototype of inferiority. The third response alludes to the power and danger of wifely fertility and sexuality within the symbolic economy of patriarchy, and thus to the necessity that a wife's will be strictly limited and subordinated to the will of her husband. The fourth response promotes the wife not as the prototype but as the paradigm of subjection: she is the exemplary inferior in a domestic and political system based upon deference.

Having thus fashioned the entire household order upon the historical and theoretical foundation of the exemplary wifely subject, Gouge concludes his catechism by indicting wives as being, in practice, the most recalcitrant and intractable of all domestic subjects. This ironic fifth and final reason "why wives duties are first taught" may also be seen to be the consequence of the contradiction latent in Gouge's paradoxical first response, that "of all other inferiours in a family, wives are farre the most excellent." If wives are "for the most part . . . most backward in yeelding subjection to their husbands," it may be because the culture in which they are formed promotes not only their moral and physical infirmity but also their virtue and excellence, not only their legal subordination but also their spiritual equality. Elsewhere in his vast tome, Gouge elaborates in great detail upon the "mutuall provident care of husband and wife," upon "such common duties as mutually respect the husband and wife, and are to be performed of each to other," and upon "other common duties which they are both jointly bound to performe to other persons"; he summarizes that, "in generall the government of the family, and the severall members thereof belongeth to the husband and the wife both . . . and a joint common dutie it is to be helpfull one to another therein" (254, 256–57). It is the intermittent presence of such reciprocal, companionate, and egalitarian elements that produces recurrent moments of rhetorical and ideological strain within Gouge's predominantly hierarchical discourse. And it is presumably because of such strains both within his own discourse and within their common culture that some of his parishioners were in a position to take "much exception" to his pronouncements from the pulpit. It is only when selectively constructed by modern criticism as an intellectual "background," against which to read a literary work of canonical status, that any such ideological/discursive field can be made to appear as a transparent, complete, and internally consistent reflection of material social practice.

Like other Shakespearean plays, *A Midsummer Night's Dream* exemplifies many of the precepts of domestic authority that were widely propounded in late sixteenth- to early seventeenth-century sermons and handbooks on marriage and household governance; and, at the same time, it foregrounds disputes and discrepancies within that prescriptive discourse, and exemplifies resistances to its prescriptions. The ideological/discursive field within which *A Midsummer Night's Dream* was initially produced and apprehended includes laws and customs for the ordering of marriage and household—norms that were subject to wide geographic and socioeconomic variation. But it also includes the widely shared and voluminously documented perception by alarmed and articulate contemporaries that their society was experiencing a crisis in household and community order—a perception that wives, children, and servants were habitually bending or breaking the scripturally sanctioned rules.[11] The social historian David Underdown has recently suggested that the study of local

11. For recent analyses by social historians of the interplay of theory and practice in Elizabethan domestic relations, see Wrightson, *English Society 1580–1680*, 66–118; D. E. Underdown, "The Taming of the Scold: The Enforcement of Patriarchal Authority in Early Modern England," in *Order and Disorder in Early Modern England*, ed. Anthony Fletcher and John Stevenson (Cambridge: Cambridge University Press, 1985), 116–36; Martin Ingram, *Church Courts, Sex and Marriage in England, 1570–1640* (Cambridge: Cambridge University Press, 1987), esp. 125–67; Amussen, *An Ordered Society*. An important recent contribution from the perspective of literary and cultural studies is Frances E. Dolan, *Dangerous Familiars: Representations of Domestic Crime in England 1550–1700* (Ithaca: Cornell University Press, 1994).

court records reveals that there existed in England between about 1560 and 1640 "an intense preoccupation with women who are a visible threat to the patriarchal system"; indeed, he goes so far as to propose that there took place "a crisis in gender relations in the years around 1600." He demonstrates that this pattern holds true for at least three distinct categories in the early modern English typology of the "rebellious woman"—namely, the witch, the scold, and the domineering wife ("The Taming of the Scold," 119–22). Underdown's explanation of this crisis accords with Keith Thomas's perspective on the extraordinary increase in witchcraft accusations between the mid-sixteenth and mid-seventeenth centuries: Underdown construes "the preoccupation with scolding women . . . as a by-product" (126) of massive and uneven socioeconomic transformations linked to the growth of capitalist market relations.[12] Underdown's perspective is illuminating and, in its broad outlines, undoubtedly correct. However, his characterization of the cultural misogyny of early modern England as a mere epiphenomenon ("a by-product") of infrastructural socioeconomic changes seems to me an inadequate conceptualization of the historical dynamic at work in the linkage he proposes. Ideologies and social practices of gender identity and relationship must have had some degree of *relative* autonomy from economic infrastructural change. The relationship that clearly did exist between epochal socioeconomic developments and local shifts and conflicts in the ideology of gender must have been exceedingly complex, variously mediated, uneven and unstable, frequently contradictory, and to some degree reciprocal in its consequences.

Underdown points out that all of the extant recorded examples in England of elaborate charivaris, "directed against couples of whom the wife had beaten or otherwise abused the husband," date from the later sixteenth and seventeenth centuries; he concludes that "the

---

12. Underdown cites Thomas, *Religion and the Decline of Magic;* and Alan Macfarlane, *Witchcraft in Tudor and Stuart England* (London: Routledge, 1970). Also see Corrigan and Sayer, *The Great Arch,* 64–65. Underdown stresses regional and local variations in the nature and degree of gender tensions that correlate with relative degrees of dislocation produced by socioeconomic change, with greater instability occurring both in urban centers and in upland wood and pasture areas, rather than in lowland farming areas.

'woman on top', like the scold and the witch, seems to be primarily a phenomenon of the century between 1560 and 1660" (121). In his analysis of *charivaris* provoked by the local community's perception of dominant or wayward wifely conduct, Martin Ingram maintains that, although such demonstrations were grounded in an ideology of patriarchal sovereignty, they nevertheless "reflected an awareness that women could never be dominated to the degree implied in the patriarchal ideal":

> A variety of sources testify that, in practice, the balance of author-
> ity between husbands and wives in marriage varied considerably.
> Equally it is plain that strong, active, able wives were often prized,
> despite the fact that the behaviour of such wives was unlikely to
> conform exactly to the stereotype of female virtue.

He concludes that "the explosive laughter of charivaris represented a cathartic release of tensions built up by . . . experience of the day-to-day conflicts between the dictates of the patriarchal ideal and the infinite variety of husband/wife relationships."[13] In other words, the normative social practice of *charivari* and the normative learned discourse of household governance evidence related forms of ideological contradiction.

The fundamental contradiction of the Elizabethan gender system that was articulated in *charivaris* may have also found controlled expression in the anxious and aggressive aspects of Elizabethan courtship comedies such as Shakespeare's. For example, like the ubiquitous jokes and fears about cuckoldry to which they are usually linked, the frequent allusions within Shakespeare's plays to the incertitude of paternity point to a source of tension, to a potential contradiction,

---

13. Martin Ingram, "Ridings, Rough Music and the 'Reform of Popular Culture' in Early Modern England," *Past & Present* 105 (November 1984), 79–113; quotation from 97–98. Also see Martin Ingram, "The Reform of Popular Culture? Sex and Marriage in Early Modern England," in *Popular Culture in Seventeenth-Century England*, ed. Barry Reay (London: Croom Helm, 1985), 129–65. In "'Rough Music': Le Charivari Anglais" (1972), E. P. Thompson indicated that by the eighteenth century, there had been a turnabout in popular morality, the targets of charivari having by then become abusive husbands and male sex offenders. This classic essay has now been published in English in an enlarged and revised version, in E. P. Thompson, *Customs in Common: Studies in Traditional Popular Culture* (New York: New Press, 1993), 467–538.

within the ostensibly patriarchal gender system of Elizabethan culture: Namely, that the dependence of the husband's masculine honor upon the feminine honor of his wife simultaneously subordinates and empowers her. In *The Merchant of Venice* and *As You Like It*—romantic comedies dominated by witty and resourceful heroines who are also socioeconomically superior to their future husbands—potential anxieties about womanly independence or dominance are focused in jokes about cuckoldry, and are only partially dispelled by uneasy laughter. As Keith Thomas points out, "laughter has a social dimension." Following the work of Mary Douglas on the anthropology of jokes, he observes that

> Jokes are a pointer to joking situations, areas of structural ambiguity in society itself, and their subject-matter can be a revealing guide to past tensions and anxieties. . . .
> Tudor humour about shrewish wives or lascivious widows was a means of confronting the anomalies of insubordinate female behaviour which constantly threatened the actual working of what was supposed to be a male-dominated marital system. Hence the . . . obsession with cuckoldry.[14]

Whether in comedy or in tragedy, Shakespearean dramatic conflicts focused upon marriage and the family frequently work upon this paradox of patriarchy. In the very process of constituting the female body as a locus of its authority, patriarchy also constitutes the female body as a locus of its vulnerability; at the same time that it imposes constraints upon women, patriarchy provides them with a means of resistance and transgression.[15]

According to William Perkins's *Christian Oeconomy*, the principal duty of the wife is "to submit herself to her husband and to acknowledge and reverence him as her head in all things." Contrary to this duty are "the sins of wives: to be proud, to be unwilling to bear the authority of their husbands, to chide and brawl with bitterness, to

14. Keith Thomas, "The Place of Laughter in Tudor and Stuart England," *Times Literary Supplement*, 21 January 1977, 77–81; quotation from 77. Also see Mary Douglas, *Implicit Meanings* (London: Routledge & Kegan Paul, 1975), 90–114. I discuss the manifestation of these tensions in *As You Like It*, in "'The Place of a Brother' in *As You Like It:* Social Process and Comic Form," *Shakespeare Quarterly* 32 (1981), 28–54.

15. For a related and more extensive discussion, see Mark Breitenberg, "Anxious Masculinity: Sexual Jealousy in Early Modern England," *Feminist Studies* 19 (1993), 377–98.

forsake their houses, etc."[16] The exposition and exchanges in the third scene of *A Midsummer Night's Dream* economically demonstrate that "proud Titania" (2.1.60) manifests all of these forms of resistance and transgression against the authority of "jealous Oberon" (2.1.61): She has "forsworn his bed and company" (62), "and now they never meet . . . / But they do square" (28, 30). Yet, to the degree that it keeps the action rigorously under the control of masculine characters throughout, *A Midsummer Night's Dream* differs markedly from the more or less contemporaneous *Merchant of Venice* and *As You Like It.* Paradoxically, Oberon goes so far as to provoke his wife's infidelity precisely in order to manifest fully his capacity to contain her agency, to subdue her pride. Using literary and dramatic sources as unproblematized forms of evidence for social practice, Underdown notes that "late Elizabethan and Jacobean writers do seem to have been uncommonly preoccupied by themes of female independence and revolt." He concludes, however, that "on the stage, as in carnival, gender inversion temporarily turns the world upside-down—but to reinforce, not subvert, the traditional order" (117); and he invokes Shakespeare's Beatrice and Rosalind in order to exemplify a containment theory of Elizabethan comedy. Nevertheless, as I shall attempt to demonstrate in the following chapters, even in so manifestly patriarchal a Shakespearean comedy as *A Midsummer Night's Dream*, the dominance of patriarchy is vulnerable to destabilization by numerous instances of dramatic contradiction and intertextual irony.

The classificatory terms of Elizabethan culture marked off symbolic actions categorized as game, play, or drama from those that were conducted and experienced as religious rites or ceremonies of state. In specific instances, such marginal symbolic actions may have constituted intervals of a creative or contestatory counter-order that generated critical perspectives upon, or rowdy parodies of, ideologically dominant forms and practices. As Robert Weimann, C. L. Barber, and others have shown, the counter-hegemonic elements of Shakespearean drama are assimilated into the playworld from an enormous range

16. William Perkins, *Christian Oeconomie: or, a short survey of the right manner of ordering a familie according to the Scriptures* (Latin original, 1590), trans. Thomas Pickering (1609); rpt. in *The Work of William Perkins*, ed. Ian Breward, The Courtenay Library of Reformation Classics 3 (Appleford, England: Sutton Courtenay Press, 1970), 429.

of available social practices and cultural forms: popular traditions of complaint, satire, and festive misrule; representative opinions and behaviors of such socially marginal figures as clowns, fools, lunatics, transvestites, beggars, criminals, aliens, children, and women; double plots and other forms of dramatic construction that create social juxta-positions, parallels, and parodies; subversions of linguistic, logical, and social categories by such folk forms as jokes, parables, riddles, and prophecies.[17]

Writing of counter-hegemonic elements in sixteenth-century French culture, Natalie Zemon Davis observes that

> the structure of the carnival form can evolve so that it can act both to reinforce order and to suggest alternatives to the existing or-der. . . . Comic and festive inversion could *undermine* as well as re-inforce . . . assent through its connections with everyday circum-stances outside the privileged time of carnival and stage-play.[18]

If this was so, it was because what carnival or dramatic comedy turned temporarily upside-down was not the totality of actual, quotidian ex-perience but rather a dominant, idealized, and coercive hierarchical model of the social order that sought to delimit and control the multi-fariousness of daily life. Play forms may have been capable of ad-dressing the complexities, contradictions, obscurities, and instabilit-ies of "everyday circumstances" that this orthodox model ignored or actively suppressed. For example, the representation of the Elizabe-than system of domestic and social relations based upon hierarchical distinctions of gender, generation, and rank is significantly different in the state homilies and in handbooks on marriage and domestic conduct from what it is in Shakespearean comedy. The dramatic in-teraction of characters is not strictly governed by a doctrinal program which the play exists merely to exemplify. In any given play, such a program may be ideologically dominant but it is never absolute and never uncontested. On the contrary, conventional and often opposing modes of thought, systems of value, and patterns of behavior are re-created within the world of the play as manifestations of human char-

17. See Barber, *Shakespeare's Festive Comedy;* and Weimann, *Shakespeare and the Popular Tradition in the Theater.* Also see Michael D. Bristol, *Carnival and Theater: Plebeian Culture and the Structure of Authority in Renaissance England* (New York: Methuen, 1985).

18. Natalie Zemon Davis, *Society and Culture in Early Modern France* (Stanford: Stanford University Press, 1975), 123, 131.

acters in conflict with each other, with the state, and with themselves. It is usually the case that the end of the play serves to reaffirm the dominant positions; nevertheless, the prior action may have opened up challenges and alternatives that subsequent attempts at closure cannot wholly efface.

CHAPTER NINE

STORIES OF THE NIGHT

The opposed domestic emphases of Brooks and Olson—the former, romantic and companionate; the latter, authoritarian and hierarchical—abstract and oversimplify what may be construed as potentially complementary or contradictory elements in the dramatic process whereby *A Midsummer Night's Dream* figures the social relationship between the sexes in courtship, marriage, and parenthood. Among the cultural materials employed in the construction of the gender system that is figured in *A Midsummer Night's Dream*, those of classical myth are perhaps the most conspicuous. The play dramatizes or alludes to numerous episodes of classical mythology that were already coded by a venerable tradition of moral allegorization, and its treatment of such mythographic traditions is, like the traditions themselves, far from unequivocal. In this chapter, I want to focus upon the mythological subtext of *A Midsummer Night's Dream* and upon its articulation with the gendered discourses of human physiology and domestic economy.

I

The beginning of *A Midsummer Night's Dream* coincides with the end of a struggle in which Theseus has been victorious over the Amazon warrior:

> Hippolyta, I woo'd thee with my sword,
> And won thy love doing thee injuries;
> But I will wed thee in another key,
> With pomp, with triumph, and with revelling.
> (1.1.16–19)

Descriptions of the Amazons or allusions to them are ubiquitous across the range of Elizabethan writing and performance genres. For example, all of the essentials are present in popular form in William Painter's "Novel of the Amazones," which opens the second book of *The Palace of Pleasure* (1575). Here we read that the Amazons "were most excellent warriors"; that "they murdred certaine of their husbands" at the beginning of their gynecocracy; and that,

> if they brought forth daughters, they norished and trayned them up in armes, and other manlik exercises.
> ... If they were delivered of males, they sent them to their fathers, and if by chaunce they kept any backe, they murdred them, or else brake their armes and legs in sutch wise as they had no power to beare weapons, and served for nothynge but to spin, twist, and doe other feminine labour.[19]

Amazonian mythology seems symbolically to embody and to control a collective (masculine) anxiety about women's power not only to dominate or to repudiate men but also to create and destroy them. It is an ironic acknowledgment by an androcentric culture of the degree to which men are in fact dependent upon women: upon mothers and nurses, for their own birth and nurture; upon chaste mistresses and wives, both for the validation of their manhood and for the birth and legitimacy of their offspring.

Shakespeare engages his wedding play in a dialectic with this mythological formation. The Amazons have been defeated shortly before the play begins, and nuptial rites are to be celebrated when it ends. *A Midsummer Night's Dream* focuses upon different crucial transitions in the masculine and feminine life cycles of early modern English society: The fairy plot focuses upon taking "a little changeling boy" from the relatively androgynous or feminized state of infancy into the more decisively gendered state of youth, from the world of mothers and nurses into the world of fathers and masters. In *The Book named The Governor,* Sir Thomas Elyot advised, "after that a [boy] child is come to seven years of age, I hold it expedient that he be taken from the company of women" and assigned "a tutor, which

19. William Painter, *The Palace of Pleasure* (1575), ed. Joseph Jacobs, 3 vols. (1890; rpt., New York: Dover Books, 1966), 2:159–61. Page citations are to volume 2 of this edition. For a sense of the ubiquity of Amazonian representations in Elizabethan culture, see the valuable survey by Celeste Turner Wright, "The Amazons in Elizabethan Literature," *Studies in Philology* 37 (1940), 433–56.

should be an ancient and worshipful man." As Stephen Orgel has recently pointed out, *à propos* of *The Winter's Tale,*

> Elizabethan children of both sexes were dressed in skirts until the age of seven or so; the 'breeching' of boys was the formal move out of the common gender of childhood, which was both female in appearance and largely controlled by women, and into the world of men. This event was traditionally the occasion for a significant family ceremony.[20]

Shakespeare's Athenian plot focuses upon conducting a young gentlewoman from the state of maidenhood to the state of matrimony, upon conveying her from her father's house to her husband's. This, too, of course, was a transition marked by significant ritual and ceremonial events—namely, betrothal, wedding, and the bedding of the bride. The pairing of the four Athenian lovers is made possible by the magical powers of Oberon and made lawful by the political authority of Theseus. Each of these rulers is preoccupied with the fulfillment of his own desires in the possession or repossession of a wife. It is only *after* Hippolyta has been mastered by Theseus that marriage may seal them "in everlasting bond of fellowship" (1.1.85). And it is only *after* "proud Titania" has been degraded by "jealous Oberon" (2.1.60, 61), has "in mild terms begg'd" (4.1.57) his patience, and has readily yielded the changeling boy to him, that they may be "new in amity" (4.1.86).

The unfolding action of *A Midsummer Night's Dream*—its diachronic structure—eventually restores the inverted Amazonian system of gender and nurture to a patriarchal norm. But the initial plans for Theseus's triumph are immediately interrupted by news of yet another unruly female. Egeus wishes to confront his daughter Her-

---

20. See Sir Thomas Elyot, *The Book named The Governor,* ed. S. E. Lehmberg (London: Dent, 1962), 19; Stephen Orgel, "Nobody's Perfect: Or, Why Did the English Stage Take Boys for Women?" *South Atlantic Quarterly* 88 (1989), 7–29; quotation from 10–11. Also see Patricia Crawford, "The Construction and Experience of Maternity in Seventeenth-Century England," in *Women as Mothers in Pre-Industrial England: Essays in Memory of Dorothy McLaren,* ed. Valerie Fildes (London and New York: Routledge, 1990), 3–38, esp. 12–13: "Contemporaries usually judged that a mother was responsible for the care of children under the age of 7. . . . In the upper levels of society, maternal education for boys was confined to their earlier years. After about the age of 7, boys from the gentry were usually entrusted to the care of a schoolmaster or tutor. . . . Although mothers were responsible for the education of daughters, they were subject to paternal authority."

mia with two alternatives: absolute obedience to the paternal will, or death. Theseus intervenes with a third alternative: If she refuses to marry whom her father chooses, Hermia must submit,

> Either to die the death or to abjure
> Forever the society of men.
> . . .
> For aye to be in shady cloister mew'd,
> Chanting faint hymns to the cold, fruitless moon.
> Thrice blessed they that master so their blood
> To undergo such maiden pilgrimage;
> But earthlier happy is the rose distill'd
> Than that which, withering on the virgin thorn,
> Grows, lives, and dies, in single blessedness.
> (1.1.65–66, 71–78)

Theseus's rhetoric concisely stages a Reformation debate on the relative virtues of virginity and marriage. He concedes praise to the former, as being exemplary of self-mastery, but nevertheless concludes that the latter more fully satisfies the imperatives of earthly existence. He implies that maidenhood is a phase in the life-cycle of a woman who is destined for married chastity and motherhood; that, when it persists as a permanent state, "single blessedness" is reduced to mere sterility.

Theseus expands Hermia's options, but only in order to clarify her constraints. In the process of tempering the father's domestic tyranny, the Duke affirms his own interests and authority. He represents the life of a vestal as a punishment, and it is one that fits the nature of Hermia's crime. The maiden is surrounded by her father, her lovers, and her lord; and each of these men claims a kind of property in her—in her body, her fantasy, her will. Yet Hermia dares to suggest that she has a claim to property in herself: She refuses to "yield [her] virgin patent up / Unto his lordship whose unwished yoke / [Her] soul consents not to give sovereignty" (1.1.80–82). Like Portia or Rosalind, Hermia wishes the limited privilege of giving herself. Theseus appropriates the sources of Hermia's fragile power, her ability to master her blood and to deny men access to her body. He usurps the power of virginity by imposing upon Hermia his own power to deny her the use of her body. If she will not submit to its use by her father and by Demetrius, she must "abjure forever the society of men," and "live a barren sister all [her] life" (1.1.65–66, 72). Her own words suggest that the female body is a supreme form of property; a locus for the contestation of authority; the site of a struggle between man and woman, and between man and man. Although displaced into the thoroughly anachronistic setting of Theseus's Athenian court, Hermia's predicament activates the vexed and contested status of Elizabethan women as conscious and willing subjects and as objects of patriarchal sovereignty. The self-possession of single blessedness is a form of resistance against which are opposed the dominant domestic values of Shakespeare's culture and the very form of his comedy.[21]

The conflict between Egeus and Hermia and its mediation by Theseus constitute a paradigm case for Northop Frye's influential theory of Shakespearean comic form. According to Frye, a Shakespearean comedy

> normally begins with an anticomic society, a social organization blocking and opposed to the comic drive, which the action of the comedy evades or overcomes. It often takes the form of a harsh or irrational law, like . . . the law disposing of rebellious daughters in *A Midsummer Night's Dream*. . . . Most of these irrational laws are preoccupied with trying to regulate the sexual drive, and so work counter to the wishes of the hero and heroine, which form the main impetus of the comic action. (*A Natural Perspective*, 73–74)

21. Linda T. Fitz, "'What Says the Married Woman?': Marriage Theory and Feminism in the English Renaissance," *Mosaic*, 13:2 (Winter 1980), 1–22, suggests that "the English Renaissance institutionalized, where it did not invent, the restrictive marriage-oriented attitude toward women that feminists have been struggling against ever since. . . . The insistent demand for the right—nay, obligation—of women to be happily married arose as much in reaction against women's intractable pursuit of independence as it did in reaction against Catholic ascetic philosophy" (11, 18). And Amy Louise Erickson, *Women and Property in Early Modern England*, points out that, "In spite of legal, demographic, economic and social shifts, an underlying continuity ties the women of 1550 and earlier to the women of 1750 and later. Men's perceived need to restrict women legally within marriage is as constant as their need to persuade women to think in terms of marriage as the natural female state" (232).

Despite the dominance and desirability of marriage as a social expectation and norm, the work of social historians and historical demographers suggests that significant numbers of Elizabethan women—and men—never married, chiefly because they were unable to accumulate the material resources necessary to establish a household.

Frye's account of Shakespearean comic action emphasizes intergenerational tension at the expense of those other forms of social and familial tension from which it is only artificially separable. The interaction of personae in the fictive societies of Shakespearean drama, like the interaction of persons in the society of Shakespeare's England, is structured by a complex interplay among culture-specific categories, not only of age and gender but also of kinship and social rank. The ideologically unstable Elizabethan gender system articulated in Shakespeare's plays is structured both in terms of *difference*—as opposition, and as complementariness; and in terms of *hierarchy*—as superiority/inferiority, and as domination/subordination.

In Shakespearean comedy, as in Shakespearean drama generally, (gentle)women are represented variously as volitional and reasonable agents, as objects of masculine desire or anxiety, and as victims of masculine aggression or slander. Frye unequivocally identifies the heroines' interests with those of the heroes. Nevertheless, the "drive toward a festive conclusion" (*Natural Perspective*, 75) that liberates and unites comic heroes and comic heroines also binds together generations of men through the giving of daughters, confers the responsibilities and privileges of manhood upon callow youths, and subordinates wives to the authority of their husbands. Women's wit may be acknowledged and accommodated in the new domestic economy that has been prepared for, or established by, the end of the comic action; however, the plays' imagined societies show little if any sign of genuine structural transformation. According to Frye, "the main impetus" of Shakespearean comic action is the defeat of attempts "to regulate the sexual drive." (Unlike more recent studies of the poetics of desire in Shakespearean drama, *A Natural Perspective* conceives of the Shakespearean erotic as exclusively heterosexual and as gender-neutral.) I would suggest a pattern different from and more equivocal than that proposed by Frye: In *A Midsummer Night's Dream*, as in other Shakespearean comedies, the *main* impetus is to regulate the concupiscible passions through the social institution of marriage, thus fabricating an accommodation between law and desire, between reason and appetite; however, a subliminal or oblique counter-impetus, of varying strength, frames these acts of regulation and accommodation as tentative, partial, or flawed.

In devising Hermia's punishment, Theseus appropriates and parodies the very condition that the Amazons sought to enjoy. They rejected marriages with men and alliances with patriarchal societies because, as one sixteenth-century writer put it, they esteemed "that Matrimonie was not a meane of libertie but of thraldome."[22] The separatism of the Amazons is a repudiation of men's claims to have property in women. But if Amazonian myth figures the inversionary claims of matriarchy, sorority, and female autonomy, it also figures the repudiation of those claims in the recuperative act of Amazonomachy. At the opening of *The Two Noble Kinsmen*, in a scene generally ascribed to Shakespeare, one of the suppliant queens addresses the about-to-be-wedded Hippolyta as

> Most dreaded Amazonian, that hast slain
> The scythe-tusk'd boar; that with thy arm, as strong
> As it is white, wast near to make the male
> To thy sex captive, but that this thy lord,
> Born to uphold creation in that honor
> First Nature styl'd it in, shrunk thee into
> The bound thou was't o'erflowing, at once subduing
> Thy force and thy affection.
>
> (*TNK*, 1.1.78–85)

The passage registers Hippolyta's imposing combination of physical beauty and physical strength as something wonderful but also as something unnatural and dangerous, and requiring masculine control. The judgment that the Amazon is monstrous and that Theseus is a champion of the natural order is given (ironically) greater credence when it is pronounced by a queen. Here, as at the beginning of *A Midsummer Night's Dream*, what seems to interest Shakespeare (and, perhaps, Fletcher) about Theseus's participation in the Amazonomachy is that it leads to his marriage with his captive. In the story of Theseus and Hippolyta, Amazonomachy and marriage coincide, reaffirming the Amazons' reputed estimation "that Matrimonie was not a meane of libertie but of thraldome."

Elsewhere in *A Midsummer Night's Dream*, Shakespeare displaces the myth of Amazonomachy into the vicissitudes of courtship. Heterosexual desire disrupts the innocent pleasures of Hermia's girlhood: "What graces in my love do dwell, / That he hath turn'd a

---

22. André Thevet, *The newefounde Worlde*, trans. T. Hacket (London, 1568), 102r.

heaven unto a hell!" (1.1.206–07). Hermia's farewell to Helena is also a farewell to their girlhood friendship, a delicate repudiation of youthful homophilia:

> And in the wood, where often you and I
> Upon faint primrose beds were wont to lie,
> Emptying our bosoms of their counsel sweet,
> There my Lysander and myself shall meet;
> And thence from Athens turn away our eyes,
> To seek new friends, and stranger companies.
>
> (1.1.214–19)

Helena is sworn to secrecy by the lovers; nevertheless, before this scene ends, in order to further her own desire, she has determined to betray her sweet bedfellow's secret to Demetrius. Before dawn comes at last to the forest, the "counsel" shared by Hermia and Helena, their "sisters' vows . . . school-days' friendship, childhood innocence" (3.2.198, 199, 202), have all been torn asunder, to be replaced at the end of the play by the primary demands and loyalties of wedlock.

On the other hand, the hostilities between the two male youths have, before dawn, dissolved into "gentle concord" (4.1.142). From the beginning of the play, the relationship between Lysander and Demetrius has been based upon aggressive rivalry for the same object of desire—first for Hermia, and then for Helena. Each youth must despise his current mistress in order to adore her successor; and a change in the affections of one provokes a change in the affections of the other. R. W. Dent has pointed out that the young women do not fluctuate in their desires for their young men, and that the ending ratifies their constant if inexplicable preferences.[23] It should be added, however, that the maidens remain constant to the objects of their desire at the cost of inconstancy to each other. On the other hand, Lysander and Demetrius are flagrantly inconstant to Hermia

---

23. Robert W. Dent, "Imagination in *A Midsummer Night's Dream*," *Shakespeare Quarterly* 15 (1964), 115–29; see 116. On the permutations of desire among the lovers of *MND*, see René Girard, "Myth and Ritual in Shakespeare: *A Midsummer Night's Dream*," in *Textual Strategies*, ed. Josué V. Harari (Ithaca: Cornell University Press, 1979), 189–212. On the relationship of Hermia and Helena, see the discussion in James L. Calderwood, *Shakespearean Metadrama* (Minneapolis: University of Minnesota Press, 1971), 126.

and Helena but the pattern of their romantic inconstancies stabilizes a relationship of rivalry between them. The romantic resolution engineered by Oberon and approved by Theseus transforms the nature of their mutual constancy from rivalry to friendship by contriving that each male will accept "his own" female. In Puck's jaunty and crude formulation:

> And the country proverb known,
> That every man should take his own,
> In your waking shall be shown:
> >   Jack shall have Jill,
> >   Nought shall go ill:
> The man shall have his mare again, and all shall
> be well.
>
> > > > (3.2.458–63)

In *A Midsummer Night's Dream*, as in *As You Like It*, the dramatic process that forges the marital couplings simultaneously weakens the bonds of sisterhood and strengthens the bonds of brotherhood.[24]

II

In the play's opening scene, Egeus claims that he may do with Hermia as he chooses because she is his property: "As she is mine, I may dispose of her" (1.1.42). This claim is based upon a stunningly simple thesis: She is his because he has made her. Charging that Lysander has "stol'n the impression" (1.1.32) of Hermia's fantasy, Egeus effectively absolves his daughter from responsibility for her affections because he cannot acknowledge her capacity for volition. If she does not—cannot—obey him, then she should be destroyed. Borrowing Egeus' own imprinting metaphor, Theseus explains to Hermia the ontogenetic principle underlying her father's vehemence:

> To you your father should be as a god:
> One that compos'd your beauties, yea, and one
> To whom you are but as a form in wax

---

24. For a detailed analysis, see my essay, "'The Place of a Brother' in *As You Like It*."

By him imprinted, and within his power
To leave the figure or disfigure it.

(1.1.47–51)

Theseus represents paternity as a cultural act, an art: The father is a demiurge or *Homo faber* who composes, in-forms, imprints himself upon, what is merely inchoate matter. Conspicuously excluded from Shakespeare's play is the relationship between mother and daughter—the kinship bond through which Amazonian society reproduces itself.[25] The mother's part is wholly excluded from this account of the making of a daughter. Hermia and Helena have no mothers; they have only fathers.[26] The central women characters of Shakespeare's comedies are not mothers but mothers-to-be, maidens who are pass-

25. In this connection, see Hobbes's interesting remarks in his discussion "Of Dominion Paternall, and Despoticall" (*Leviathan*, pt. 2, ch. 20): Hobbes construes the parent-child relationship as the condition of dominion or sovereignty by generation, with the proviso that this dominion is not established through mere procreation but rather by contract. Hobbes reasons that, because "there be alwayes two that are equally Parents: the Dominion therefore over the Child, should belong equally to both"; however, this "is impossible; for no man can obey two Masters." Hobbes notes that "in Common-wealths, this controversie is decided by the Civill Law: and for the most part, (but not alwayes) the sentence is in favour of the Father; because for the most part Common-wealths have been erected by the Fathers, not by the Mothers of families." However, in the (hypothetical) state of "meer Nature, either the Parents between themselves dispose of the dominion over the Child by Contract; or do not dispose thereof at all. . . . We find in History that the *Amazons* Contracted with the Men of the neighboring Countries, to whom they had recourse for issue, that the issue Male should be sent back, but the Female remain with themselves: so that the dominion of the Females was in the Mother." See Thomas Hobbes, *Leviathan* (1651), ed. C. B. Macpherson (Harmondsworth, Middlesex: Penguin Books, 1968), 253–54.

26. I first emphasized this point in "Shaping Fantasies" (1983). Now see Mary Beth Rose, "Where Are the Mothers in Shakespeare? Options for Gender Representation in the English Renaissance," *Shakespeare Quarterly* 42 (1991), 291–314. In her meticulous study, Rose sketches a range of attitudes toward, and representations of, motherhood in Elizabethan-Jacobean England; she concludes that Shakespearean maternal representations are almost exclusively of the most traditional and conservative sort. In this construction, motherhood, "lagging behind the altering definitions of other family roles . . . remains most resolutely limited to the private realm, inscribed entirely in terms of early love and nurture. As a result, motherhood in this formulation can be dramatized only as dangerous or as peripheral to adult, public life" (313). For an excellent overview of the early modern representation and practice of motherhood, based primarily on diaries, letters, and

ing from fathers to husbands in a world made and governed by men. Here, the proprietary claims of patriarchy are taken to their logical extreme, and the female subject is wholly denied the capacity to have property in herself.[27]

In effect, Theseus's lecture on the shaping of a daughter is a fantasy of male parthenogenesis. Titania's votaress is the only biological mother in *A Midsummer Night's Dream*. But she is an absent presence who must be evoked from Titania's memory because she has died in giving birth to a son. Assuming that they do not maim or kill their sons, the Amazons are only too glad to give them away to their fathers. In Shakespeare's play, however, Oberon's paternal dominance must be directed against Titania's maternal possessiveness:

> For Oberon is passing fell and wrath,
> Because that she as her attendant hath
> A lovely boy, stol'n from an Indian king—
> She never had so sweet a changeling;
> And jealous Oberon would have the child
> Knight of his train to trace the forest wild;

---

guidebooks, see Crawford, "The Construction and Experience of Maternity in Seventeenth-Century England"; and, for a powerful psychoanalytic reading of the problematic representation of motherhood in Shakespeare's later plays, see Janet Adelman, *Suffocating Mothers: Fantasies of Maternal Origin in Shakespeare's Plays, "Hamlet" to "The Tempest"* (New York and London: Routledge, 1992).

27. This may be an extreme form of the proprietary fantasy of patriarchy but it is nevertheless securely grounded in the gender ideology and customary and legal practices of early modern England. See, for example, the observations of Amy Louise Erickson:

Many men would have liked to regard women as property in and of themselves; but while married women's legal disabilities put them in the same category as idiots, convicted criminals and infants, they were never legally classed with chattels. Nonetheless, there are ways in which women were treated as a form of property. The specious theory of the "unity" of husband and wife, and the constant threat of legal incapacitation; the association of a woman's marriage portion with her sexual honour; the view of rape as a form of theft, not from the victim but from her husband or male relatives; the prosecution of adultery only in cases where the woman was married; and the implications of even a practice as apparently innocuous as losing one's name upon marriage—all of these smack of men's ownership of women. Certainly in the seventeenth century a number of women (and a very few men) protested that women were treated little better than slaves. (*Women and Property in Early Modern England*, 232–33)

But she perforce withholds the loved boy,
Crowns him with flowers, and makes him all her joy.

(2.1.20–27)

In his *De Pueris,* Erasmus approves of the mothers of infants, who "swaddle their children and bandage their heads, and keep a watchful eye on their eating and drinking, bathing and exercising"; however, he excoriates those who would prolong infancy into later childhood: "What kind of maternal feeling is it that induces some women to keep their children clinging to their skirts until they are six years old and to treat them as imbeciles?"[28] A boy's transition from the woman-centered world of his early childhood to the man-centered world of his youth is given a kind of phylogenetic sanction by myths recounting a cultural transition from matriarchy to patriarchy.[29] Such a mythic charter is represented at the very threshhold of *A Midsummer Night's Dream:* Oberon attempts to take the boy from what Puck suggests is an indulgent and infantilizing mother, and this attempt is sanctioned by Theseus's defeat of the Amazons, a matriarchate that maims and effeminizes its male offspring. Oberon will make a man of the boy by subjecting him to service as his "henchman" and "Knight of his train," thus exposing him to the challenges of "the forest wild." Yet, "jealous" Oberon is not only Titania's rival for the child but also the child's rival for Titania: Making the boy "all her joy," "proud" Titania withholds herself from her husband; she has "forsworn his bed and company" (2.1.62–63). Oberon's preoccupation is to gain possession not only of the boy but also of the woman's desire and obedience; he must master his own dependency upon his wife.[30]

---

28. *De pueris statim ac liberaliter instituendis declamatio* ("A Declamation on the Subject of Early Liberal Education for Children"), trans. Beert C. Verstraete, in *Collected Works of Erasmus,* vol. 26 (Literary and Educational Writings, vol. 4), ed. J. K. Sowards (Toronto: University of Toronto Press, 1985), 295–346; quotations from 300, 309.

29. See Joan Bamberger, "The Myth of Matriarchy: Why Men Rule in Primitive Society," in *Woman, Culture and Society,* ed. Michelle Zimbalist Rosaldo and Louise Lamphere (Stanford: Stanford University Press, 1974), 262–80, esp. 266, 277.

30. Some of the play's (masculine) critics have approved of Oberon's actions as undertaken in the best interests of a growing boy and a neurotic mother. Two of the play's most rewarding critics must be included among them: see Barber,

In his pioneering essay on "the double standard" in regard to sexual conduct, Keith Thomas notes that the importance of legitimate heirs to Englishmen of the property-owning classes has frequently been cited to explain and justify the emphasis on wifely chastity. However, he concludes that the property issues involved include not only "the property of legitimate heirs, but the property of men in women." Virginity before and chastity during marriage have been regarded as of paramount importance in women because "the absolute property of the woman's chastity was vested not in the woman herself but in her parents or her husband."[31] This perspective on the persistence of "the double standard" in English law and custom helps to focus more sharply the gendered thematics of power and possession that characterize both of the conflict-generating plots in *A Midsummer Night's Dream*, those contesting the statuses of Hermia and the changeling. Thus, the conflict between the King and Queen of Faeries, like those between Egeus and Hermia and between Theseus and Hippolyta, revolves around issues of authority and autonomy, around claims to have property in others and in oneself, as these claims are generated in relations between husbands and wives, parents and children.

Titania has her own explanation for her fixation upon the changeling:

> His mother was a votress of my order
> And in the spiced Indian air, by night,
> Full often hath she gossip'd by my side;
> And sat with me on Neptune's yellow sands,
> Marking th'embarked traders on the flood:
> When we have laugh'd to see the sails conceive
> And grow big-bellied with the wanton wind,

Shakespeare's Festive Comedy, 119–62, esp. 137; Calderwood, *Shakespearean Metadrama*, 120–48, esp. 125.

31. Keith Thomas, "The Double Standard" (1959), rpt., with revisions, in *Ideas in Cultural Perspective*, ed. Philip P. Wiener and Aaron Noland (New Brunswick, New Jersey: Rutgers University Press, 1962), 446–67; quotations from 461, 464. Thomas quotes Juan Luis Vives's influential Tudor treatise, *The Instruction of a Christen Woman*, to the effect that "A woman hath no power of her own body, but her husband; thou dost the more wrong to give away that thing which is another body's without the owner's licence" (trans. R. Hyrde [1541], 66r).

Which she, with pretty and with swimming gait
Following (her womb then rich with my young squire),
Would imitate, and sail upon the land
To fetch me trifles, and return again
As from a voyage rich with merchandise.
But she, being mortal, of that boy did die,
And for her sake do I rear up her boy;
And for her sake I will not part with him.

(2.1.123–37)

Titania's attachment to the changeling boy embodies her attachment
to the memory of his mother. As is later the case with Bottom, Titania
both dotes upon and dominates the child; her bond to the child's
mother attenuates his imprisonment to the womb: "And for her sake
I will not part with him." What Oberon accomplishes by substituting
Bottom for the boy is to break Titania's solemn vow. As in the case
of the Amazons, or of Hermia and Helena, here again the play enacts
a masculine disruption of an intimate bond between women—first
by the boy, and then by the man. It is as if, in order to be freed and
enfranchised from the prison of the womb, the male child must kill
his mother: "She, being mortal, of that boy did die." Titania's words
suggest that mother and son are potentially mortal to each other.
Thus, embedded within the changeling plot are transformations of
the collective masculine fantasies of powerful and dangerous motherhood that are figured in Amazonian myth. The matricidal male infant
has a reciprocal relationship to the infanticidal Amazon. Elizabethan
family life was characterized by a high incidence of spontaneous and
induced abortion and of infant mortality, and a pervasive perception
that pregnancy and parturition were life-threatening to the mother.
Material conditions of existence such as these are given imaginative
articulation in Shakespeare's play as an inherently dangerous relationship between mother and son.[32]

32. For evidence regarding infant mortality, see R. S. Schofield and E. A.
Wrigley, "Infant and Child Mortality in the Late Tudor and Early Stuart Period,"
in *Health, Medicine and Mortality in the Sixteenth Century*, ed. Charles Webster (Cam-
bridge: Cambridge University Press, 1979), 61–95; on spontaneous and induced
abortion, and fears of pregnancy, see Linda A. Pollock, "Embarking on a Rough
Passage: The Experience of Pregnancy in Early-Modern Society," in *Women as
Mothers in Pre-Industrial England*, 39–67; also, Crawford, "The Construction and
Experience of Maternity in Seventeenth-Century England," *ibid.*, 21–23.

Titania represents her bond to her votaress as one that is rooted in an experience of female fertility. The women "have laugh'd to see the sails conceive / And grow big-bellied with the wanton wind"; and the votaress has parodied such false pregnancies by sailing to fetch trifles, at the same time that she herself bears a treasure within her womb. The riches of the maternal womb and those of the merchant venturer provide the dramatic poet's rich wit with matter for similitudes. Yet, in part because of the gendered perspective of the similitude's fictive speaker, the passage not only gives priority to the woman's (fatal) generativity but also gives voice to women's proprietary relationship to their own bodies and to the products of their maternal labor. In this sense, the passage provides a lyrical counter-statement to the paternal and patriarchal claims upon Hermia. Specifically, the notion of maternity implied in Titania's speech counterpoints the notion of paternity formulated by Theseus in the opening scene. In Theseus's description, neither biological nor social mother—neither *genetrix* nor *mater*—plays a role in the making of a daughter; in Titania's description, neither *genitor* nor *pater* plays a role in the making of a son. The father's daughter is shaped from without; the mother's son comes from within her body: Titania dwells upon the physical bond between mother and child, as manifested in pregnancy and parturition. Like an infant of the Elizabethan upper classes, however, the changeling is nurtured not by his natural mother but by a surrogate. Here it is worth remembering that in early modern social practice, men were rarely present during labor and birth; and that the work of midwives and wetnurses, and the custom of female visitations during the period of lying-in, strongly reinforced the sense of childbirth as a collectively and exclusively feminine modality of experience. As Adrian Wilson has characterized it, "the social space of the birth . . . was a collective female space, constituted on the one hand by the presence of gossips and midwife, and on the other hand by the absence of men."[33] By emphasizing her own role as a foster mother to the offspring of the votary who "gossip'd by [her] side," Titania links the biological and social aspects of parenthood together

33. Adrian Wilson, "The Ceremony of Childbirth and Its Interpretation," in *Women as Mothers in Pre-Industrial England*, 68–107; quotation from 73. Also see Crawford, "The construction and experience of maternity in seventeenth-century England," *ibid.*, 21, 25–29.

within a wholly maternal world, a world in which the relationship between women has displaced the relationship between wife and husband.

In *A Midsummer Night's Dream*, the mother is represented as a vessel, as a container for her son; she is not his maker. Lemnius' *Secret Miracles of Nature*, a sixteenth-century treatise translated in 1658, demystifies the lyrical similitude for maternal fecundity that Shakespeare gives to Titania. Lemnius attacks such a conception of conception, one that teaches women that

> Mothers afford very little to the generation of the child, but onely are at the trouble to carry it . . . as if the womb were hired by men, as Merchants Ships are to be straited by them; and to discharge their burden . . . women grow luke-warm, and lose all humane affections towards their children.[34]

In contrast to such a representation of maternity, the implication of Theseus's description of paternity is that the male is the only begetter; a daughter is merely a token of her father's potency. Such an implication reverses the putative Amazonian practice, in which women use men merely for their own reproduction. Taken together, the speeches of Theseus and Titania may be said to formulate in poetic discourse, a proposition about the genesis of gender and power: Men make women and make themselves through the medium of women.[35]

Despite the exclusion of a paternal role from Titania's speech, the embryological notions represented in *A Midsummer Night's Dream* have a recognizably Aristotelian coloring. In the Aristotelian tradition, the actively in-forming *sperma* of the male is the efficient cause of generation, and the passively receptive *catamenia* of the female is the material cause of generation.[36] Whereas Aristotle emphasizes two

---

34. L. Lemnius, *The Secret Miracles of Nature* (London, 1658), 23; quoted in Crawford, "The Construction and Experience of Maternity in Seventeenth-Century England," 7.

35. In *Love's Labour's Lost*, such an assertion seems to be implied in Berowne's ostensible paean to the ladies of France: "Or for men's sake, the authors of these women, / Or for women's sake, by whom we men are men" (*LLL*, 4.3.355–56).

36. On classical embryological theory, I have found the following useful: F. J. Cole, *Early Theories of Sexual Generation* (Oxford: Clarendon Press, 1930); Joseph Needham, *A History of Embryology*, 2nd ed., rev. (New York: Abelard-Schuman, 1959); Maryanne Cline Horowitz, "Aristotle and Woman," *Journal of the History of Biology* 9 (1976), 183–213; Thomas Laqueur, *Making Sex: Body and Gender from the*

distinct sexes, Galenic anatomy and physiology emphasize what Thomas Laqueur calls a "one-sex" model: There is a homology between the genital organs of man and woman, the latter being an inverted and internalized version of the former. Accordingly, both sexes contribute their "seed" to conception, and both have to experience orgasm and ejaculation in order for conception to take place.[37] However, when Angus McLaren writes that, in Galenic medicine, "both sexes were presented as contributing *equally* in conception" (*Reproductive Rituals*, 17; emphasis added), he may give the wrong impression that this implies an egalitarian sex/gender system. It would be more accurate to say that, in Galenic theory, males and females contribute to conception according to their homologous but inherently unequal abilities: The Galenic "one-sex" model is based upon the norm of male anatomy and physiology; the female is an imperfect version of the male, unable to realize the *telos* of masculinity due to a lack of vital heat in her constitution. The act of generation brings man and woman into a relationship that is both complementary and hierarchical. Thus, there exists a homology between ideologies of sexual and domestic relations: genitor is to genetrix as husband is to wife.

According to *The Problemes of Aristotle*, a popular Elizabethan medical guide that continued to be revised and reissued well into the nineteenth century,

> The seede [i.e., of the man] is the efficient beginning of the childe, as the builder is the efficient cause of the house, and therefore is not the materiall cause of the childe.... The seedes [i.e., both male and female] are shut and kept in the wombe: but the seede of the man doth dispose and prepare the seed of the woman to receive the forme, perfection, or soule, the which being done, it is converted into humiditie, and is fumed and breathed out by the pores of the matrix, which is manifest, bicause onely the flowers

---

Greeks to Freud (Cambridge, Mass.: Harvard University Press, 1990), and also his earlier essay, "Orgasm, Generation, and the Politics of Reproductive Biology," *Representations* 14 (Spring 1986), 1–41.

37. On theories of sexuality and conception in early modern English culture, see Audrey Eccles, *Obstetrics and Gynaecology in Tudor and Stuart England* (Kent, Ohio: Kent State University Press, 1982); and Angus McLaren, *Reproductive Rituals: The Perception of Fertility in England from the Sixteenth to the Nineteenth Century* (London: Methuen, 1984). Also see Laqueur, *Making Sex*.

[i.e., the menses] of the woman are the materiall cause of the yoong one.[38]

Incorporating Galenic elements into its fundamentally Aristotelian perspective, this text registers some confusion about the nature of the inseminating power and about its attribution to the woman as well as to the man. Although the contributions of both man and woman are necessary, the female seed is nevertheless materially inferior to that of the male. The notion of woman as an unperfected, an inadequate, version of man extends to the analogy of semen and menses: "The seede ... is white in man by reason of his greate heate, and because it is digested better.... The seede of a woman is red ... because the flowers is corrupt, undigested blood" (*Problemes of Aristotle*, E3r). Although Laqueur insists upon a sharp theoretical distinction between a "one-sex" and a "two-sex" model, in practice such distinctions may have been neither clear nor absolute to most men and women in early modern England. A widely read medical text like *The Problemes of Aristotle* suggests the existence of a syncretic and sometimes internally contradictory popular discourse, both written and oral, extending beyond the confines of a learned discourse that was based almost exclusively upon the Galenic corpus.

What most people today tend to think of as the "facts of life" have been established on the basis of observations and hypotheses made relatively recently in human history, since the development of microbiology that began in Europe in the late seventeenth century.[39] Whatever unexamined assumptions and hidden agendas motivate and skew the quest for "objective truth" in modern scientific research, few would dispute that present-day knowledge of anatomy and physiology is not merely different from but also quantitatively and qualitatively superior to that possessed by Shakespeare's contemporaries. In Elizabethan England, it seems to have been widely held that seminal and menstrual fluids are relevant to generation, and that people have a natural father as well as a natural mother. Nevertheless, the configuration and articulation of such beliefs, and their epistemologi-

38. *The Problemes of Aristotle, with other Philosophers and Phisitions* (London, 1597), E3v–E4r.

39. The following discussion is indebted to J. A. Barnes, "Genetrix : Genitor :: Nature : Culture?" in *The Character of Kinship*, ed. Jack Goody (Cambridge: Cambridge University Press, 1973), 61–73.

cal foundations, differed—sometimes, radically—from our own. Biological maternity has always been a readily observable material datum, a natural and universal fact—yet one, nevertheless, that is subject to widely varying, culture-specific representation, experience, and understanding. Outside the modern laboratory, however, biological paternity has everywhere remained a cultural construct for which ocular proof is unavailable.

This consequence of biological asymmetry calls forth an explanatory—and compensatory—cultural asymmetry in many traditional embryological theories, both learned and popular: Paternity is procreative, the formal and/or efficient cause of generation; maternity is nurturant, the material cause of generation. The quasi-Aristotelian procreative propositions of *A Midsummer Night's Dream* work against some of those Galenic propositions that were dominant in the learned tradition of Shakespeare's culture, propositions that are represented or implied elsewhere in his plays.[40] *A Midsummer Night's Dream* articulates a relatively extreme—but, nevertheless, not wholly anomalous—perspective on the Elizabethan system of gender and sex. Whatever the particular and subjective occasion of its invention by the playwright, this culturally inscribed phallocentric rhetoric overcompensates for the observable natural fact that men do indeed come from the bodies of women. Furthermore, it overcompensates for the cultural fact that consanguineal and affinal ties between men were established through their mutual but differential relationships to women, who were variously positioned as mothers, wives, or daughters.

Whether in folk medicine or in philosophy, notions of maternity have a persistent natural or material bias, while notions of paternity have a persistent social or spiritual bias. And such notions are articulated within a belief-system in which nature is subordinated to civility, and matter is subordinated to spirit. Thomas Hobbes avers that, "in the condition of meer Nature, where there are no Matrimoniall

40. For a reading of Shakespearean comedy and Elizabethan theatrical cross-dressing that is based upon Galenic theories of sexuality and is much influenced by the perspective of Laqueur, see "Fiction and Friction," in Stephen Greenblatt, *Shakespearean Negotiations*, 66–93. As I have already suggested, I believe that the Elizabethan discourse of sexuality and generation was wider and significantly more heterogeneous than Greenblatt's provocative essay implies.

lawes, it cannot be known who is the Father, unlesse it be declared by the Mother: and therefore the right of Dominion over the Child dependeth on her will" (*Leviathan*, 254). Traditional sex/gender systems impose law upon mere nature in order to secure a conceptual space for paternity. However, the legitimation of paternity as a general principle does not guarantee the establishment of specific and individual paternity, the physiological link between a particular man and child. This bond has always been highly tenuous—at least, until very recent advances in forensic genetics. The role of *genetrix* is self-evident but the role of *genitor* is not. As Launcelot Gobbo puts it, in *The Merchant of Venice*, "it is a wise father that knows his own child" (2.2.76–77).

A cynical quip attributed to Sir Henry Wotton summarizes the modalities in which a man's relationship to matrimony and paternity might be realized: "Next to no wife and children, your own wife and children are best pastime; another's wife and your children worse; your wife and another's children worst."[41] Man's worst condition is to be made a cuckold by his wife and the unwitting provider for another man's offspring; less bad, to make another man a cuckold by begetting one's own bastards upon his adulterous spouse; better, to be secure in the chasteness of one's spousal relationship and the legitimacy of one's offspring; but, best of all, to be a bachelor and thus invulnerable to the degrading temptations of the flesh and to the threat of contaminated blood lines, one's own and others'. In Shakespearean drama, the uncertain linkage of father and child is frequently a focus of anxious concern, whether the motive is to validate paternity or to call it into question. For example, Lear tells Regan that if she were not glad to see him, "I would divorce me from thy mother's tomb, / Sepulchring an adult'ress" (*King Lear*, 2.4.131–32). And Leontes exclaims, upon first meeting Florizel, "Your mother was most true to wedlock, Prince, / For she did print your royal father off, / Conceiving you" (*Winter's Tale*, 5.1.124–26). In the former speech, a father who is vulnerable to perceived acts of "filial ingratitude" invokes his previously unacknowledged wife precisely when he wishes to repudiate his female child. In the latter speech, a husband who is subject to cuckoldry anxieties rejoices in the ocular proof of paternity; he celebrates wifely chastity as the instrument of mascu-

41. Logan Pearsall Smith, *The Life and Letters of Sir Henry Wotton*, 2:490.

line self-reproduction. *A Midsummer Night's Dream* dramatizes a set of claims that are repeated in various registers—and not without challenge—throughout the Shakespearean canon: claims for a spiritual kinship among men that is unmediated by women; for the procreative powers of men; and for the autogeny of men.

III

While Shakespeare's plays reproduce such legitimating structures, they also produce challenges to their legitimacy. Within the course of a given dramatic action, representatives of opposition and difference are usually defeated, banished, converted, or otherwise apparently contained by the play's ideologically dominant forces and forms. Nevertheless, in its very representation of alternatives and resistances, the play articulates and disseminates fragments of those socially active heterodox discourses that the politically dominant discourse seeks, with only limited success, to appropriate, repudiate, or suppress. The play may try to impose symbolic closure upon the heterodoxy to which it also gives voice, but that closure can be neither total nor final. And such ideological instability or permeability in the drama may be a consequence not only of its performance but also of its inscription. It is obvious that theatrical productions and critical readings originating from beyond the cultural time and place of the text's own origin may work against the grain to achieve radically heterodox meanings and effects. But it may also be the case that the appropriative potential of such subsequent acts of interpretation is enabled by Elizabethan cultural variations and contradictions that have been sedimented in the text of the play at its originary moment of production.

I want to turn now to some of those instances in which *A Midsummer Night's Dream* produces challenges to its own legitimating structures, a focus to which I shall return at greater length in chapter 11. At the close of the play, Oberon's epithalamium represents procreation as the union of man and woman and marriage as a relationship of mutual affection:

> To the best bride-bed will we,
> Which by us shall blessed be;
> And the issue there create
> Ever shall be fortunate.

> So shall all the couples three
> Ever true in loving be.
>
> (5.1.389–94)

This benign and communal vision is predicated upon the play's prior reaffirmation of the father's role in generation and the husband's authority over the wife. Nevertheless, although *A Midsummer Night's Dream* reaffirms essential elements of a patriarchal ideology, it continues to call that reaffirmation into question, thus intermittently undermining its own comic propositions. The all-too-human struggle between the fairy king and queen—the play's already married couple—provides an ironic prognosis for the new marriages. As personified in Shakespeare's fairies, the divinely ordained imperatives of Nature call attention to themselves as the humanly constructed imperatives of culture; Shakespeare's naturalization and legitimation of the domestic economy deconstructs itself. Oberon assures himself that, by the end of the play, "all things shall be peace" (3.2.377). But the continuance of the newlyweds' loves and the good fortune of their issue are by no means assured. As soon as the lovers have gone off to bed, the rustic and sylvan Puck appears within the confines of the ducal court; he remains a central presence there until the end of the play, and then speaks the epilogue. Now, at the close of the wedding day and while the marriages are being consummated, Puck begins to evoke an uncomic world of labor, fear, pain, and death (5.1.357–76): "The hungry lion roars"; "the heavy ploughman snores, / All with weary task fordone"; "the screech-owl . . . / Puts the wretch that lies in woe / In remembrance of a shroud" (357, 359–60, 362–64). Puck's invocation of night alludes to the heritage of the Fall and the burden of Eve's transgression—a grim prelude that gives some urgency to Oberon's blessing of the bridal beds (389–400). The dangers are immanent and the peace is most fragile.

The play ends upon the threshhold of another generational cycle, in which the procreation of new children will also create new mothers and new fathers. This ending contains within it the potential for renewal of the forms of strife exhibited at the opening of the play. The promised end of romantic comedy is not only undermined by dramatic ironies but is also contaminated by a kind of intertextual irony. I do not mean to imply that such ironies necessarily registered in the minds of most members of Shakespeare's audience, nor that it was the playwright's intention that they should. Rather, I am trying to (re)construct an intertextual field of representations, resonances, and pressures that constitutes an ideological matrix from which—and against which—Shakespeare shaped the mythopoeia of *A Midsummer Night's Dream*. The mythology of Theseus is well supplied with examples of terror, lust, and jealousy; and these are prominently recounted and censured by Plutarch in his *Life of Theseus* and in his subsequent comparison of Theseus with Romulus. Shakespeare uses Plutarch as his major source of Theseus lore but does so selectively, for the most part down-playing those events "not sorting with a nuptial ceremony" (5.1.55) nor with a comedy. At their first entrance, Oberon accuses Titania of abetting (or actually compelling) Theseus's abuses—an accusation she dismisses as "the forgeries of jealousy" (81):

> Didst not thou lead him through the glimmering night
> From Perigouna, whom he ravished;
> And make him with fair Aegles break his faith,
> With Ariadne and Antiopa?
>
> (2.1.77–80)

This is perhaps the play's only explicit reference to Theseus's checkered past.[42] However, as Harold Brooks's Arden edition has convincingly demonstrated, the text of *A Midsummer Night's Dream* is permeated by echoes, not only of Plutarch's parallel lives of Theseus and

---

42. Compare Plutarch, "The Life of Theseus," in *The Lives of the Noble Grecians and Romanes*, trans. Thomas North (1579) from Amyot's French trans., 6 vols., The Tudor Translations (1895; rpt., New York: AMS Press, 1967):

The Poet telleth that the Amazones made warres with Theseus to revenge the injurie he dyd to their Queene Antiopa, refusing her, to marye with Phaedra. . . . We finde many other reportes touching the mariages of Theseus, whose beginnings had no great good honest ground, neither fell out their endes very fortunate: and yet for all that they have made no tragedies of them, neither have they bene played in the Theaters. For we reade that he tooke away Anaxo the Troezenian, and after that he had killed Sinnis and Cercyon, he tooke their daughters perforce: and that he dyd also marye Peribaea, the mother of Ajax, and afterwards Pherebaea, and Ioppa the daughter of Iphicles. And they blame him much also, for that he so lightly forsooke his wife Ariadne, for the love of Aegles the daughter of Panopaeus. . . . Lastly, he tooke awaye Hellen: which ravishement filled all the Realme of Attica with warres, and finally was the very occasion that forced him to forsake his countrye, and brought him at the length to his ende. (1:58–59)

Romulus but also of Seneca's *Hippolitus* and his *Medea*—by an archaeological record of the texts that shaped the poet's fantasy as he was shaping his play.[43] Thus, sedimented within the verbal texture of *A Midsummer Night's Dream* are traces of those forms of sexual and familial violence that the ethos of romantic comedy seeks to neutralize or to evade: acts of bestiality and incest, of parricide, uxoricide, filicide, and suicide. In the mythological record, such sexual fears and urges erupt into cycles of violent desire that stretch from Pasiphaë's consummated taurophilia to Phaedra's frustrated lust for her stepson.[44] It is precisely this lurid mythological subtext of unchecked,

43. For a review and analysis of the play's sources and analogues, see Brooks's edition, lviii–lxxxviii; 129–53; and the notes throughout the text. D'Orsay W. Pearson, "'Vnkinde' Theseus: A Study in Renaissance Mythography," *English Literary Renaisance* 4 (1974), 276–98, provides an informative survey of Theseus's "classical, medieval, and Renaissance image as an unnatural, perfidious, and unfaithful lover and father" (276). Olson characterizes the traditional Theseus as uneqivocally embodying "the reasonable man and the ideal ruler of both his lower nature and his subjects" ("*A Midsummer Night's Dream* and the Meaning of Court Marriage," 101), thus oversimplifying both the tradition and the play.

44. Many details in the texts of Plutarch and Seneca that have not been considered previously as "sources" for Shakespeare's play are nevertheless relevant to problems of gender, generation, filiation, and licit desire, which seem to me to be central to *MND*. Here I can do no more than enumerate a few of these details. The following discussion cites Shakespeare's classical sources from the following editions: Plutarch, *The Lives of the Noble Grecians and Romanes,* trans. Sir Thomas North (1579), Tudor Translations, cited by page numbers in volume 1; Seneca, *Tragedies,* trans. F. J. Miller, Loeb Classical Library, 2 vols. (London: Heinemann, 1960–61), cited by line numbers in the Latin texts.

   In his *Lives,* Plutarch relates that Theseus was "begotten by stealth, and out of lawfull matrimony" (30); that, "of his father's side," he was descended from the "Autocthones, as much to say, as borne of them selves" (30); that, having been abandoned by Theseus on Cyprus, the pregnant Ariadne "dyed . . . in labour, and could never be delivered" (48); that, because the negligently joyful Theseus forgot to change his sail as a sign of success upon his return from Crete, his father Egeus, "being out of all hope evermore to see his sonne againe, tooke such a griefe at his harte, that he threw him selfe headlong from the top of a clyffe, and killed him selfe" (49). In Seneca's *Hippolytus,* Hippolytus reminds Phaedra that she has come from the same womb that bore the Minotaur, and that she is even worse than her mother, Pasiphaë (688–93). At the end of the play, Theseus's burden is to refashion his dead son from the "disiecta . . . membra" of his torn body (1256–70). Now a filicide, as well as a parricide and uxoricide, Theseus has perverted and destroyed his own house (1166).

violent, and polymorphous desire that the play text's dominant discourse seeks to contain.

Shakespeare's play actually calls attention to its own mechanisms
of mythological suppression, however, by an ironic metadramatic gesture: Theseus demands "some delight" with which to "beguile / The
lazy time" (5.1.40–41) before the bedding of the brides. The list of
available entertainments includes "The battle with the Centaurs, to
be sung / By an Athenian eunuch to the harp," as well as "The riot
of the tipsy Bacchanals, / Tearing the Thracian singer in their rage"
(5.1.44–45, 48–49). Theseus rejects both on the grounds that they are
already too familiar. These brief scenarios encompass the extremes
of reciprocal violence between the sexes. The first offering narrates
a wedding that degenerates into rape and warfare; the singer and his
subject—emasculated Athenian and phallic Centaur—are two anti-
thetical kinds of male monster. In the second offering, what was often
regarded as the natural inclination of women toward irrational behavior is manifested in the Maenads' terrible rage against Orpheus.
The tearing apart and decapitation of the misogynistic Ur-poet at
once displaces and vivifies the Athenian singer's castration. It also
evokes the fate of Hippolytus, the misogynistic offspring of Theseus and Hippolyta: Hippolytus' body was torn apart upon the rocks
when his horses bolted at the instigation of his father, who had been
deceived by Phaedra's charge that her stepson had attempted to rape
her.

The seductive and destructive powers of women figure centrally
in Theseus's career; and his habitual victimization of women, the
chronicle of his own rapes and disastrous marriages, is a discourse of
anxious misogyny that persists as an echo within Shakespeare's text,
despite its having been variously muted or transformed. In Seneca,
as in Plutarch, the mother of Hippolytus is named Antiopa. Shakespeare's deliberate choice of the alternative, Hippolyta (an apparent
back-formation from the name of her son) obviously evokes the future Hippolytus. A profoundly ironic context is thus provided for the
royal wedding, for Oberon's intention to bless "the best bride-bed,"
and for his prognosis that "the issue there create / Ever shall be fortunate." (In a related example of intertextual irony, by choosing the
name of Theseus's father, Egeus, for the Athenian patriarch whose
will is overborne by the Duke, Shakespeare effects a displacement
within his comedy of Theseus's negligent parricide.) Seneca's Hip-

polytus emphasizes Theseus's abuse of women; Phaedra's invective gives voice to his victims. At this point in his sordid career, Theseus has forsaken (or, perhaps, killed) Antiopa/Hippolyta and married Phaedra. Hippolytus, as Phaedra's nutrix reminds him, is the only living son of the Amazons (Seneca, *Hippolytus*, 577). It is by his very misogyny—his scorn of marriage, and his self-dedication to virginity, hunting, and the cult of Diana—that Hippolytus proves himself to be his mother's son; he is "genus Amazonium" (*Hippolytus*, 231). Oberon's blessing of the marriage bed of Theseus and Hippolyta evokes precisely that which it seeks to suppress: the cycle of sexual and familial desire, fear, violence, and betrayal that will begin again at the very engendering of Hippolytus, whose fate is already written in his name.

In *The Palace of Pleasure*, Painter recounts the battle between the Amazons, led by Menalippe and Hippolyta (both sisters of Queen Antiopa), and the Greeks, led by Hercules and Theseus. Hercules returned Menalippe to Antiopa in exchange for the queen's armor, "but Theseus for no offer that she coulde make, woulde he deliver Hippolyta, with whom he was so farre in love, that he carried her home with him, and afterward toke her to wyfe, of whom hee had a sonne called Hipolitus" (163). Plutarch reports that Antiopa (conflated with Hippolyta in Shakespeare's play) was not conquered in personal combat but was captured by Theseus with "deceit and stealth" (55). Hippolyta is divorced from her sisters and from the society of Amazons as a consequence of Theseus's possessive passion—the deceitful, violent, and insatiable lust that North's Plutarch suggestively calls his "womannishenes" (116). To term masculine concupiscence "womannishenes" implies that a man who continually lusts after women is behaving like a woman; he has become enslaved to his passions. Indeed, "womannishenes" suggests that masculine heterosexual desire is itself, in its essence, effeminizing; that concupiscence weakens and degrades manly virtue. Ironically, the very opening of *A Midsummer Night's Dream* finds Hippolyta counseling restraint and patience to Theseus, who restlessly longs for his wedding night (1.1.1–11). Shortly thereafter, we are introduced to Oberon, who is jealous and vengeful because his wife has "forsaken his bed and company," and has made the changeling "all her joy." Sir Thomas Elyot's counsel regarding the education of boys, partially quoted above, is impelled by a fear of incipient womanishness:

After that a child is come to seven years of age . . . he [should] be taken from the company of women . . . for though there be no peril of offence in that tender and innocent age, yet in some children nature is more prone to vice than to virtue, and in the tender wits be sparks of voluptuosity which, nourished by any occasion or object, increase in time to so terrible a fire that therewith all virtue and reason is consumed. Wherefore, to eschew that danger, the most sure counsel is to withdraw him from all company of women, and to assign him to a tutor, which should be an ancient and worshipful man. (*The Book named The Governor*, 19)

It is fear of the consequences of womanishness, too, that makes Wotton consider "no wife and children" to be a man's best option. The term "womannishenes" suggests that there exists within the Elizabethan ideology of gender, a complementary and compensatory relationship between attitudes of uxoriousness and misogyny.

CHAPTER TEN

THE IMPERIAL VOTARESS

The foregoing analysis has suggested that a counter-discourse is active in *A Midsummer Night's Dream*, and that this counter-discourse intermittently disrupts and destabilizes the normative discourse of patriarchy that dominates both Elizabethan culture and Shakespeare's play. Through its production of textual and performative ironies, dissonances, and contradictions, *A Midsummer Night's Dream* pinpoints some of the joints and stresses in the ideological structures that shaped the culture of which it is an instance; and it discloses—perhaps, in a sense, despite itself—that patriarchal norms are compensatory for men's perceptions that they are vulnerable to the powers of women. Such moments of textual disclosure also illuminate the interplay between gender politics in the Elizabethan household and gender politics in the Elizabethan state, for the woman to whom *all* Elizabethan men were subject and vulnerable was Queen Elizabeth herself. As summarized by Thomas Wilson in 1600, it was the exclusive privilege of the Queen to

> pardon and give lyfe to the condemned or to take away the life or member of any subject at her pleasure, and none other in all ye Kingdom hath power of life and member but onely the Prince, noe not so much as to imprison or otherwise to punish any other, unless it be his servant, without expresse comission from the Queen.[45]

Within legal and fiscal limits, this female prince held the power of life and death over every Englishman; the power to advance or frustrate the worldly desires of all her subjects. In this chapter, I explore the modes in which that gendered royal power is figured and medi-

45. Thomas Wilson, *The State of England Anno Dom. 1600*, ed. F. J. Fisher, Camden Miscellany vol. 16 (London: Camden Society, 1936), 37–38.

ated in *A Midsummer Night's Dream*. Since the play's figures are complex reworkings of already existing representations, to study them is also to locate the play in the Elizabethan cultural intertext that constituted "the Queen."

I

At the beginning of her reign, Elizabeth formulated the strategy by which she turned the political liability of her gender to advantage for the next half century. She told her first parliament that she was content to have as her epitaph, "that a Queene, having raigned such a tyme, lived and dyed a virgin"; and she assured her second, "that though after my death yow may have many stepdames, yet shall yow never have any a more naturall mother then I meane to be unto you all." [46] She appropriated not only the suppressed cult of the Blessed Virgin but also the Tudor conception of the Ages of Woman. Thus, the queen's self-mastery and mastery of others were enhanced by an elaboration of her maidenhood into a cult of eroticized virginity that "allows of amorous admiration but prohibits desire";[47] the displacement of her wifely duties from a household to a nation; and the sublimation of her temporal and ecclesiastical authority into a nurturing maternity. By fashioning herself into a singular combination of maiden, matron, and mother, the Queen transformed the normative domestic life-cycle of an Elizabethan woman into what was at once a social paradox and a quasi-religious mystery.

At the very beginning of her reign, Elizabeth's parliaments and counselors boldly but unsuccessfully urged her to marry and to produce an heir. In her delicately balanced response to her first parliament, she pointedly contrasted a petition "that is simple and conteineth no limytacion of place or person" to one that seeks to constrain the sovereign; of the latter sort, she declared, with obvious irritation and disdain,

> I muste nedes have myslyked it verie muche and thought it in yow
> a verie great presumption, being unfitting and altogether unmete

46. See *Proceedings in the Parliaments of Elizabeth I*, vol. 1: *1558–1581*, ed. T. E. Hartley (Leicester: Leicester University Press, 1981), 45, 95.

47. Francis Bacon, *In Felicem Memoriam Elizabethae* (ca. 1608), in *The Works of Francis Bacon*, ed. James Spedding et al., 15 vols. (Boston: Brown & Taggard, 1860), 11:425–42 (Latin text), 443–61 (English trans.); quotation from 460.

for yow to require them that may commande, or those to appoynte
whose partes are to desire, or such to bynde and lymite whose
duties are to obaye, or to take upon yow to drawe my love to your
lykinges or frame my will to your fantasies. (*Proceedings in the Parliaments of Elizabeth I*, 45)

Despite the royal warning, Elizabethan masculine subjects were to
continue, by various and sometimes highly elaborate or subtle rhetorical and performative means, to seek to draw the queen's love to their
likings and to frame her will to their fantasies. Throughout the reign,
Queen Elizabeth's marital status and her sexual condition remained
matters of state, but ones more safely negotiated through the oblique
strategies of fictive forms and actions than through parliamentary pe-
titions and printed tracts.

There was a deeply felt and loudly voiced need to insure a legitimate succession, upon which the welfare of the whole people depended. But there may also have been another, more obscure motivation that amplified these requests. The political nation, which was
wholly a nation of men, seems at times to have found it frustrating
or degrading to serve a female prince—a woman who was herself
unsubjected to any man. Late in Elizabeth's reign, the French ambassador observed that "her government is fairly pleasing to the
people, who show that they love her, but it is little pleasing to the
great men and nobles; and if by chance she should die, it is certain
that the English would never again submit to the rule of a woman." [48]
Elizabeth's rule was not intended to undermine the masculine hegemony of her society. The emphasis upon her *difference* from other
women seems to have been designed, in part, to neutralize the appearance of such a threat; it was a strategy for personal survival and
political legitimation within a social and political culture that was
pervasively patriarchal. That the threat nevertheless remained quite
real is apparent from the evidence that at least some of her masculine subjects worked very hard to contain or contest it. This attitude
was an affective consequence of a fundamental cultural contradiction
specific to Elizabethan society: namely, the expectation that English
gentlemen would manifest loyalty and obedience to their sovereign

48. André Hurault, Sieur de Maisse, *A Journal of all that was accomlished by Mon-
sieur de Maisse Ambassador in England from King Henry IV to Queen Elizabeth anno
domini 1597*, trans. and ed. G. B. Harrison and R. A. Jones (Bloomsbury: Nonesuch
Press, 1931), 11–12.

at the same time that they exercised masculine authority over women. It would be naïvely reductive to suggest that either the person or the cult of Queen Elizabeth provides an adequate causal explanation for the heightened social perception of women's challenge to the patriarchal order, the beginnings of which perception coincide with the beginning of her reign. However, without going so far as to redefine history as the biography of great women, I think it may reasonably be claimed that there existed an indirect but nevertheless reciprocally influential relationship between the widespread social perception that Elizabethan women were more apt to be out of place than their predecessors and the contemporaneous political and cultural reality that the throne was occupied by a woman of remarkable skills and accomplishments who was unmarried and thus not subjected to any man.

During the 1560s and 1570s, Elizabeth witnessed allegorical entertainments boldly criticizing her attachment to a life of what Shakespeare's Theseus calls "single blessedness." For example, in a play devised by George Gascoigne for the Kenilworth entertainments sponsored by the Earl of Leicester in 1575, Diana praised the state of fancy-free maiden meditation and condemned the "wedded state, which is to thraldome bent." But Juno had the last word in the pageant: "O Queene, O worthy queene / Yet never wight felt perfect blis / But such as wedded beene." Leicester was still trying to frame Elizabeth's will to his fantasy but she would have none of it: Though readied for performance before the queen, the play "never came to execution"; sponsor and deviser had the last word, however, by seeing the annotated text into print.[49] Thomas Churchyard, in devising shows with which to entertain the Queen upon her visit to the city of Norwich in 1578, effectively answered the allegorical program

49. "A briefe rehearsall, or rather a true Copie of as much as was presented before her majesti[e] at Kenelworth, during her last aboade there" (1576), in *The Complete Works of George Gascoigne*, ed. John W. Cunliffe, 2 vols. (Cambridge: Cambridge University Press, 1910), 2:91–131; quotations from 107, 120. Following the play in the printed text, Gascoigne coyly notes that "This shew was devised and penned by M. Gascoigne, and being prepared and redy (every Actor in his garment) two or three dayes together, yet never came to execution. The cause whereof I cannot attribute to any other thing, then to lack of opportunitie and seasonable weather" (120). There is an innuendo that the queen, having wind of the subject, prevented occasion for its presentation.

of Gascoigne and/or Leicester by celebrating the Queen as being impervious to passion. At Norwich, she was the unmoved mover of desire. "Dame Chastitie and hir maydes" routed Cupid, confiscated his bow and arrows, and presented them to the queen: "Bycause (sayd Chastitie) that the Queene had chosen the best life, she gave ye Queene CUPIDS bow, to learn to shoote at whome she pleased, since none coulde wounde hir highnesse hart."[50] Like Shakespeare's, Churchyard's imperial votaress remained impervious to Cupid's arrows, "fancy free"; unlike Theseus, Queen Elizabeth, although a woman, was not womanish. In 1579, Simier, the Duke of Alençon's representative in his marriage negotiations with the queen, witnessed a masque of Amazons and knights at the English court. Surviving records indicate that, after a page representing each group made a speech to the queen, the six Amazons and six knights danced together, and also fought at barriers. A dispatch describing "an entertainment in imitation of a tournament, between six ladies and a like number of gentlemen *who surrendered to them*" indicates that this unconventional Amazonomachy was devised to assert the power and autonomy of the English virago.[51]

By the early 1580s, the Queen was past childbearing, and any serious prospect of a royal marriage was rapidly waning. Diana and her virginal nymph, Eliza, now carried the day in such courtly entertainments as George Peele's *Araygnment of Paris*. Although "as fayre and lovely as the queene of Love," Peele's Elizabeth was also "as chast as Dian in her chast desires."[52] By the early 1590s, the cult of the unaging royal virgin had entered its last and most extravagant phase. In the 1590 Accession Day pageant, there appeared "a Pavilion . . .

---

50. Thomas Churchyard, *A Discourse of The Queenes Majesties entertainement in Suffolk and Norffolk* (London, 1578), rpt. in *Records of Early English Drama: Norwich 1540–1642*, ed. David Galloway (Toronto: University of Toronto Press, 1984), 292–330; quotation from 305.

51. See Chambers, *Elizabethan Stage*, 1:166. Chambers cites Albert Feuillerat, *Documents relating to the Office of the Revels in the Time of Queen Elizabeth* (Louvain, 1908), 286, 294; and *Calendar of Letters and State Papers, relating to English Affairs, principally in the Archives of Simancas*, ed. M. A. S. Hume, 4 vols. (London, 1892–99), 2:627, 630. I have added the emphasis in the quotation.

52. George Peele, *The Araygnment of Paris* (printed 1584), ed. R. Mark Benbow, in *The Dramatic Works of George Peele*, C. T. Prouty, general editor (New Haven: Yale University Press, 1970), lines 1172–73.

like unto the sacred Temple of the Virgins Vestal."[53] Upon the altar there were presents for the queen—offerings from her votaries. At Elvetham, during the royal progress of 1591, none other than "the Fairy Quene" gave to Elizabeth "a garland, made in fourme of an imperiall crowne" that she herself had received from "Auberon, the Fairy King." After her presentation speech to Queen Elizabeth, "the Faery Quene and her maides daunce[d] about the Garden," singing a song lavishly praising "Elisa . . . the fairest Quene." Queen Elizabeth was always alert to pageants encoding unwanted advice; on this occasion, however, she must have liked what she heard, for "shee commanded to heare it sung and to be danced three times over, and called for divers Lords and Ladies to behold it: and then dismist the Actors with thankes, and with a gracious larges."[54] In the words of her ducal surrogate from Athens, "never anything can be amiss / When simpleness and duty tender it" (*MND*, 5.1.82–83).

The ambiguously filial and erotic metaphors frequently employed by the queen's courtiers could accommodate expressions of desire for disinterested service and self-interested advancement; and, at the same time, they could insinuate that stifled desire/ambition might lead to disaffection, resistance, and even rebellion. The nobility, gentlemen, and hangers-on of the court generated a variety of pressures that constantly threatened the fragile stability of the Elizabethan regime. At home, personal rivalries and political dissent might be sublimated into the strategically neo-feudal chivalric pageantry of courtly culture; abroad, they might be expressed in warfare and colonial enterprise—displaced into the conquest of lands that had yet their maidenheads.[55] Throughout the middle years of the reign, the

53. Described in Sir William Segar, *Honor Military, and Civill* (1602), 197–200; rpt. in John Nichols, *The Progresses and Public Processions of Queen Elizabeth*, 3 vols. (1823; rpt., New York: Burt Franklin, 1966), 3:41–50; quotation from Nichols, 3:46. One of the most popular iconographic attributes of Queen Elizabeth was the sieve, which identifies her with the vestal virgin Tuccia. See Roy Strong, *Portraits of Queen Elizabeth I* (Oxford: Clarendon Press, 1963), 66–69, and paintings nos. 43–49; Yates, *Astraea*, 112–20.

54. *The Honorable Entertainment gieven to the Quene's Majestie, in Progresse, at Elvetham in Hampshire, by the Right Hon'ble the Earle of Hertford, 1591* (London, 1591), rpt. in Nichols, *Progresses and Public Processions of Queen Elizabeth*, 3:101–21; quotations from 118–19.

55. The latter phrase is Sir Walter Ralegh's: "Guiana is a countrey that hath yet her maydenhead, never sackt, turned, nor wrought. . . . It hath never bene

elaborate play-forms of aristocratic culture provided a relatively effective means of containing the potential for rebellion. But by the turn of the century, in the deep social discontent and political instability of Elizabeth's last years, the queen's most brilliant courtier-client led a short-lived revolt of desperate malcontents. Of the Earl of Essex's insatiable thirst for those offices and honors which were in the queen's gift, Sir Robert Naunton later wrote that "my lord . . . drew in fast like a child sucking on a uberous breast."[56] Naunton's simile suggests that the queen's prior bountifulness was now her greedy and overweening subject's undoing. That most observant of ornamental courtiers, Sir John Harington, wrote "that ambition thwarted in its career, dothe speedilie leade on to madnesse; herein I am strengthened by what I learned in my Lord of Essex, who shyftethe from sorrowe and repentaunce to rage and rebellion so suddenlie, as well provethe him devoide of goode reason or righte mynde." Like the special performance of *Richard II* that was intended to be its prologue, the Essex rebellion was a political failure. Nevertheless, the very fact that it came to performance was itself evidence of a dysfunction in the Elizabethan system of cultural and political containment. Harington's meditation on Essex closed with an image of political desperation that had been twisted out of the amorous discourse of sonnet-courtships: "The Queene well knowethe how to humble the haughtie spirit, the haughtie spirit knoweth not how to yield, and the mans soule seemeth tossede to and

---

entred by any armie of strength, and never conquered or possessed by any christian Prince." See *The Discoverie of the large, rich and beautifull Empire of Guiana* (1596), rpt. in Richard Hakluyt, *The principle navigations voyages traffiques & discoveries of the English nation* (1598–1600); I quote from the modern edition of Hakluyt, *Principle Navigations*, 12 vols. (Glasgow: James MacLehose & Sons, 1904), 10:428. For further discussion of Ralegh and Elizabethan masculine subject-formation in "the New World," see my essay, "The Work of Gender in the Discourse of Discovery," *Representations* 33 (Winter 1991), 1–41; rpt. in *New World Encounters*, ed. Stephen Greenblatt (Berkeley: University of California Press, 1993), 177–217.

On the chivalric revival and other aspects of the strategic "re-feudalization" of Elizabethan aristocratic culture, see Yates, *Astrea*, 88–111; Strong, *The Cult of Elizabeth*, 114–91; McCoy, *The Rites of Knighthood*.

56. Sir Robert Naunton, *Fragmenta Regalia or Observations on Queen Elizabeth, Her Times & Favorites* (written ca. 1630; printed 1641), ed. John S. Cerovski (Washington, D.C.: Folger Shakespeare Library, 1985), 75.

fro, like the waves of a troubled sea."[57] Maternal and erotic discourses did not merely provide materials for an allegorical encodement of political messages; they were the affective languages in which Elizabethans thought and experienced the relationship between sovereign and subject.

Perhaps four or five years before the first production of *A Midsummer Night's Dream*, in a pastoral entertainment enacted before the Queen at Sudeley during the progress of 1591, the royal presence changed Ovid's metamorphosis of Daphne into an emblem of Constancy. Daphne, pursued by Apollo, was transformed into a tree; Apollo's ensuing song concluded that "neither men nor gods, can force affection." "The song ended, the tree rived, and DAPHNE issued out, APOLLO ranne after," himself apparently unregenerate. "DAPHNE running to her Majestie uttred this": "I stay, for whether should chastety fly for succour, but to the Queene of chastety." Daphne was then reprieved from the potential consequences of Apollo's lust and craft simply by the power of Elizabeth's presence, "that by vertue, there might be assurance in honor."[58] As "the Queene of chastety," Elizabeth incarnated Diana, to whom Ovid's Daphne was votary. In Ovid's *Metamorphoses*, when Daphne cried for succour to her father Peneus, she was changed into the laurel. At Sudeley, Daphne's metamorphosis into a tree was less an escape than a demonic incarceration from which she had to be liberated. The queen's virtuous magic derived from a kind of matriarchal virginity; her powers transcended those of the lustful and paternal pagan gods. In Elizabethan royal iconography, the Queen was made responsible for the fate of only one victim of Ovidian metamorphosis: namely, Actaeon, the transgressing masculine devotee of a virgin goddess.

From early in the reign, Elizabeth had been directly addressed and engaged by such performances as the one at Sudeley. Distinc-

57. "Breefe Notes and Remembrauncer," in Harington, *Nugae Antiquae*, 2:225–26.

58. The text of the Sudeley entertainment was printed in *Speeches Delivered to Her Majestie this Last Progresse* (Oxford, 1592), rpt. in *The Complete Works of John Lyly*, ed. R. Warwick Bond, 3 vols. (Oxford: Clarendon Press, 1902), 2:477–84; quotations from 479–80. For a more detailed analysis of the Sudeley entertainments, see my essay, "'Eliza, Queene of Shepheardes' and the Pastoral of Power," *English Literary Renaissance* 10 (1980), 168–80.

tions were effaced between the spatio-temporal locus of the royal
spectator/actor and that of the characters being enacted before her.
Debates were referred directly to her arbitration; the magic of her
presence civilized savage men, restored the blind to sight, released
errant knights from enchantment, and rescued virgins from defile-
ment. These social dramas of celebration and coercion played out the
delicately balanced relationship between the monarch and those of
her subjects who constituted the political nation—nobility, gentry,
and urban elites. A significant collateral effect of these events must
have been to evoke reverence and awe in the local common folk who
assisted in and witnessed them. And because texts and descriptions
of most of these processions, pageants, and shows were in print
within a year—sometimes, within just a few days—of their performance, they may have had a cultural impact far more extensive and
enduring than their occasional and ephemeral character might at first
suggest. The scenarios of such royal pageantry as was presented at
Kenilworth, Norwich, Elvetham, and Sudeley appropriated materials
from popular late medieval romances, from Ovid, Petrarch, and other
literary sources; and when late Elizabethan plays and poems such as
A Midsummer Night's Dream and *The Faerie Queene* reappropriated those
sources, they were now inscribed by the allegorical discourse of Elizabethan royal courtship, panegyric, and political negotiation. Thus,
the deployment of Ovidian, Petrarchan, and allegorical romance
modes by late Elizabethan writers must be read in terms of an intertextuality that includes both the discourse of European literary history and the discourse of Elizabethan state power.

II

As has long been recognized, *A Midsummer Night's Dream* has affinities
with Elizabethan royal iconography and courtly entertainments. Harold Brooks cautiously endorses two familiar and frequently conflated
hypotheses regarding the play's occasion: that it was "designed to
grace a wedding in a noble household," and that "it seems likely that
Queen Elizabeth was present when the *Dream* was first acted. . . . She
delighted in homage paid to her as the Virgin Queen, and receives it
in the myth-making about the imperial votaress" (Arden *MND*, liii,
lv). It should be noted that both of these hypotheses make originary
claims for a royal or aristocratic occasion. Nevertheless, it seems to

have been common practice for the professional players to perform at court or in noble houses plays that were already part of their repertory in the public playhouse, perhaps revising or cutting them for a special occasion and venue. Although attractive, the widely accepted general hypothesis of the play's occasion is without substantiation. Furthermore, scholars have advanced competing candidates for the specific occasion, the evidence in each case being entirely conjectural.[59] My own perspective on the play's connection to the monarch and to the culture of the court construes their relationship as dialectical rather than causal, as structural rather than incidental. Whether or not Elizabeth was physically present at the first performance of *A Midsummer Night's Dream*, and whether or not the play was first (or ever) performed for an aristocratic wedding, the pervasive cultural presence of the Queen was a condition of the play's imaginative possibility. And, in the sense that the royal presence was itself represented within the play, the play appropriated and extended the imaginative possibilities of the queen. Thus, I construe Shake-

---

59. The leading contenders are the wedding of William Stanley, Earl of Derby, and Lady Elizabeth Vere, daughter of the Earl of Oxford and granddaughter of Lord Burghley, on 26 January 1594/5; and the wedding of Thomas, son of Lord Berkeley, and Elizabeth, daughter of Sir George Carey and granddaughter of Lord Hunsdon, the Lord Chamberlain and patron of Shakespeare's company, on 19 February 1595/6. For a summary of the arguments, see the Arden *MND*, liii–lvii. The claim for the Stanley-Vere wedding has been restated in James P. Bednarz, "Imitations of Spenser in *A Midsummer Night's Dream*," *Renaissance Drama*, n. s. 14 (1983), 79–102; and the claim for the Berkeley-Carey wedding, in Steven W. May, "*A Midsummer Night's Dream* and the Carey-Berkeley Wedding," *Renaissance Papers* (1983), 43–52. See Marion Colthorpe, "Queen Elizabeth I and *A Midsummer Night's Dream*," *Notes and Queries* 232 (June 1987), 205–7, for a careful and skeptical assessment of the various claims.

In a recent study, which I encountered only after my own was already in final form, David Wiles has learnedly and suggestively reconsidered the issue of the play's occasion. Wiles adds to the list of contenders the marriage of Henry, Earl of Northumberland to Dorothy Devereux, widow of Sir Thomas Perrot and sister of the Earl of Essex, in late 1594, but finally suggests the Berkeley-Carey wedding as the occasion with the strongest claim. See David Wiles, *Shakespeare's Almanac: "A Midsummer Night's Dream," Marriage and the Elizabethan Calendar* (Cambridge: D. S. Brewer, 1993), 137–75. Wiles's is the most extended and sophisticated "occasionalist" approach to the play, giving it a "double context: first within a tradition of private dramatic entertainment in the ambit of the court of 'Cynthia', and second within the literary tradition of the epithalamium and its related dramatic mode, the wedding masque" (177).

speare's *A Midsummer Night's Dream* as calling attention to itself, not only as an end but also as a source of cultural production.

At Sudeley, it was in the power of the royal virgin to undo the metamorphosis, to release Daphne from her arboreal imprisonment and to protect her from the advances of Apollo. In *A Midsummer Night's Dream*, however, magical power is invested not in the Queen but in the King, her husband. Immediately after invoking the royal vestal and vowing to torment the Fairy Queen, Oberon encounters Helena in pursuit of Demetrius. In Shakespeare's metamorphosis of Ovid—and, perhaps, his metamorphosis of Sudeley—"the story shall be chang'd / Apollo flies, and Daphne holds the chase" (2.1.230–31). Oberon's response is neither to extinguish desire nor to make it mutual but rather to restore the normal pattern of pursuit: "Fare thee well, nymph; ere he do leave this grove / Thou shalt fly him and he shall seek thy love" (2.1.245–46). Unlike Elizabeth, Oberon uses his mastery over Nature to subdue others to their passions. The festive conclusion of *A Midsummer Night's Dream* depends upon the success of a process by which the feminine pride and power manifested in Amazon warriors, possessive mothers, unruly wives, and willful daughters are brought under the control of lords and husbands. When the contentious young lovers have been sorted into pairs by Oberon, then Theseus can invite them to share his own wedding day. If the Duke finally overbears Egeus' will (4.1.178), it is because the father's obstinate claim to "the ancient privilege of Athens" (1.1.41) threatens to obstruct the very process by which Athenian privilege and Athens itself are reproduced. The desires of Hermia and Helena are, of course, fulfilled; nevertheless, those apparently subjective individual choices have been shaped by a social imperative. Thus, neither for Oberon nor for Theseus does a contradiction exist between mastering the desires of a wife and patronizing the desires of a maiden.

There is an obvious dramaturgical contrast between *A Midsummer Night's Dream* and the progress pageants or such panegyrical court plays as Peele's *Araygnement of Paris*. In such courtly performance genres, the resolution of the action, the completion of the form, is dependent upon the actual presence of the monarch as privileged auditor/spectator. Her judgment may be actively solicited, or, *in propria persona*, she may become the focus of the characters' collective celebration and veneration; frequently, as in Peele's play, the two strategies are combined. There are also, however, Elizabethan plays that do not require the queen's active participation but instead refer the dramatic resolution to an on-stage character who is an allegorical personage readily if not wholly identifiable with the queen. Such formal strategies are presumably motivated by the practical concern to make the play playable in more than one venue and for more than one audience. The professional players had more people to please than the monarch alone. In any case, the Queen was frequently unavailable to play her part; and for someone else to have personated her explicitly would have been a potentially dangerous offense.[60] The formal and dramaturgical responses to such manifestly practical and commercial concerns may have had significant ideological consequences. Such plays preserve the theatrical illusion of a self-contained play-world. In doing so, they necessarily produce a more mediated—and, thus, a potentially more ambiguous, more unstable—mode of royal reference and encomium than do those plays which open the frame of the fiction to accommodate a direct resolution of the dramatic action by the Queen herself. In this sense, plays performed in the commercial playhouses had a relatively greater degree of both formal and ideological autonomy than did exclusively courtly entertainments, and such repertory plays would have maintained a relatively greater autonomy even when performed at court.

Perhaps the most obvious example of such a play is John Lyly's *Endimion, The Man in the Moone. Endimion* was printed in 1591, with the title-page announcement that it had been "Playd before the Queenes Majestie at Greenewich on Candlemas day at night [1588?], by the Chyldren of Paules"; we may assume that they also played it

60. On controversies involving stage representations of the Queen as well as prominent courtiers, see Dutton, *Mastering the Revels*, 127–40. As Dutton and others have noted, Jonson was apparently compelled to change the original ending of *Every Man Out of His Humour* because of some objection to the necessary impersonation of the Queen when it was performed at the Globe. In "'So Sudden and Strange a Cure': A Rudimentary Masque in *Every Man Out of His Humour*," *English Literary Renaissance* 22 (1992), 315–32, Helen M. Ostovich cites a number of other performance texts in which Queen Elizabeth appears to have been represented explicitly; however, almost all of these were in pageants presented before the queen.

at the "private" theatres in Blackfriars and Paul's, as was their practice.[61] The printed text includes a prologue and epilogue that are directly addressed to the queen. In the Prologue, Lyly coyly repudiates allegorical intent: "We hope in our times none will apply pastimes, because they are fancies. . . . We present neither Comedie, nor Tragedie, nor storie, nor anie thing, but that whosoever heareth may say this, Why heere is a tale of the Man in the Moone."[62] In a typical scenario for a courtly entertainment, such as might have been presented during a royal progress, the release of Endimion from his charmed sleep would have been accomplished by the charismatic physical presence of Queen Elizabeth herself. In Lyly's play, however, it is accomplished by the kiss of Cynthia, an enacted character who is ambiguously monarch and personified abstraction, woman and deity: "Shee whose figure of all is the perfectest, and never to bee measured—alwaies one, yet never the same—still inconstant, yet never wavering" (3.4.155–57). Lyly's Cynthia restores the youth of the reawakened Endimion when he demonstrates that he has fully understood the cardinal lesson for courtiers of Queen Elizabeth: he must acknowledge that "Such a difference hath the Gods sette between our states, that all must be dutie, loyaltie, and reverence; nothing (without it vouchsafe your highnes) be termed love" (*Endimion*, 5.3.168–70).

Endimion has been enchanted by an old witch, Dipsas, at the behest of a jealous lady, Tellus, who seeks revenge upon Endimion because he has shifted his devotion from herself to Cynthia. Tellus tells us that "Hee shall knowe the mallice of a woman to have neither meane, nor ende; and of a woman deluded in love, to have neither

61. See G. K. Hunter, *John Lyly: The Humanist as Courtier* (London: Routledge & Kegan Paul, 1962), 97–98.

62. *Endimion* is quoted by act, scene, and line from *The Complete Works of John Lyly*, ed. R. Warwick Bond, 3: 17–79. See G. K. Hunter, *John Lyly*, for discussion of *Endimion* (184–94), and for a comparison of Shakespeare's technique in *MND* with that of Lyly in his court comedies (318–30). For a reading of *Endimion* in the context of Christian and Neoplatonic allegory, see Peter Saccio, *The Court Comedies of John Lyly: A Study in Allegorical Dramaturgy* (Princeton: Princeton University Press, 1969), 169–86; and, for a reading of Lyly's court plays in terms of gender and politics, Phillipa Berry, *Of Chastity and Power: Elizabethan Literature and the Unmarried Queen* (London and New York: Routledge, 1989), 111–33.

rule, nor reason" (1.2.52–54). A strong current of misogyny runs through the play, as manifested in the variously malign and peevish characters of Tellus, Dipsas, and Semele. Cynthia herself is repeatedly described or represented as remote, threatening, and inscrutable. Endimion warns Tellus "that of the gods we are forbidden to dispute, because theyr deities come not within the compasse of our reasons; and of *Cynthia* we are allowed not to talke but to wonder, because her vertues are not within the reach of our capacities" (2.1.75–78). At the beginning of the play, Endimion proclaims to his friend Eumenides that he is "setled, eyther to die, or possesse the Moone herselfe." This dangerous and foredoomed desire Eumenides declares to be "a dotage no lesse miserable then monstrous" (1.1.14–15, 25). Following Endimion's mysterious enchantment, Cynthia explains that she has understood the politic necessity that she arrest and manage his ambitions: "I favoured thee *Endimion* for thy honor, thy vertues, thy affections: but to bring thy thoughts within the compasse of thy fortunes, I have seemed strange, that I might have thee staied" (4.3.78–81). The deathlike sleep inflicted upon Endimion by the jealous Tellus is the indirect consequence of his improper devotion to Cynthia. From this perspective, Tellus and Dipsas may be construed as oblique aspects or obscure agents of the inconstant yet all-powerful virgin moon-goddess. As a consequence of the surplus of meaning and resonance emanating from Lyly's Cynthia, she is contaminated by her apparent opposites. The impassioned and vengeful Tellus and the diabolically powerful Dipsas are apprehensible as the terrestrial and infernal aspects of the triform Cynthia.

A similar effect of allegorical contamination is evident in other ostensibly panegyrical late Elizabethan texts—in Spenser's polymorphous figurations of the queen, for example, or in the relationship between the imperious Cynthia and vain Philautia of Jonson's *Cynthias Revels*.[63] Ben Jonson's *The Fountaine of Selfe-Love, or Cynthias Revels* harks back to Lyly's court comedies in its dramaturgy, in its enactment by one of the (newly revived) boys' companies, and in its naming of the monarch's surrogate as Cynthia. Nevertheless, the play is distinctively Jonsonian in its internalization of a surrogate for the

---

63. On this aspect of Spenser's poem, see my essay, "The Elizabethan Subject and the Spenserian Text," in *Literary Theory/Renaissance Texts*, ed. Patricia Parker and David Quint (Baltimore: Johns Hopkins University Press, 1986), 303–40.

playwright, named Criticus, who threatens to displace Cynthia as the locus of the play's moral and intellectual initiative and authority.[64] Although the play is labelled "a comicall satyre" only in the 1616 Folio, the description also holds true for the version printed in the 1601 Quarto, the satire being explicitly directed against the pride, folly, and luxury of Cynthia's court. Philautia, one of the allegorical court characters finally repudiated by Cynthia, is, in her own fantasy, a dark and dangerous parody of Jonson's queen:

> Onely I would wish my selfe a little more command, and soveraig-netie; that all the court were subject to my absolute becke, and all things in it depending on my looke; as if there were no other heaven, but in my smile, nor other hell, but in my frowne; that I might send for any man I list, and have his head cut off, when I have done with him; or made an *eunuch*, if he denyed me: and if I saw a better face then mine owne, I might have my doctor to poyson it. (4.1.161–69)

The imperious and (self-)righteous Cynthia is herself much con-cerned to repudiate and to punish unattributed charges that she is "too severe, and sowre": "Let't suffice, / That we take notice, and can take revenge, / Of these calumnious, and lewd blasphemies" (5.11.10, 31–33).

Processes of disenchantment are increasingly evident in Elizabe-than cultural productions of the 1580s and 1590s. In *A Midsummer Night's Dream*, as in *The Faerie Queene*, *Endimion*, or *Cynthias Revels*, the project of elaborating Queen Elizabeth's personal mythology has a recurrent tendency to subvert itself. These complex fictions generate ironies, contradictions, and resistances that undo the royal magic they

64. The 1601 Quarto titles the play, *The Fountaine of Selfe-Love. Or Cynthias Revels*, adding "As it hath beene sundry times privately acted in the Black-Friers by the Children of her Majesties Chappell." The 1616 Folio titles the play, *Cynthias Revels, Or The Fountayne of selfe-Love. A Comicall Satyre*, adding "Acted, in the yeere 1600. By the then Children of Queene Elizabeths Chappel." Aside from the reversal of the play's running title and the name change from Criticus to Crites, the folio text differs most notably from the quarto in the extensive enlarge-ment of Act 5 to include an elaborate, masque-like courtship competition. (The usual and reasonable assumption that this represents Jonson's Jacobean revision of his late Elizabethan entertainment tends to rely upon a prior assumption that the quarto text preserves the Elizabethan version uncut.) I cite the text, based upon the folio, printed in *Ben Jonson*, ed. C. H. Herford and Percy and Evelyn Simpson, 11 vols. (Oxford: Clarendon Press, 1925–53).

ostensibly celebrate. And, frequently, the means of this undoing is a contamination of the virtuous royal magic by counter-representations of feminine lasciviousness, sorcery, and witchcraft. Gender-specific intimations and denials of witchcraft and demonism in fact form a persistent undercurrent in *A Midsummer Night's Dream*. Oberon insists that he and Puck "are spirits of another sort" (3.2.388) than the damned. The play is rich, however, in intertextual allusions to the sorceresses of the classical world: Titania's evocation of the cosmic disharmony caused by her conflict with Oberon (2.1.104 ff.) and Puck's invocation of "the triple Hecate's team" (5.1.370) both echo passages in Ovid (*Metamorphoses*, 7.179–219) and Seneca (*Medea*, 750 ff.) in which Medea invokes Hecate.[65] In its asinine metamorphosis of Bottom, and in its descriptions of female sorcery, the play evokes not only the Medea of both Ovid and Seneca but also the enchantresses in Apuleius's *Golden Ass*, Meroë, Panthia, and Pamphile.[66] Perhaps most strikingly, in Ovid's *Metamorphoses*, in two of its three occurrences in the entire work (14.382, 438), "Titania" is an

---

65. See Arden edition of *MND*, ed. Brooks, lxxxv, 144–45. Citations in my text are to Ovid, *Metamorphoses*, trans. F. J. Miller, Loeb Classical Library, 2 vols. (London: Heinemann, 1964–66), cited by book and line numbers in the Latin text; *Medea*, in Seneca, *Tragedies*, ed. F. J. Miller, Loeb Classical Library, cited by line numbers in the Latin text.

Also clearly relevant to the mythological subtext of *MND* is the domestic violence of Seneca's *Medea:* Medea's betrayal of her father; the sparagmos of her brother; and, after Jason's unfaithfulness, her slaughter of their two young sons. But Medea also has a significant place in the history of Theseus, as recorded by Plutarch (*Lives*, 1:39) and by Seneca (*Hippolytus*, 696–97): Fleeing Corinth after destroying Creusa and her own two boys, Medea seeks asylum in Athens with old Egeus, whose power to beget offspring she promises to renew by her magic. Finding that young Theseus has come to Athens in disguise, Medea attempts unsuccessfully to trick the suspicious Egeus into poisoning his own son. Thus, as Seneca's Hippolytus points out (*Hippolytus*, 558–64), Medea has been to his father what Phaedra is to himself: the impassioned and barbaric female who seeks to pervert the bonds between father and son, between man and man.

66. See *The XI. Bookes of The Golden Asse containing The Metamorphosie of Lucius Apuleius*, trans. William Adlington (1566), The Tudor Translations (1893; rpt. New York: AMS Press, 1967). For Meroë and Panthia, see Bk. 1, chs. 3–5; for Pamphile, Bk. 3, chs. 15–16. In Bk. 10, ch. 46, in telling about a certain noble and rich matron who lusted for and coupled with him in his incarnation as an ass, Apuleius twice alludes to Pasiphaë (see 217, 219).

epithet for Circe. As exemplars of the dangerous—and explicitly sexual—power of women, it is logical that these witches should share a place with the Amazons in the man-made system of sex and gender that is articulated in *A Midsummer Night's Dream*.

In their study of English state formation as cultural revolution, Philip Corrigan and Derek Sayer point out the significance of the inclusion of witchcraft among a number of other acts that became classified as felonies and thus as capital crimes during the Tudor period. The witches' compact with Satan and with each other constituted a conspiracy against the godly state. Noting that witchcraft in this period was perceived to be a crime overwhelmingly (although not exclusively) committed by women, they suggest that witchcraft prosecutions exemplify the "structuring by gender of society and its self-images through state routines." Beliefs that all women were potentially dangerous, and that "women not under patriarchal authority were particularly dangerous," are reflected in the datum that "the largest single category of convicted witches, who were ritually burned to death, were old, single women."[67] As the Virgin Queen—and, by the 1590s, as an old, single woman—Elizabeth was, uniquely, a ruler whose political power, personal mythology, and physical condition bore a disquieting resemblance to those associated with Amazons, witches, and other unruly women. In *A Midsummer Night's Dream*, the conjuncture of the witch and the Virgin Queen is effected through a mythological displacement, and activated through the trope of "the triple Hecate" invoked by Puck. The multiform goddess was ubiquitous not only in Roman mythological poetry and drama but in the Renaissance mythography that pervaded the learned culture of Elizabethan England. As Abraham Fraunce describes this triune goddess, "in heaven she is called *Luna*, in the woods *Diana*, under the earth *Hecate*, or *Proserpina*."[68] It is by means of this mythological collocation

67. Corrigan and Sayer, *The Great Arch*, 64–65. Corrigan and Sayer rely, in particular, upon the work of Christina Larner and Keith Thomas. See Thomas, *Religion and the Decline of Magic;* Larner, *Witchcraft and Religion: The Politics of Popular Belief*, ed. Alan Macfarlane (Oxford: Basil Blackwell, 1984). Corrigan and Sayer cite Acts of 1542 and 1563 classifying witchcraft as a felony.

68. Abraham Fraunce, *The Third part of the Countesse of Pembrokes Yvychurch: Entituled, Amintas Dale* (London, 1592), facsimile ed. The Renaissance and the Gods, 13 (New York: Garland, 1976), 42v.

that Lyly's *Endimion* insinuates Cynthia's affinity with Tellus and Dipsas. And, at the same time that Shakespeare's play evokes Queen Elizabeth through its allusions to Cynthia and Diana, by the same means it insinuates her malign and dangerous aspect.

As I have already noted, in two of its three occurences in Ovid's *Metamorphoses*, Titania is an epithet for Circe. In its only other occurence, Ovid uses it as an epithet for Diana; and he does so precisely at that moment in Book Three in which her hapless votary Actaeon sees her naked, coming from her bath (3.173). Actaeon's punishment for being in the wrong place at the wrong time is to be metamorphosed into a stag which is then torn apart by his own hounds. Shakespeare's strategic choice of the name Titania for his Faery Queen thus fuses Circe, the powerful seductress who metamorphoses men into swine, with Diana in her threatening and vindictive aspect, as the patroness who metamorphoses her devotee into a stag which is then hunted and killed. In this aspect, as in others, Diana is the primary mythological persona of England's imperial votaress. The fable of Diana and Actaeon was a story of compelling and perhaps unique relevance and resonance in the Elizabethan context, in which the prince was a woman whose cult had appropriated the mythology of Diana.[69] This Ovidian episode was associated with the militant virginity of Queen Elizabeth not only in written texts but also in the iconography of royal gardens, as is confirmed by several travelers' accounts of depictions of Diana and Actaeon at two of the queen's residences.[70] Thus, Jonson was working within an already established

69. Such a scenario may well be represented on the title page of the cryptic book of poems, *Willobie his Avisa* (1594). At the bottom of the page, in an oval inset, Diana and her nymphs stand in a rectangular, artificial fountain, and splash water at Actaeon, whose head has already been transformed into a stag's; at the top of the page is the head of a stag, crowned with a crescent moon. B. N. de Luna, *The Queen Declined: An Interpretation of Willobie his Avisa, with the Text of the Original Edition* (Oxford: Clarendon Press, 1970), makes a fairly convincing argument for the book as an elaborate cipher of Queen Elizabeth's courtships. An identification of Actaeon with the Earl of Essex is based upon the latter's armorial bearings, which contain a stag and a hunting dog, and upon contemporaneous allusions (see 88–89).

70. See *The Diary of Baron Waldstein, A Traveller in Elizabethan England*, trans. and annotated by G. W. Groos (London: Thames & Hudson, 1981), 159, 161. These statues, gardens, and inscriptions are also described in *Thomas Platter's*

context of political mythopoeia when, in *Cynthias Revels*, he allegorized the disgrace of the Earl of Essex as the fate of Actaeon.[71] Having thus invested Titania with such powerful and ominous associations, Shakespeare proceeds to divest her of her autonomy and power, to put her under the spell of her husband, and to make the asinine metamorphosis of her mortal minion—at once her paramour and infant—the very instrument of her own degradation and containment.

III

In the third scene of Shakespeare's play, after Titania has remembered her Indian votaress (2.1.123–37), Oberon remembers his "imperial votress." He has once beheld,

Travels in England 1599, trans. Clare Williams (London: Jonathan Cape, 1937), 195–97, and are mentioned in the "Diary of the Journey of Philip Julius, Duke of Stettin-Pomerania, through England in the year 1602," ed. Gottfried von Bülow, *Transactions of the Royal Historical Society*, n. s., 6 (1892), 1–67; 57.

71. At the beginning of the play, Cupid announces the occasion of Cynthia's revels: "The Huntresse, and Queene of these groves, DIANA (in regard of some black and envious slanders hourely breath'd against her, for her divine justice on ACTAEON, as shee pretends) hath here in the vale of *Gargaphy*, proclaim'd a solemne revells, which (her god-head put off) shee will descend to grace" (1.1.91–96). At the beginning of the final scene, Cynthia justifies herself:

> For so ACTAEON, by presuming farre,
> Did (to our griefe) incurre a fatall doome;
> . . .
> But are we therefore judged too extreme?
> Seemes it no crime, to enter sacred bowers,
> And hallowed places, with impure aspect,
> Most lewdly to pollute? Seemes it no crime,
> To brave a *deitie?*
> . . .
> To men, this argument should stand for firme,
> "A Goddesse did it, therefore it was good."
> (5.11.14–15, 18–22, 25–26)

The polluting offense alluded to is presumably the unauthorized return of the Earl of Essex from his post in Ireland and his presumptuous, unannounced entry into the Queen's privy chamber at Nonsuch. (See Dutton, *Mastering the Revels*, 132–33.) These notorious, dangerous, and unstable actions marked the beginning of the end for Essex: As a consequence of his indiscretion, he incurred the fatal doom that he forfeit all of his royal offices. This loss of power, prestige, and revenue precipitated his revolt.

> Flying between the cold moon and the earth,
> Cupid all arm'd; a certain aim he took
> At a fair vestal, throned by the West,
> And loos'd his love-shaft smartly from his bow
> As it should pierce a hundred thousand hearts.
> But I might see young Cupid's fiery shaft
> Quench'd in the chaste beams of the watery moon;
> And the imperial votress passed on,
> In maiden meditation, fancy-free.
> Yet mark'd I where the bolt of Cupid fell:
> It fell upon a little western flower,
> Before milk-white, now purple with love's wound:
> And maidens call it 'love-in-idleness'.
> . . .
> The juice of it, on sleeping eyelids laid,
> Will make or man or woman madly dote
> Upon the next live creature that it sees.
>
> 　　　　　　　　　　(2.1.156–68, 170–72)

The evocative monologues of Titania and Oberon are carefully matched and contrasted: The Faery Queen speaks of a mortal mother from the east; the Faery King speaks of an invulnerable virgin from the west. Their memories express two myths of origin: Titania provides a genealogy for the changeling and an explanation of why she will not part with him; Oberon provides an aetiology of the metamorphosed flower that he will use to make her part with him.

Subsequently, the deluded Titania treats Bottom as if he were both her child and her lover—which seems entirely appropriate, since he is a substitute for the changeling boy, who is, in turn, Oberon's rival for Titania's attentions. Titania herself is ambivalently benign and sinister, imperious and enthralled. She dotes upon Bottom, and indulges in him all those desires to be fed, scratched, and coddled that render Bottom's dream recognizable to us as a parodic fantasy of infantile narcissism and dependency. But it is also, at the same time, a parodic fantasy of upward social mobility. Titania mingles her enticements with threats:

> Out of this wood do not desire to go:
> Thou shalt remain here, whether thou wilt or no.
> I am a spirit of no common rate;

The summer still doth tend upon my state;
And I do love thee: therefore go with me.
I'll give thee fairies to attend on thee;
And they shall fetch thee jewels from the deep,
And sing, while thou on pressed flowers dost sleep:
And I will purge thy mortal grossness so,
That thou shalt like an airy spirit go.

(3.1.145–46).

The sublimation of matter into spirit is identified with the social elevation of the base artisan into the gentry: Titania orders her attendants to "be kind and courteous to this gentleman" (3.1.157), to "do him courtesies" (167), and to "wait upon him" (190); she concludes the scene, however, with an order to enforce her minion's passivity, thus reducing him to the demeanor prescribed for women, children, and servants: "Tie up my love's tongue, bring him silently" (104).[72] This order is, perhaps, a sinister glance at the dangerously powerful feminine personages of Diana and Circe, with whom Titania shares her name.

In the liaison between Titania and Bottom, Shakespeare restores Lyly's metamorphosis of the myth of Endimion and Phoebe to its usual form, that of a goddess who dotes upon a mortal. At the same time, Shakespeare transgresses the separation of high and low plots, which is carefully observed by Lyly. The farcical element in *Endimion* is provided by Sir Tophas, a comical, cowardly braggart soldier who falls in love with Dipsas, the play's crone. At the behest of Cynthia, he is eventually matched with Bagoa, who had been metamorphosed into a tree by Dipsas and who, in the celebratory conclusion of *Endimion*, is restored to her own shape by the benign magic of Cynthia. We could say that, in Shakespeare's rewriting of Lyly's *En-*

---

72. Gail Kern Paster has recently made the ingenious suggestion that "Titania's plans to 'purge' Bottom of mortal grossness seem . . . equally poised between, or inclusive of, ethical and physical reference, just as her interest in his physical state seems poised between the erotic and maternal. Like an overcontrolling mother focused upon the body processes of her infant, Titania prescribes a *literal* purge. . . . The idea of the purge has the general effect . . . of identifying Titania's mastery and Bottom's passivity with the structure of early childhood experience of the body, especially infantile experience of maternal stimulation" (*The Body Embarrassed: Drama and the Disciplines of Shame in Early Modern England* [Ithaca: Cornell University Press, 1993], 132, 138).

dimion, it is Cynthia who falls a-doting upon Sir Tophas. Shakespeare further degrades the omnipotent and omniscient Lylian maiden queen/goddess by rendering her a wayward matron whose doting is under the observation and control of her husband. This play's metamorphoses are not subject to charismatic queenship; rather, they are the mischievous work of the wayward servant of the Faery King and serve to further the ridiculousness of the Faery Queen's affection. Shakespeare's representation of Titania in her relationship to Bottom may also be seen to parody the erotic scenarios of the 1590 *Faerie Queene* in which superhuman feminine figures both dominate and dote upon their young, mortal lovers. Spenser's scenarios of Acrasia and Verdant (*FQ*, 2.12.72–82) and of Venus and Adonis (*FQ*, 3.6.46–49) are evocative of those played out by the aging Queen and her courtiers. In contrast to Spenser's *Faerie Queene* and Lyly's *Endimion*, Shakespeare's theatrical representation is strongly marked by transgressions of social rank and stylistic decorum. To find equivalent transgressions in the Spenserian text, we must look to the encounter between Belphoebe and Braggadocchio (*FQ*, 2.3). Even in that comically grotesque scenario, however, the royal virtue is externally threatened rather than internally compromised. Shakespeare's caricature has two dimensions, both of which operate at the expense of the Faery Queen: On the one hand, Bottom is impervious to Titania's blandishments and unshakeably earthbound in his desires; on the other, Titania's powers are circumscribed by Oberon's.

Unlike the inviolable vestal, or the already espoused Titania, Shakespeare's comic heroines are in transition between the conditions of maiden and wife, daughter and mother. These transitions are mediated by the wedding rite and the act of defloration, which are brought together at the end of *A Midsummer Night's Dream:* When the newlyweds have retired for the night, Oberon and Titania enter the court in order to bless the "bride-bed" where the marriages are about to be consummated. By the act of defloration, the husband takes physical and symbolic possession of his bride. The sexual act in which the man draws blood from the woman is already implicit, at the beginning of the play, in Theseus's vaunt: "Hippolyta, I woo'd thee with my sword, / And won thy love doing thee injuries" (1.1.16–17). In the play-within-the-play, which wears away the hours "between our after-supper and bedtime" (5.1.34), the impending injury is evoked by malapropism and is thus dismissed with laughter: Pyramus finds Thisbe's mantle "stain'd with blood," and concludes that "lion vile hath here deflower'd [his] dear" (5.1.272, 281). The image in which Oberon describes the flower's metamorphosis suggests the immanence of defloration in the very origin of desire: "The bolt of Cupid fell / . . . Upon a little western flower, / Before milk-white, now purple with love's wound." Cupid's shaft violates the flower when it has been deflected from the vestal: Oberon's purple passion flower is procreated in a displaced and literalized defloration.

The change suffered by the flower—from the pristine whiteness of milk to the purple wound of love—juxtaposes maternal nurturance and erotic violence. For Elizabethan auditors and readers, the metamorphosis may have carried a suggestion not only of defloration but also of menstruation—and, perhaps, of the menarche, which was taken to be the sign of female sexual maturity, the advent of womanhood and potential motherhood.[73] In Elizabethan popular gynecology, the observed relationship between lactation and amenorrhea was explained by the belief that mother's milk is a transubstantiation and refinement of menstrual blood: "Why have not women with childe the flowers? . . . Because that then the flowers turne into milke, and into the nourishment of the childe" (*Problemes of Aristotle*, E5r). An awareness that the commonest Elizabethan term for menses was "flowers" adds a peculiar resonance to certain occurrences of flower imagery in Renaissance texts.[74] This is especially the case in *A Midsummer Night's Dream*, in which flowers are conspicuously associated

73. See the summary of popular Elizabethan notions in Crawford, "The Construction and Experience of Maternity in Seventeenth-Century England," 6: "The onset of menstruation showed a woman to be fertile and was thought necessary for conception. After the menarche, she developed seed in her blood and longed for sex because she wanted to be a mother."

74. See *Oxford English Dictionary* (*OED*), s. v. "flower," sense 2. b. See Patricia Crawford, "Attitudes to Menstruation in Seventeenth-Century England," *Past & Present* 91 (May 1981), 47–73, for a useful historical introduction to this subject. See Barbara B. Harrell, "Lactation and Menstruation in Cultural Perspective," *American Anthropologist* 83 (1981), 796–818, for an analysis of the interplay between physiological and cultural factors in the "preindustrial reproductive cycle"; and also, Dorothy McLaren, "Marital Fertility and Lactation 1570–1720," in *Women in English Society 1500–1800*, ed. Mary Prior (London: Methuen, 1985), 22–53. For a general discussion of the cultural symbology of blood and bleeding in Shakespearean drama and early modern culture, see the stimulating recent study by Gail Kern Paster, *The Body Embarrassed*, 64–112.

with female sexuality and with the moon. Consider Titania's observation:

> The moon, methinks, looks with a watery eye,
> And when she weeps, weeps every little flower,
> Lamenting some enforced chastity.
>
> (3.1.101–03)

The answer to the question, "Why do the flowers receive their name *Menstrua*, of this word *Mensis* a moneth?" constitutes a gloss on Titania's speech:

> Bicause it is a space of time which doth measure the Moone.... Now the Moone hath dominion over moist things, and bicause the flowers are an humiditie, they take their denomination of the moneth, and are called monethly termes: for moist things do increase as the Moone doth increase, and decrease as she doth decrease. (*Problemes of Aristotle*, E5r).

Such oblique menstrual symbolism suggests that a subliminal discourse on female sexuality pervades Shakespeare's text.[75] The imagery of the text insinuates that, whatever its provenance in horticultural lore, Oberon's maddening love-juice is also a sublimation of vaginal blood. It conflates menstrual blood with the blood of defloration: The former is the ambivalent sign of women's generative power and of their sexual pollution, of the dangers they pose to men's potency, to their reason, and to their honor; the latter is the sign of

---

75. In the quoted passage, Brooks follows previous editors in glossing "enforced" (l. 193) as "violated by force" (Arden *MND*, 62; cf. cxxix). However, the opposite reading—"enforced" as compulsory chastity—seems equally possible. (See *OED*, s.v. "enforced," sense 1: "That is subjected to force or constraint"; and sense 2: "That is forced upon or exacted from a person; that is produced by force.") In one sense, then, the allusion is to sexual violation; in the other, it is to compulsory abstinence. In the present context, the latter sense may suggest the injunction against sexual relations during menstruation (Leviticus 20:18; Ezekiel 18:6), which was commonly repeated by sixteenth- and seventeenth-century writers on domestic relations, and provided a scriptural basis for attitudes toward the polluting powers of the female body. See, for example, Gouge, *Of Domesticall Duties*, 223–24, who cites Leviticus and Ezekiel in referring to "polluted copulation," "when husbands require this duty in that time, which under the Law was called *the time of a wives separation for her disease*." (For a rare piece of evidence that such injunctions were not necessarily observed in early modern English sexual practice, see Pollock, "Embarking on a Rough Passage: The Experience of Pregnancy in Early-Modern Society," 41–42.)

men's assertion of control over women's bodies, the sign of masculine mastery over potentially dangerous feminine generative and erotic powers.

Unlike the feminine *dramatis personae* of *A Midsummer Night's Dream*, Oberon's vestal virgin is not subject to Cupid's shaft, to the frailties of the flesh and the fancy. Nor is she subject to the mastery of men. Isolated from the experiences of desire, marriage, and maternity, she is immune to the pains and pleasures of human mutability. But it is precisely her bodily and mental impermeability which make possible Oberon's pharmacopoeia. The floral symbolism of female sexuality that is begun in Oberon's description of "love-in-idleness" is completed when he names "Dian's bud" (4.1.72) as its antidote. With Cupid's flower, Oberon can make the Fairy Queen "full of hateful fantasies" (2.1.258); and with Dian's bud, he can win her back to his will.[76] In the very act of preserving "Dian's bud," the "fair vestal" is indirectly responsible for the creation of "love-in-idleness." Thus, her invulnerability to desire becomes doubly instrumental to Oberon in his reaffirmation of romantic, marital, and parental norms that have been inverted during the course of the play. Ironically, the vestal's very freedom from fancy guarantees the subjection of others. She is necessarily excluded from the erotic world of which her own chastity is the efficient cause.

In royal pageantry, the Queen was always the cynosure; her virginity was the source of magical potency. And in courtly plays such as Lyly's *Endimion*, dramatic representation of the charismatic royal virgin continued to enact such a role—although the limitations and resources of such representation opened up new and perhaps unintended possibilities for equivocation and ambiguity in the apparent affirmation of royal wisdom, power, and virtue. Like Lyly's *Endimion*, *A Midsummer Night's Dream* is permeated by images and devices that suggest characteristic forms of Elizabethan court culture. But Shakespeare's ostensibly courtly wedding play is neither focused upon the

---

76. On the identification of "love-in-idleness" with the purple pansy and of "Dian's bud" with mugwort or St. John's Plant, see Anca Vlasopolos, "The Ritual of Midsummer: A Pattern for *A Midsummer Night's Dream*," *Renaissance Quarterly* 31 (1978), 21–29; esp. 23–26. Vlasopolos notes that mugwort belongs to the genus *Artemisia* and that, according to the *Herbarium* of Apuleius, the properties of the genus were discovered by the goddess Diana, who entrusted the knowledge to Chiron, the centaur.

Queen nor structurally dependent upon her actual presence or her intervention in the action.[77] Nor does it include among its on-stage and speaking characters a transparent allegorical representation of the queen—a character who enjoys a central and determing authority over the action. Even in *Love's Labour's Lost*—which the 1598 Quarto claims on its title page to reproduce "as it was presented before her Highnes this last Christmas"—the Princess of France bears a more mediated relationship to Shakespeare's queen than do the Cynthias of Lyly's *Endimion* and Jonson's *Cynthia's Revels*.

My point is not that the structure and ethos of *A Midsummer Night's Dream* are indifferent to the cultural resonance of the Queen but rather that the play's own cultural resonance may be said to depend precisely upon the dramaturgical exclusion of the queen, upon her *conspicuous* absence. It has been the norm for critics and editors of *A Midsummer Night's Dream* to identify the "imperial votress" as an allusion to Queen Elizabeth, and to interpret it as an incidental, topical compliment, rather than as an integral element of the play's dramaturgy and ideology. From the latter perspective, however, Shakespeare's ostensible royal compliment may be seen as a complex mediation of the charismatic royal presence that pervaded late Elizabethan culture and as an appropriation of the cult of the Virgin Queen. The poetic texts of Spenser often fragment the royal image, refracting aspects of the Queen "in mirrours more then one" (*FQ*, 3.Proem.5). In a similar way, Shakespeare's play text splits the triune Elizabethan cult image between the fair vestal, who is an unattainable *virgin*, and the Fairy Queen, who is represented as both an intractable *wife* and a dominating *mother*. Oberon uses one against the other in order to reassert masculine prerogatives.

Within Elizabethan society, relationships of authority and dependency, of desire and fear were characteristic of both the public and the domestic domains. Domestic relations between husbands and wives, parents and children, masters and servants were habitually politicized: the household was a microcosm of the state; at the same time, socioeconomic and political relationships of patronage and clientage were habitually eroticized: the devoted suitor sought some loving return from his master-mistress. The collective and individual impact of Elizabethan symbolic forms frequently depended upon an

77. Compare Hunter, *John Lyly*, 329–30.

interplay between these domains. Indeed, the political transactions of Elizabeth's reign were so fundamentally individual and interpersonal in character that it is perhaps anachronistic to distinguish any exclusively public domain of Elizabethan political life.

Within *A Midsummer Night's Dream*, the public and domestic domains of Elizabethan culture converge in the absent figure of the imperial votaress. Queen Elizabeth was a woman ruler officially represented, by herself and by others, as the virgin mother of her subjects. When those same Elizabethan subjects employed the themes of masculine procreative power, autogeny, and mastery of women in their own speech and writing, the familiar tropes of misogyny and patriarchy could acquire a seditious resonance, a resonance that was specific to the gendered discourse of Elizabethan state power. In this sense, the ruler and the ruled, the Queen and the playwright, are construable as subjects differentially shaped within a shared conjuncture of language and social relations, who jointly reshape that conjuncture in the very process of performing it.

All of Shakespeare's plays may have been written with the possibility in mind of courtly as well as commercial performances, and there is evidence that a number of them during both the Elizabethan and Jacobean reigns were performed in both venues. Some plays may have received their most lucrative performances at court or in aristocratic households, but there is no evidence that any of them was originally written for such a performance. Certainly, the potential for both courtly and public performances provides evidence for the shared tastes of Queen and commoner. And, needless to say, the advertisement that a play had been performed at court or before the Queen was intended to enhance the interest of Elizabeth's theatre-going or play-reading subjects, who might thereby vicariously share the source of her majesty's entertainment. Nevertheless, despite the very broad social appeal of Shakespearean and other plays, we should resist any consequent impulse to homogenize Elizabethan culture and society into an organic unity. Shakespeare's plays played to both courtly and popular audiences, and these audiences constituted frequently overlapping but nevertheless distinct and potentially contradictory sources of socioeconomic support and ideological constraint.

The writing of plays that would be playable in both the commercial playhouses and in the royal court points toward the transitional nature of the material and ideological conditions in which the Elizabethan theatre emerged and thrived. That *A Midsummer Night's Dream* was originally (or ever) performed as an aristocratic wedding entertainment, at which the Queen herself was present, is an attractive but unproven hypothesis. What we know for certain is that the title page of the first quarto, printed in 1600, claims to present *A Midsummer Night's Dream* "As it hath been sundry times publickely acted, by the Right honourable the Lord Chamberlaine his servants." Shakespeare's play was not itself a product of the court but rather of a professional and commercial theatre that existed in an ambiguous and delicate relationship to the court. Despite the legal fiction that public performances served to keep the privileged players of the Lord Chamberlain's Men in readiness for performance at court, and despite whatever adaptions may have been made in repertory plays to suit them to the conditions of particular court performances, the dramaturgical and ideological matrix of the Shakespearean drama was located not in the royal court but in the professional playhouse.

☽

CHAPTER ELEVEN

BOTTOM'S DREAM

In *A Midsummer Night's Dream*, the interplay among characters is structured by an interplay among categories—namely, the unstable Elizabethan hierarchies of gender, rank, and age. Differences *within* the mortal and faery courts of *A Midsummer Night's Dream* are structured principally in terms of gender and generation. However, by the end of the fourth act, the multiple marriages arranged within the Athenian aristocracy and the marital reconciliation arranged between the King and Queen of Faeries have achieved domestic harmony and reestablished hierarchical norms. When Bottom and his company are introduced into the newly concordant courtly milieu in the play's final scene, social rank and social calling displace gender and generation as the play's most conspicuous markers of difference. The dramatic emphasis is now upon a contrast between the socially and stylistically refined mixed-gender communities of court and forest, and the "crew of patches, rude mechanicals" (3.2.9), who "have toil'd their unbreath'd memories" (5.1.72) in order to honor and entertain their betters. In the coming together of common artisan-actors and the leisured elite for whom they perform, sociopolitical realities and theatrical realities converge. The nature and consequences of this convergence are the subject of this chapter.

I

Like their companion Bottom in his liaison with Titania, the mechanicals are collectively presented in a childlike relationship to their social superiors. They characterize themselves, upon two occasions, as "every mother's son" (1.2.73, 3.1.69); however, they hope to be "made men" (4.2.18) by the patronage of their lord, Duke Theseus. Just as Bottom is made an explicit substitute for the changeling, so the mechanicals collectively parody the changeling's gender-specific transition from the matriarchal world of infancy to the patriarchal world of manhood. Titania vows that she will purge Bottom's mortal grossness and will make him her "gentle joy" (4.1.4); Bottom's own company hope that the Duke will grant him a pension of sixpence a day for his performance as Pyramus. It is surely more than dramatic economy that motivated Shakespeare to make the artisan who is the queen's complacent paramour also an enthusiastic amateur actor who performs before the Duke. Bottom is a comically exorbitant figure for the common masculine subject of Queen Elizabeth. His interactions with the Queen of Faeries and with the Duke of Athens represent distinct modes of relationship to his sovereign: in the former, that relationship is figured as erotic intimacy; in the latter, it is figured as public homage.

The immediate reason for the presence of Bottom and his companions in *A Midsummer Night's Dream* is to rehearse and perform an "interlude before the Duke and the Duchess, on his wedding-day at night" (1.2.5–7). However, their project simultaneously evokes what had been a central aspect of civic and artisanal culture in England scarcely a generation before the production of Shakespeare's play—namely, the Feast of Corpus Christi, with its ceremonial procession and its often elaborate dramatic performances. The civic and artisanal status of the amateur players is insisted upon with characteristic Shakespearean condescension: Puck describes them to his master, Oberon, as "rude mechanicals, / That work for bread upon Athenian stalls" (3.2.9–10); and Philostrate describes them to his master, Theseus, as "Hard-handed men that work in Athens here, / Which never labour'd in their minds till now" (5.1.72–73). In the most material way, Bottom's name relates him to the practice of his craft—the "bottom" was "the core on which the weaver's skein of yarn was wound" (Arden *MND*, 3, n. 11). Among artisans, weavers in particular were associated with Elizabethan food riots and other forms of social protest that were prevalent during the mid 1590s, the period during which *A Midsummer Night's Dream* was presumably written and first performed.[78] Bottom's name also relates him, more generally, to his

78. On the connection between weavers and social protest, see Theodore B. Leinwand, "'I believe we must leave the killing out': Deference and Accommodation in *A Midsummer Night's Dream*," *Renaissance Papers* (1986), 11–30, esp. 14–21;

relatively lowly position in the temporal order, to his social baseness. But if we construe Bottom as the spokesman for the commons in this play, we must add the proviso that his *vox populi* is not merely that of a generalized *folk*. His is not the voice of the dispossessed or the indigent—of rogues, vagabonds, or sturdy beggars; he is rather the comic representative of the middling sort—a broad grouping of socioeconomically self-sufficient artisans, yeomen, merchants, and tradespeople, with its own highly articulated culture.

It was in such a civic, artisanal, and entrepreneurial ethos that Shakespeare had his own roots. His father, John Shakespeare, was a glover and whittawer (a curer and whitener of skins), a craft for which he would have served an apprenticeship, and also a dealer in such commodities as wool, timber, and grain. He held an increasingly prestigious series of civic offices in Stratford, from constable, to alderman, to high bailiff.[79] During his childhood in Stratford, the younger Shakespeare would have had the opportunity and the occasion to experience the renowned Corpus Christi play that was performed annually in nearby Coventry, until its suppression after 1579. Bottom himself, the most enthusiastic of amateur thespians, makes oblique allusion to the figures and acting traditions of the multipageant mystery plays.[80] Thus, resonating through the dramatic persona of Nick Bottom, the weaver, are not only a generalized common voice but also the particular socioeconomic and cultural origins of Master Wil-

---

also Annabel Patterson, *Shakespeare and the Popular Voice*, 56–57. On Elizabethan food riots, see John Walter and Keith Wrightson, "Dearth and the Social Order in Early Modern England," *Past & Present* 71 (May 1976), 22–42; Buchanan Sharp, *In Contempt of All Authority: Rural Artisans and Riot in the West of England, 1586–1660* (Berkeley: University of California Press, 1980); John Walter, "A 'Rising of the People'? The Oxford Rising of 1596," *Past & Present* 107 (May 1985), 90–143.

79. On the playwright's social origins and his father's position in Stratford, see S. Schoenbaum, *William Shakespeare: A Compact Documentary Life* (Oxford: Oxford University Press, 1977), 14–44. See Theodore Leinwand, "Shakespeare and the Middling Sort," for an important recent statement regarding Shakespeare's relationship to issues of social rank. On Elizabethan classifications of social rank, see the studies cited above in part 1, n. 75.

80. See Clifford Davidson, "'What hempen home-spuns have we swagg'ring here?' Amateur Actors in *A Midsummer Night's Dream* and the Coventry Civic Plays and Pageants," *Shakespeare Studies* 19 (1987), 87–99. On the end of the Coventry play, see R. W. Ingram, "Fifteen Seventy-nine and the Decline of Civic Religious Drama in Coventry."

liam Shakespeare, the professional player-playwright—and, too, the collective sociocultural origins of his craft.[81] *A Midsummer Night's Dream* simultaneously acknowledges those origins and frames them at an ironic distance; it educes connections, only to assert distinctions. In part 1 of this study, I have noted that the Elizabethan regime sought to curtail performances of the civic Corpus Christi plays and to inhibit other forms of popular pastime, to institute state holidays and ceremonial events that were focused upon the sovereign, and to extend patronage and protection to the companies of professional players who performed in the commercial theatres. I have suggested that the implementation of such policies was part of a broad strategy to secure and enhance the Elizabethan regime and to further the work of Tudor state formation. The beginning of the fully professional, secular, and commercial theatre of Elizabethan London coincided with the effective end of the religious drama and the relative decline of local amateur acting traditions in the rest of England. By incorporating Bottom and his company of amateur thespians into *A Midsummer Night's Dream*, Shakespeare creates a sharply comic metadramatization of this profoundly consequential cultural conjuncture.

In the case of Coventry, the decay of traditional civic culture during the middle and late sixteenth century paralleled the city's economic decline.[82] Such cultural changes were abetted, however, by the active suppression or co-optation of popular ceremonies and recreations undertaken by the Tudor state and by Reformist civic and ecclesiastical authorities. Some specific instances of this general process can provide a context for construing Shakespeare's comic representation of civic, artisanal culture and its relationship to the state. Queen Elizabeth visited Coventry during her progress of 1566. In his speech of welcome, the City Recorder alluded to the role of Coventry in the overthrow of the Danes, "a memoriall whereof is kept unto this day

---

81. On the relationship of Shakespearean drama and dramaturgy to the late medieval Mystery cycles, see Emrys Jones, *The Origins of Shakespeare* (Oxford: Clarendon Press, 1977), 31–84; Weimann, *Shakespeare and the Popular Tradition in the Theater*, 49–97.

82. See Charles Phythian-Adams, "Ceremony and the Citizen: The communal Year at Coventry, 1450–1550"; and his monograph, *Desolation of a City: Coventry and the Urban Crisis of the Late Middle Ages* (Cambridge: Cambridge University Press, 1979).

by certaine open shewes in this Citty yearely"; the reference is to the elaborate and rowdy annual Hock Tuesday play, in which the role of women combatants was prominent. Upon her actual entrance into the city, the Queen viewed the pageants of the Tanners, Drapers, Smiths, and Weavers that formed parts of the Corpus Christi play.[83] Two years later, under the pressure of reformist preachers, the civic celebrations of the Hocktide shows were banned. Despite this, the Queen had a subsequent opportunity to witness them at first hand. According to a putative eyewitness account, this was in 1575, during her celebrated visit to the Earl of Leicester's estate at Kenilworth. Led by a mason who styled himself Captain Cox, the "good harted men of Coventree" daringly presented their quaint show among the spectacular entertainments and displays with which the earl courted and counseled his royal mistress. The Coventrymen intended to make "theyr humbl peticion untoo her highnes, that they might have theyr playz up agayn."[84] According to Langham's vivid account, the performance of the Coventrymen's Hocktide show was preceded by a rustic Brideale, complete with such village pastimes as morris dancing and running at quintain (49–52). The presentation of such quaint shows within the context of Kenilworth's spectacular courtly pageants suggests that they were being framed and displayed for the amusement of an elite that was already in the process of withdrawing itself from direct participation in the popular.

Significantly, none of these common and amateur entertainments is mentioned in George Gascoigne's self-promoting courtly account, *The Princely Pleasures at the Courte at Kenelwoorth*, printed in 1576. It is probable that the Kenilworth entertainments penned by Gascoigne and others in Leicester's pay were performed by Leicester's Men, led by none other than James Burbage.[85] Thus, a peer's calculated

83. See the documents printed in *Records of Early English Drama: Coventry*, ed. R. W. Ingram (Toronto: University of Toronto Press, 1981), 233–34. Also see Ingram, "Fifteen seventy-nine and the Decline of Civic Religious Drama in Coventry."

84. See Robert Langham, *A Letter*, with Introduction, Notes, and Commentary by R. J. P. Kuin (Leiden: E. J. Brill, 1983), 52–55.

85. See Chambers, *Elizabethan Stage*, 2: 88–89: "From 9 to 27 July 1575 Elizabeth paid her historic visit to Kenilworth, and there is no proof, but much probability, that the company were called upon to take their part in her entertain-

wooing of his royal mistress provided a fleeting occasion for the as-
cendant professional theatre and the declining civic drama to cross
paths. Despite the Coventrymen's "humbl peticion untoo her highnes," it appears that, after 1579, the citizens of Coventry ceased to
entertain themselves with either their Hocktide show or their Corpus
Christi play. At about the same time, in the city records for 1578,
there occurs the first of a number of extant entries for payments in
connection with celebrations "on the quee[n']s hollyedaye" (*Records
of Early English Drama: Coventry*, 286). In these fragmentary records,
we glimpse instances of the complex ideological process by which
traditional ceremonial forms and events focused upon the articulation
and celebration of the civic community became occasions for the city's celebration of a royal visit, or else were displaced outright by a
newly instituted calender of holidays that promoted the cult of the
Queen by honoring her birthday and her accession day.

A *Midsummer Night's Dream* incorporates allusions to a changed and
diminished world of popular civic play forms. Within the play, Titania
evokes the "vigorous and variegated popular culture, the matrix of
everyday life" that, according to Charles Phythian-Adams, "was
eroded and began to perish" during the mid and late sixteenth century ("Ceremony and the Citizen," 57). Within his marriage play,
however, Shakespeare assimilates the disruption of traditional cultural practices to elemental disorder and attributes such cosmic disharmony to the marital discord, the debate and dissension, between
the King and Queen of Faeries:

> The nine-men's morris is fill'd up with mud,
> And the quaint mazes in the wanton green
> For lack of tread are indistinguishable.
> The human mortals want their winter cheer:
> No night is now with hymn or carol blest.
>
> (2.1.98–102)

Here the first three lines are concerned with collective, secular recreations, while the last two are evocative of the good tidings to poor

---

ment. . . . They played at Court on 28 December 1575 and 4 March 1576, and
are described in the account for their payment as 'Burbag and his company'."
Gascoigne's account, which also records for posterity his own putatively im-
promptu performances before the queen, is reprinted in *The Complete Works of
George Gascoigne*, ed. John W. Cunliffe, 2: 91–131.

"human mortals" that were at the core of the Nativity pageants. In its very title and in passing allusions—to the festivals of Midsummer Eve and Saint John's Day, to the rites of May, and to Saint Valentine's Day—the play gestures toward a larger context of popular holiday occasions and customs that mixed together pagan and Christian traditions. In this context, it is significant that Corpus Christi, though a moveable feast, was nevertheless an early summer festival, occurring between 21 May and 24 June—a circumstance that made possible its extensive open-air ceremonies and entertainments.[86]

The institutional basis of civic ritual drama in the craft guilds survives in *A Midsummer Night's Dream* in the names of the "rude mechanicals, / That work for bread upon Athenian stalls" (3.2.9–10). In the play's second scene, Peter Quince enumerates them as "Nick Bottom, the weaver," "Francis Flute, the bellows-mender," "Robin Starveling, the tailor," "Tom Snout, the tinker," and "Snug the joiner"; in the original stage directions for this scene, in both the first quarto and the folio, Quince himself is identified as a carpenter. The identification of the mechanicals in terms of both their particular crafts or "mysteries" and their collective dramatic endeavor amplifies the evocation of the mystery plays of the Corpus Christi tradition. Nevertheless, despite the conspicuous title of Shakespeare's play, and despite the oblique allusions to the guild structure of the civic community, the occasion for the artisans' play-within-the-play is not the marking of the traditional agrarian calendar nor the articulation of the collective urban social body through the celebration of customary holidays. Neither is it the observance of the ecclesiastical calendar, the annual cycle of holy days, nor the dramatization of the paradigmatic events of sacred history, from the Creation and Fall to the Final Doom. Instead, the rude mechanicals pool their talents and strain their wits in order to dramatize an episode from classical mythology, a learned and courtly tradition, and the purpose of their playing is to

---

86. For allusions to the rites of May in *MND*, see 1.1.167, 4.1.132; on St. Valentine's Day, 4.1.138. On the inseparability of St. John's Day and Midsummer Night "in the religious and folk consciousness of the sixteenth century," see Anca Vlasopolos, "The Ritual of Midsummer: A Pattern for *A Midsummer Night's Dream,*" 21–29; esp. 23–26. On rites and games of May Day and Midsummer Eve and Day, also see Barber, *Shakespeare's Festive Comedy,* 119–24; Young, *Something of Great Constancy,* 16–24; Laroque, *Shakespeare's Festive World,* passim. On Corpus Christi as a summer festival, see Rubin, *Corpus Christi,* 208–9, 213, 243, 271, 273.

celebrate the wedding of Duke Theseus, an event that focuses the collective interests of the commonwealth upon the person of the ruler.

In *A Midsummer Night's Dream*, the playwright's ironic imagination bodies forth the ruler and patron in the personage of Theseus. Shakespeare's antique duke holds clear opinions on the purpose of playing, and these opinions take two forms. One is that the drama should serve as a pleasant pastime for the sovereign, as an innocuous respite from princely care:

> Come now; what masques, what dances shall we have,
> To wear away this long age of three hours
> Between our after-supper and bed-time?
> Where is our usual manager of mirth?
> What revels are in hand? Is there no play
> To ease the anguish of a torturing hour?
> Call Philostrate. . . .
> Say, what abridgement have you for this evening,
> What masque, what music? How shall we beguile
> The lazy time, if not with some delight?
>
> (5.1.32–41)

In the personage of Philostrate, Shakespeare's play incorporates the courtly office of Master of the Revels, but limits it to its original charge, which was to provide entertainments for the monarch. Like the ambivalent term *license*, Philostrate's alliterative title as Theseus's "manager of mirth" suggests an official concern simultaneously to allow and to control the expression of potentially subversive festive, comic, and erotic energies.[87]

---

87. In the first quarto of *MND* (1600), Egeus is absent from 5.1; in the folio text, he is present in 5.1 and is assigned the lines that Q1 gives to Philostrate. It has recently been pointed out that whether Egeus is absent or present in 5.1 can have a significant impact on the final effect of the comic action—especially upon the stage. Briefly, his absence reinforces the sense of unresolved generational difference, whereas his presence and participation in the festivity indicates his approval of his daughter's match and his incorporation into the new community. See Barbara Hodgdon, "Gaining a Father: The Role of Egeus in the Quarto and the Folio," *Review of English Studies* 37 (1986), 534–42. Hodgdon argues with some justice that the F variants "complicate and enrich the performance possibilities for *A Midsummer Night's Dream*" (541). Nevertheless, it seems to me that the Q1 readings are more logical and more consistent with Shakespeare's comic practice:

Of the four proffered entertainments, the first two—"The battle with the Centaurs, to be sung / By an Athenian eunuch to the harp"; and "the riot of the tipsy Bacchanals, / Tearing the Thracian singer in their rage" (5.1.44–45; 48–49)—are dismissed by Theseus, ostensibly because their devices are overly familiar. As I have suggested above, both allude to the sexual and familial violence pervading the play's classical mythological subtext and Theseus's own mythic biography—a network of allusions over which the play's patriarchal comedy keeps a precarious control. The third prospect is excluded because it smacks of social protest:

> 'The thrice three Muses mourning for the death
> Of learning, late deceas'd in beggary'?
> That is some satire, keen and critical,
> Not sorting with a nuptial ceremony.
>
> (5.1.52–55)

This conspicuous irrelevance has two operative points: the first, that its subject is the familiar complaint of Elizabethan cultural producers that they lack generous and enlightened patronage from the great; the second, that Duke Theseus—the play's personification of courtly patronage—doesn't want to hear about it. His taste is for the entertainment that promises to be the least challenging, and he persists in his choice despite the recommendation of his Master of the Revels, who has already auditioned it:

> No, my noble lord,
> It is not for you: I have heard it over,
> And it is nothing, nothing in the world;
> Unless you can find sport in their intents,
> Extremely stretch'd and conn'd with cruel pain
> To do you service.

This is the play that Theseus will hear, "For never anything can be amiss / When simpleness and duty tender it" (5.1.76–83).

The lines assigned to Philostrate in both 1.1 and 5.1 are entirely and precisely appropriate to his office and to no one else's; the conversion of Egeus implied by F is wholly unprepared for (cf. his sentiments in 4.1.153–58, his last words in Q1); it is characteristic of Shakespearean comedy either conspicuously to refuse the paradigm of a final reconciliation, conversion, and inclusion, or to grant it in such a way as to problematize or to delegitimize it.

Thus, the other form taken by Theseus's opinions concerning the drama is that it should serve as a gratifying homage to princely power, one that simultaneously provides an occasion for the exercise of royal magnanimity:

> Our sport shall be to take what they mistake:
> And what poor duty cannot do, noble respect
> Takes it in might, not merit.
> Where I have come, great clerks have purposed
> To greet me with premeditated welcomes;
> Where I have seen them shiver and look pale,
> Make periods in the midst of sentences,
> Throttle their practis'd accent in their fears,
> And, in conclusion, dumbly have broke off,
> Not paying me a welcome. Trust me, sweet,
> Out of this silence yet I pick'd a welcome,
> And in the modesty of fearful duty
> I read as much as from the rattling tongue
> Of saucy and audacious eloquence.
> Love, therefore, and tongue-tied simplicity
> In least speak most, to my capacity.
>
> (5.1.90–105)

As is characteristic of Shakespearean drama's dialogical mode, Theseus's self-gratifying sense of his subjects' love and simplicity is counterpointed by those subjects' own voicings of the material interests and personal fantasies that have motivated their desire to perform before their lord. In the brief scene before Bottom rejoins his companions with the news that their "play is preferred" (4.2.36–37), Snug asserts that, "If our sport had gone forward we all had been made men"; and Flute laments that Bottom has "lost sixpence a day during his life; he could not have 'scaped sixpence a day. And the Duke had not given him sixpence a day for playing Pyramus, I'll be hanged. He would have deserved it" (17–23). What the ruler chooses to take as a spontaneous act of homage is the subject's calculated means to acquire a pension.

In regard to the purpose of playing, the opinions of Shakespeare's Athenian duke bear a strong likeness to those of his own sovereign, as these were represented in her policies and in her own public performances. Thus, in the metatheatrical context of the play's long final scene, Duke Theseus is not so much Queen Elizabeth's *masculine antithesis* as he is her *princely surrogate.* Theseus's attitude toward his subjects' offerings has analogues in the two printed texts that describe the queen's visit to the city of Norwich during her progress of 1578. In a curiously metadramatic speech directly addressed to Elizabeth, the figure of Mercury describes the process of creating and enacting entertainments for the queen—such as the one in which he is presently speaking:

> And that so soone as out of dore she goes
> (If time do serve, and weather waxeth fayre)
> Some odde device shall meete hir highnesse streight,
> To make hir smyle, and ease hir burthened brest,
> And take away the cares and things of weight
> That Princes feele, that findeth greatest rest.[88]

On another occasion, as the Queen returned toward her lodgings,

> within Bishops gate at the Hospitall dore, master Stephan Limbert, master of the Grammer schoole in Norwich stoode readie to render her an Oration: her majestie drew neare unto him, and thinking him fearefull, saide graciously unto him: Bee not afeard. He answered her againe in English: I thanke your majestie, for your good encouragement: and then with good courage entred into this Oration.

After printing the oration in the original Latin and in English translation, the account continues by describing the Queen as "very attentive, even untill the end therof. And the Oration ended, after she had given great thanks therfore to Maister Lymbert, she saide to him: It is the best that ever I heard." [89] The tone in which Theseus responds to the mechanicals' "palpable gross play" catches the element of hyperbole in the queen's reported speech, and turns its gracious condescension toward mockery. For example, as Theseus says to Bottom: "Marry, if he that writ it had played Pyramus, and hanged himself in Thisbe's garter, it would have been a fine tragedy—and so it is, truly,

---

88. Thomas Churchyard, *A Discourse of The Queenes Majesties entertainement in Suffolk and Norffolk* (London, 1578), rpt. in *Records of Early English Drama: Norwich, 1540–1642,* ed. David Galloway, 302.

89. B[ernard] G[arter], *The Joyfull Receyving of the Queenes most excellent Majestie into hir Highnesse Citie of Norwich* (London, 1578), rpt. in *Records of Early English Drama: Norwich,* 266–67, 271.

and very notably discharged" (5.1.343–47). I have suggested analogues from royal pageantry—which was frequently performed by children and amateurs as well as by professional players—because such performances most clearly equate to the mechanicals' performance of *Pyramus and Thisbe* within Shakespeare's play. However, the queen's attitude toward the plays and players of the adult, professional, and commercial theatre seems to have differed little from what it was toward other forms of royal entertainment and their performers. As I have noted in part 1, as early as 1574, a company of professional players under the patronage of the Earl of Leicester and led by James Burbage were licensed by the Queen to perform in public so that they would be in readiness to play at court, "aswell for the recreacion of oure loving subjectes, as for oure solace and pleasure when we shall thincke good to see them." [90]

II

Despite the apparently indifferent attitude of the sovereign—or, perhaps, precisely because of it, in *A Midsummer Night's Dream*, Shakespeare calls attention to the artistic distance between the professional players and their putatively crude predecessors, and he does so by incorporating a comic representation of such players into his play. This professional self-consciousness is the very hallmark of the play's celebrated metatheatricality—its calling of attention to its own artifice, to its own artistry. *A Midsummer Night's Dream* parodies antecedent dramatic forms and performance styles: the amateur acting traditions that had largely declined along with the civic drama by the end of the 1570s and the work of the professional companies active during the 1570s and earlier 1580s, and it juxtaposes to them the representational powers of The Lord Chamberlain's Men and their playwright. [91] This contrast was made manifest by Shakespeare's company in the

90. Patent of 10 May 1574, rpt. in Chambers, *Elizabethan Stage*, 2: 87–88.

91. Davidson convincingly suggests that the mechanicals' rehearsal and performance of *Pyramus and Thisbe* is designed to burlesque "the older dramatic styles (including . . . the theatrical styles of the public theatre fashionable before c. 1585) with their tendency toward bombastic language and clumsy use of mythological subjects"; and to conjoin this burlesque with one directed toward the acting capacities of the amateurs who performed in the civic religious drama, which had been largely suppressed by the early 1580s ("'What hempen home-spuns have we swagg'ring here?'," 88). Also see Young, *Something of Great Constancy*, 34–41.

very process of performing *A Midsummer Night's Dream*. In particular, it was demonstrated in what we may presume was their consummately professional comic enactment of the mechanicals' vexed rehearsals and inept performance of *Pyramus and Thisbe*. The dramaturgical problems with which the mechanicals struggle show them to be incapable of comprehending the relationship between the actor and his part: They have no skill in the art of personation; they lack an adequate conception of playing. The contrast between amateur and professional modes of playing is incarnated in the *performance* of Bottom—by which I mean the professional player's performance of Bottom's performance of Pyramus. Bottom is the amateur actor who wants to be cast in all the parts—the tyrant, the lover, the lady, the lion. And he is the only character in this play of nocturnal and lunatic changes who is literally metamorphosed. Yet, despite his translations into an ass-headed monster and a fabled lover, Bottom remains immutably—*fundamentally*—Bottom. The fully professional collaboration between the imaginative playwright and the protean player of the Lord Chamberlain's Men—between Will Shakespeare and the celebrated comedian and dancer, Will Kemp—creates the illusion of Bottom precisely by creating the illusion of his incapacity to translate himself into other parts.[92]

The play-within-the-play device calls attention to the theatrical transaction between the players and their audience. In the process of foregrounding the imaginative and dramaturgical dynamics of this transaction, *A Midsummer Night's Dream* also calls attention to its sociopolitical dynamics. Shakespeare's Duke Theseus formulates policy when he proclaims that "The lunatic, the lover, and the poet / Are of imagination all compact"; that "Lovers and madmen have such seething brains, / Such shaping fantasies, that apprehend / More than cool reason ever comprehends" (5.1.7–8, 4–6). The social order of Theseus's Athens depends upon his authority to name the forms of

---

92. On Bottom as "the latest of a series of vehicles for Will Kempe," see Brooks, Arden ed. of *MND*, lxxxii. Kemp was one of the sharers in the Lord Chamberlain's Men from its inception until 1599. For a detailed and suggestive analysis of Kemp's popular artistry, see David Wiles, *Shakespeare's Clown: Actor and Text in the Elizabethan playhouse* (Cambridge: Cambridge University Press, 1987), esp. 24–60, 73–82. Wiles points out that many of the speech headings for Bottom in Q1 merely indicate "Clowne" (74–75); his brief discussions of *MND* take for granted that Kemp created the role of Bottom.

mental disorder and his power to control its subjects. Theseus's anal-
ogizing of the hyperactive imaginations of lunatics, lovers, and poets
accords with the orthodox perspective of Elizabethan medical and
moral discourses. These insisted that the unregulated passions and
disordered fantasies of the ruler's subjects—from Bedlam beggars to
melancholy courtiers—were an inherent danger to themselves, to
their fellows, and to the state.[93] For Theseus, no less than for the
Elizabethan Privy Council, the ruler's task is to *comprehend*—to un-
derstand and to contain—the energies and motives, the diverse, unstable, and potentially seditious apprehensions of the ruled. But the
Duke—so self-assured and benignly condescending in his comprehension—might also have some cause for *apprehension*, for he himself
and the fictional society over which he rules have been shaped by
the fantasy of a poet. Theseus's deprecation of lunatics, lovers, and
poets is his unwitting exposition of the scope and limits of his own
wisdom.

The wonderful musings of the newly awakened Bottom provide
a seriocomic prelude to the Duke's set-piece. Fitfully remembering
his nocturnal adventure, Bottom apprehends something strange and
admirable in his metamorphosis and his liaison with Titania:

> I have had a most rare vision. I have had a dream, past the wit of
> man to say what dream it was. Man is but an ass if he go about to
> expound this dream. . . . The eye of man hath not heard, the ear
> of man hath not seen, man's hand is not able to taste, his tongue
> to conceive, nor his heart to report, what my dream was. I will
> get Peter Quince to write a ballad of this dream: it shall be called
> "Bottom's Dream," because it hath no bottom; and I will sing it in
> the latter end of a play, before the Duke. (4.1.203–16)

Bottom's (non-)exposition of his dream is a garbled allusion to a passage in Saint Paul's First Epistle to the Corinthians:

---

93. Among modern critical and historical studies, see Lawrence Babb, *The
Elizabethan Malady: A Study of Melancholia in English Literature from 1580 to 1642*
(East Lansing, Michigan: Michigan State College Press, 1951); Michael MacDon-
ald, *Mystical Bedlam: Madness, Anxiety, and Healing in Seventeenth-Century England*
(Cambridge: Cambridge University Press, 1981); Lacey Baldwin Smith, *Treason in
Tudor England: Politics and Paranoia* (Princeton: Princeton University Press, 1986);
Karin Coddon, "'Suche Strange Desygns': Madness, Subjectivity, and Treason in
Hamlet and Elizabethan Culture," *Renaissance Drama*, n. s., 20 (1989), 51–75.

And we speake wisdome among them that are perfite: not the wisdome of this worlde, nether of the princes of this worlde, which
come to noght.

But we speake the wisdome of God in a mysterie, even the
hid wisdome, which God had determined before the worlde, unto
our glorie.

Which none of the princes of this worlde hathe knowen: for had
thei knowen it, thei wolde not have crucified ye Lord of glorie.

But as it is written, The things which eye hathe not sene,
nether eare hathe heard, nether came into mans heart, are, which
God hathe prepared for them that love him.

But God hath reveiled them unto us by his Spirit: for the Spirit
searcheth all things, yea, the deepe things of God. (1 Corinthians
2: 6–10; *Geneva Bible*, 1560 ed.)

This allusion has often been remarked. Insufficiently remarked,
however, is the political resonance that the passage may have had for
Elizabethan playgoers and readers and the possibility that, in select-
ing it for parody, the playwright may have had a point to make, however oblique its expression.[94] The New Testament passage is built
upon an opposition between the misconceived and misdirected profane knowledge possessed by "the princes of this worlde" and the
spiritual wisdom accessible only to those who humble themselves
before a transcendent source of power and love. The biblical text
does more than construct a generalized opposition between the profane and the sacred: It gives that abstract moral opposition a political
edge by proposing an inverse relationship between the temporal hierarchy of wealth and power and the spiritual hierarchy of wisdom
and virtue.

---

94. The "context of profound spiritual levelling" implied by Shakespeare's
biblical parody is noted in Patterson, *Shakespeare and the Popular Voice*, 68. Patterson
pursues the "genial thesis" that *MND* imagines "an idea of social play that could
cross class boundaries without obscuring them, and by those crossings imagine
the social body whole again" (69); accordingly, she focuses upon the integrative
"Christian communitas" suggested in I Corinthians 12: 14–15, rather than upon
the obvious and immediate oppositional context of I Corinthians 2: 6–10. For another recent study of the relationship between late Elizabethan social conflict and
the tensions of rank within *MND*, see Leinwand, "'I believe we must leave the
killing out': Deference and Accommodation in *A Midsummer Night's Dream*." Less
sanguine than Patterson, Leinwand concludes that "Shakespeare criticizes the relations of power in his culture, but does so with remarkable sensitivity to the
nuances of threat and accommodation which animate these relations" (30).

It is fitting that the play's chosen instrument for its scriptural message of sociospiritual inversion be a common artisan and amateur player named Bottom. Early in the play (1.2.19, 24, 36), Bottom alludes obliquely to the raging tyrant of the Nativity pageants in the Mystery cycles, whose nemesis is "ye Lord of glorie," the King of Kings. Although, he tells us, his "chief humour is for a tyrant" (1.2.24), Bottom is cast to play a lover in "an interlude before the Duke ... on his wedding-day" (1.2.5–7). Thus, Shakespeare's play firmly records the redirection of the popular dramatic impulse toward the celebration of "the princes of this worlde." At the same time, however, the comical garbling of the allusion and its farcical dramatic context have the effect of mediating the sacred text, thereby allowing Shakespeare to appropriate it for his own dramatic ends: An opposition between sacred and profane knowledge is displaced into an opposition between Bottom's capacity to apprehend the story of the night and Theseus's incapacity to comprehend it. Through such rhetorical strategies, Shakespeare's professional theatre implicitly repudiates Theseus's attitude toward the entertainer's art, and does so precisely by incorporating and ironically circumscribing it. I am suggesting, then, that Shakespeare's evocation of the scriptural context functions to provide a numinous resonance for the play's temporal, metatheatrical concerns; that these concerns are rooted in the distinction and relationship between the instrumental authority of the state, as personified in the sovereign, and the imaginative authority of the public and professional theatre, as personified in the common player-playwright; and that Bottom—artisan, amateur player, and clown—serves as a comic mediator of that relationship.

Philostrate comments to Theseus that, "unless you can find sport in their intents," the purport of the artisans' play is "nothing"; and Theseus responds, with congenial condescension, that "our sport shall be to take what they mistake." However, the artisans' lament that, "If our sport had gone forward we all had been made men," has already revealed to the audience that "their intents" exceed the comprehension of the court. Something other than "simpleness and duty" prompts them to tender their play to the prince; and the mistakes that the playwright gives them to make are something more than nothing. Consider Quince's mispointed Prologue:

If we offend, it is with our good will.
That you should think, we come not to offend,
But with good will. To show our simple skill,
That is the true beginning of our end.
Consider then, we come but in despite.
We do not come, as minding to content you,
Our true intent is. All for your delight,
We are not here. That you should here repent you,
The actors are at hand; and by their show,
You shall know all, that you are like to know.

(5.1.108–17)

It seems to me that, in devising this metatheatrical Prologue, the playwright's serious sport, his playful purpose, is only incidentally directed toward the grammatical shortcomings of the artisan-actors. When it has been "rightly" punctuated, the Prologue reads as a subject's appropriately deferential, if slightly stilted, address to his superiors; it now observes decorum.[95] As it stands, however, the Prologue reads as a potential act of impudent effrontery—but one that is rendered excusable and enjoyable by its construal as a well-intentioned instance of vulgar error. The sly and witty ambivalence or duplicity of the text that the professional playwright has invented for his incompetent amateur players—a text construable in contrary senses, depending upon pointing—pointedly puts into question the determination of "true intent" in dramatic performance. In this darker or more oblique sense, Shakespeare's metatheatrical Prologue is an interpretive challenge, immediately directed toward the regulatory authority of the Duke and his Master of the Revels; and, beyond them, mediately directed to the Elizabethan authorities—the queen, her Master of the Revels, and her Privy Council, to whose interpretive findings and takings the intentions of the players and their playwrights were always ultimately subject.

Theseus finds Quince's speech to be "like a tangled chain; nothing impaired, but all disordered" (5.1.124–25). But the order of this

95. In a final appendix to his Arden edition of *MND* (165), Harold Brooks presents "QUINCE'S PROLOGUE (V.i.108–16) RIGHTLY PUNCTUATED." Conscientiously righting Shakespeare's comic malapropisms, Brooks shares Theseus's perspective that our sport shall be to take what the artisans mistake.

disorder, the concord of this discord, forms a riposte to Theseus's own princely perspective on the purpose of playing. Immediately preceding Quince's Prologue, Theseus proclaims that he desires to "beguile / The lazy time . . . with some delight"; and that, when judging such performances, "Love . . . and tongue-tied simplicity / In least speak most, to [his] capacity." The response of Shakespeare's Player to Shakespeare's Prince is that, "All for your delight, / We are not here." In a witty reformulation of the Horatian/Elizabethan commonplace of instruction through delight, the players' "true intent" is not "minding to content you" but rather "that you should think." The purpose of playing begins in the performative impulse—"to show our simple skill"—but its end is to claim for the world of the theatre a privileged mode of knowing in the theatre of the world: "The actors are at hand; and by their show, / You shall know all, that you are like to know." The metatheatricality of *A Midsummer Night's Dream* frequently operates so as to distinguish the mechanicals' art from that of the Lord Chamberlain's Men. But it also, and sometimes simultaneously, operates so as to present the amateur players as the professionals' strategically comic parody of themselves in their relationship to their patrons and to the state.

Many of the play's critics have seen in the play-within-the-play, and in the presentation of Bottom and his colleagues more generally, a satire upon amateur theatricals and a ridicule of the plebs by a theatrical professional whose own sensibilities and social pretensions were fundamentally gentle and courtly, and who on this occasion was writing for an exclusively gentle and courtly audience. It seems to me, however, that Shakespeare is no more clearly aristocratic in his biases here than he is plebian and that, in any case, in this instance as in most others, he is writing primarily for the commercial theatre and only incidentally, if at all, for the court. Indeed, in performance in the Elizabethan playhouse, this popular strain may have been more immediately striking than is now readily apparent from the text. For example, at the conclusion of the performance of *Pyramus and Thisbe*, the resurrected Pyramus/Bottom asks the Duke, "Will it please you to see the epilogue, or to hear a Bergomask dance between two of our company?" To which Theseus replies, "No epilogue, I pray you; for your play needs no excuse. Never excuse; for when the players are all dead, there need none to be blamed. . . . But come, your Bergomask; let your epilogue alone" (5.1.338–43, 347–48). At this point, two in the artisans' company perform what was presumably a rough peasant dance, a fitting conclusion to what Theseus calls "this palpable-gross play" (353); immediately afterwards, the artisans exit the play, quickly followed by the newlyweds. Earlier in the play, upon his awakening in the forest, Bottom decides to "get Peter Quince to write a ballad of this dream"; it will be called "Bottom's Dream" and he "will sing it in the latter end of a play, before the Duke" (4.1.13–16). Bottom's invitation "to see the epilogue, or to hear a . . . dance" evokes the synesthesia of his awakening speech: "The eye of man hath not heard, the ear of man hath not seen" (4.1.209–10). Theseus preempts such an epilogue to "Pyramus and Thisbe." As I have already suggested, the Duke would likely have found the theme of "Bottom's Dream" uncongenial. But as David Wiles has intriguingly suggested, Bottom's offer of an epilogue to the play-within-the-play may also have been intended as a metadramatic anticipation of the jig that Nick Bottom/Will Kemp would have danced and sung at the Curtain playhouse at the conclusion of *A Midsummer Night's Dream* (Wiles, *Shakespeare's Clown*, 55). Wiles describes the Elizabethan jig as a product of English folk culture that "occupies an ambiguous terrain somewhere between patriotism and subversion," as a virtuosic stylization of misrule enacted beyond the confines of the play-text, and as "an essential component in the fragile balance which the Elizabethan theatre set up between popular and courtly modes" (43–46).[96] Such an extra-textual possibility forcefully reminds us of the collective nature of theatrical production and of the scripted play's embeddedness within a larger setting of cultural performance. These dimensions of the theatrical experience, now largely irrecoverable except in isolated or fragmentary instances, would likely have been critical elements in any determination of a given play's "intent."

96. Wiles explains the departure of Kemp from the Lord Chamberlain's Men as precipitated by their move to the Globe, and by the courtship of a more prosperous and less overtly popular audience that this move implied: "Kemp would have come to realize that the move to the Globe stood to deprive him of the free hand and the receptive audiences to which he had been accustomed at the Curtain" (47–48). For an interesting, if sometimes forced, argument regarding the opposition of popular and elite forms and practices of dancing in *MND*, see Skiles Howard, "Hands, Feet, and Bottoms: Decentering the Cosmic Dance in *A Midsummer Night's Dream*," *Shakespeare Quarterly* 44 (1993), 325–42.

Like that of the jig itself, the ideological positioning of Shakespeare's play is more complex and more equivocal than can be accommodated by the terms of an elite/popular opposition. The attitude that the professional player-playwright displays toward Bottom, and toward the artisanal culture that he personifies, is a mixture of affection, indulgence, condescension, and ridicule, and the complexity and ambivalence of that mixture is nowhere more conspicuous than in the speech about Bottom's dream. At the same time, it is through the mediation of Bottom—weaver, player, and dreamer—that the upwardly mobile Master William Shakespeare—artist-entrepreneur, and subsequently, landowner, investor, civic leader, and gentleman— is related to his popular and artisanal roots. The scenes involving Bottom and his companions provide Shakespeare's *Dream* with a perspective from below that might be called Bottom's *Dream*. In particular, it is through the subject, occasion, and execution of the playwithin-the-play that Shakespeare metadramatizes a fundamental shift in the cultural politics of playing that had occurred during the course of Elizabeth's reign. When, in 1584, the Queen's Players petitioned the Privy Council to be allowed to play publicly in the City of London, the Recorder for the Corporation of the City of London objected that

> it hath not ben used nor thought meete hertofore that players shold make their lyving on the art of playing, but men for their lyvings using other honest and lawfull artes, or retteyned in honest service, have by companies learned some enterludes for some encreasce to their profit by other mens pleasures in vacant time of recreation.[97]

A decade later, in the artisans' performance of *Pyramus and Thisbe* for Theseus's wedding, *A Midsummer Night's Dream* gestures toward the shift of focus of civic culture from Corpus Christi to the politic body of the prince; and the performance of the artisans themselves by the Lord Chamberlain's Men gestures toward the ascendancy of the professional and commercial theatre over occasional and amateur forms

---

97. Petition of the Queen's Players to the Privy Council, ca. November 1584, and Answer of the Corporation of London, enclosing the Act of Common Council of 6 December 1574; rpt. in Chambers, *Elizabethan Stage,* 4: 298–302; quotation from 300.

of playing. The social origins of those who created the professional Elizabethan theatre were, like Shakespeare's, of the middling sort and were, specifically, artisanal. James Burbage's original occupation was as a joiner; his brother-in-law, John Brayne, who financed the Red Bull and The Theatre, was a freeman of the Grocers' Company; and his brother, Robert Burbage, who may well have built The Theatre, was a freeman of the Carpenter's Company.[98] The artisanal affinity between the Burbages and Shakespeare's "rude mechanicals" is not merely a topical curiosity. From within this relatively well-educated, respectable, and prosperous grouping of urban commoners came the skills, capital, and initiative that—in conjunction with the interests of the state—produced the cultural and socioeconomic innovation of a professional and commercial theatre. Bottom's *Dream* is an incongruous evocation, an oblique marker, of a popular and artisanal ethos that *A Midsummer Night's Dream* and its playwright have ostensibly left behind—a lingering trace of cultural, social, and spiritual filiation.

III

Leaving aside the possibility that Kemp performed a jig as postlude to *A Midsummer Night's Dream*, it still remains the case that Shakespeare's play-text incorporates an epilogue, and that the last word is not given to the ruler—whether the Duke of Athens or the King of Faeries—but rather to Puck, the retainer and entertainer who "jest[s] to Oberon, and make[s] him smile" (2.1.44). Throughout the play, Oberon's power to shape a patriarchal order meets resistance not only from the matriarchal force personified in his spouse but also from the consequential occurrences of accident, coincidence, and impulse. Within *A Midsummer Night's Dream*, the radically destabilizing concept of contingency is personified in the King of Faeries' own wayward and mischievous servant, "that shrewd and knavish sprite / Call'd Robin Goodfellow" (2.1.33–34).[99] It is he

98. See William Ingram, *The Business of Playing*, 92–112, 185–95.
99. See *MND*, 2.1.33–57; 3.2.88–91, 120–21, 345–53. On Robin Goodfellow and his companions as personifications functioning to motivate and thus to rationalize the otherwise inexplicable accidents of traditional village life, see Barber, *Shakespeare's Festive Comedy*, 143; Thomas, *Religion and the Decline of Magic*, 611–13. For the relationship of Shakespeare's Puck to folklore, popular ballads, and the

That frights the maidens of the villagery,
Skim milk, and sometimes labour in the quern,
And bootless make the breathless housewife churn,
And sometimes make the drink to bear no barm,
Mislead night-wanderers, laughing at their harm.

(2.1.34–39)

A figure of folklore and village life, Puck also waits court upon a king. Intervening in the courtships of the young Athenian gentles, disrupting the artisans' rehearsal, endowing Bottom with the head of an ass—the capricious and errant nature of Puck's actions, even when under orders from his master, suggests that he embodies a will to maximize confusion:

Oberon.   This is thy negligence; still thou mistak'st,
           Or else committ'st thy knaveries wilfully.
Puck.   Believe me, king of shadows, I mistook.
           . . .
           And so far am I glad it so did sort,
           As this their jangling I esteem a sport.

(3.2.345–47, 352–53)

As Master of the Revels to Oberon, Puck is an antithesis to Philostrate—no "manager of mirth" but rather a promoter of carnivalesque inversions: "And those things do best please me / That befall prepost'rously" (3.2.120–21).[100]

---

earlier dramatic figure of the Vice, see Weimann, *Shakespeare and the Popular Dramatic Tradition in the Theater*, 192–96. On fairy traditions in the play, see also Young, *Something of Great Constancy*, 25–32.

100. For a richly learned and wide-ranging study of the trope of preposterousness in Shakespeare—the reversal of normative narrative, logical, and ideological orders—see Patricia Parker, "Preposterous Events," *Shakespeare Quarterly* 43 (1992), 186–213. She comments that

comic structures of preposterous reversal in Shakespeare involve . . . not just temporary carnival overturning but reversals of sequence that expose what is invested in priority, order, and "righting" even as it is often forms of re-righting that enable a play to move toward an orderly end. This would be my reading . . . of the simultaneous emphasis on what Theseus terms the ordered "chain" of discourse and the parodic scrambling of it by the "rude mechanicals" of *A Midsummer Night's Dream*, where a middle in which things "befall preposterously" . . . is finally replaced by the "righting" of a patriarchal end, heterosexual joinings, and movement to a "point" that par-

It is to this faintly malign entertainer, this equivocator between service and roguery, between court and town, that Shakespeare assigns the Epilogue to *A Midsummer Night's Dream:*

> If we shadows have offended,
> Think but this, and all is mended,
> That you have but slumber'd here
> While these visions did appear.
> And this weak and idle theme,
> No more yielding but a dream,
> Gentles, do not reprehend;
> If you pardon, we will mend.
> And, as I am an honest Puck,
> If we have unearned luck
> Now to 'scape the serpent's tongue,
> We will make amends ere long;
> Else the Puck a liar call.
> So good night unto you all.
> Give me your hands, if we be friends,
> And Robin shall restore amends.
>
> (5.1.409–24)

Puck's reference to "we shadows" implies not only the personified spirits in the play but also the players of Shakespeare's company who have performed the play.[101] On behalf of the whole company, Puck begs pardon of the audience for any offenses that might provoke reprehension. His Epilogue lightly touches the theme of intent and regulation that is the mispointed point of Quince's Prologue, but it does so in the context of a different kind of theatrical transaction. The play's final couplet—"Give me your hands, if we be friends, / And Robin shall restore amends"—is suited to the relatively egalitarian

allels the echoes within it of the proper "mechanics" or construction of order in discourse (201).

This reading of *MND* is elaborated in a forthcoming study entitled "Rude Mechanicals"; my thanks to Prof. Parker for allowing me to read this essay in manuscript.

101. For "shadow" as "applied rhetorically . . . to an actor or a play in contrast to the reality represented," see *OED,* s. v. "Shadow," sense I.6.b. The earliest usages cited by *OED* are in Lyly, *Euphues;* and Shakespeare, *MND* and *TGV.*

decorum of the playhouse, where the professional players entertained their customers, rather than to a royal court or noble hall, where subjects and retainers performed in homage to their betters.

As the Chorus who speaks the Prologue to *Henry V* begs "pardon, gentles all" (*H5*, Prologue, 8), so Puck ingratiates himself with the audience whose "pardon" he seeks by addressing them collectively as "gentles." In *Henry V*, the status of the popular audience is elevated in acknowledgment of the imaginative authority that the theatre confers upon them: "For 'tis your thoughts must deck our kings" (Prologue, 28). In *A Midsummer Night's Dream*, gentility is conferred upon those empowered to judge the quality of the play and its performance. In both plays, the power to confer such gentility resides with the players themselves. And in each play, the liminal, metatheatrical choric address marks out the theatre as an alternative site of cultural authority, reciprocally constituted by the professional players and their paying audiences, and based upon a contract freely entered into by the parties, rather than upon traditional hierarchical relations of patronage and clientage, dominance and deference. The contractual relationship between the players and their audience that is figured in the final couplet of Puck's Epilogue—"Give me your hands, if we be friends, / And Robin shall restore amends"—is simultaneously imaginative and commercial; it is the play's parting gesture toward the material location of its dreams and visions in the playhouse and in the social world beyond its walls.[102]

Theseus registers Puck's use of "shadows" when he says of the mechanicals' acting in *Pyramus and Thisbe*, that "The best in this kind are but shadows; and the worst are no worse, if imagination amend them" (5.1.208–09). The ducal statement itself is, however, belied on two counts: on the one hand, the rehearsal and performance of the play-within-the-play do invite the audience to make qualitative distinctions between the best and the worst of shadows, and, on the other hand, the on-stage audience at the Athenian court refuses to amend imaginatively the theatrical limitations of the mechanicals.

---

102. As Jean-Christophe Agnew well observes, "Renaissance dramatists did not shrink from comparing their own conventions of performance to the new contractual relationships arising outside the theater. A conditional credibility, not faith, was the playwright's aim, much as it was for his fellow artisans . . . who sought credit in the marketplace" (*Worlds Apart*, 111–12).

When Puck addresses his master as "King of shadows" (3.2.347), the appellation recognizes Oberon as the principal player in the action, whose powers of awareness and manipulation also mark him as the play's internal dramatist. Although Titania has a limited power to manipulate Bottom, an artisan and an amateur actor, she herself is manipulated by this "King of shadows," who is also her husband and her lord. Thus, in the triangulated relationship of Titania, Oberon, and Bottom, a fantasy of masculine dependency upon woman is expressed and contained within a fantasy of masculine control over woman. And, more specifically, the social reality of the Elizabethan players' dependency upon Queen Elizabeth is inscribed within the imaginative reality of a player-playwright's control over The Faery Queen.

To the extent that the cult of Elizabeth informs the play, it is itself transformed within the play. The playwright re-mythologizes the royal cult in such a way as to sanction a relationship of gender and power that affirms masculine authority in the state, the family, and the theatre. Within the imagined world of *A Midsummer Night's Dream*, Oberon and Theseus—the King of Shadows and the Duke of Athens—work toward a common goal: to restabilize, if only temporarily, the patriarchal ordering of the public and domestic domains. This assertion of an equivalence between the patriarchal family and the patriarchal state effectively suppresses the anomalous relationship between gender and power that is incarnated in Shakespeare's sovereign. It is in this sense that the structure of Shakespeare's comedy may be said to neutralize symbolically the gendered forms of royal power to which it ostensibly pays homage. It is in this sense, too, that the dramaturgical conditions of London's professional theatre may be seen to present a *formal* resistance to the absolutist pretensions of late Elizabethan court culture. *A Midsummer Night's Dream* does more than analogize the powers of prince and playwright: it dramatizes—or, rather, it metadramatizes—the relations of power between prince and playwright.

These conclusions may seem to imply a claim for the play as "subversion"; however, its ideological import is not by any means so easily or unequivocally specified. To contextualize the ideological effect produced by the royal allusion—to ask what is being subverted, and what contained—is to make manifest the inadequacy of an analytical paradigm based upon putatively stable and mutually exclusive terms of dominance and opposition. From a perspective that construes Queen Elizabeth as the personification of the state, of royal prerogative, and of courtly culture, the play's handling of her iconography does indeed have a resonance that is both resistant to and subversive of the authorizing myths of power and privilege. Nevertheless, from a perspective that construes the dominant institutional and ideological structures of Elizabethan society as pervasively and resolutely patriarchal, the play's representational strategies appear to be working to contain or to repudiate a perceived challenge to that dominance that is personified in the anomalous feminine sovereign herself. *A Midsummer Night's Dream* both internalizes and resists a princely claim to cultural generativity and social authority; and it does both in terms of the gendered figurative discourse that was the collective medium of the Elizabethan political imagination. By comically enacting the contestation and reaffirmation of authority in the family and in the state, the play enacts a claim for the cultural generativity of the playwright's imagination and for the social authority of the professional theatre.

In construing *A Midsummer Night's Dream* as a *production* of Elizabethan culture, I have in mind the process by which it gives a distinctive and compelling imaginative form to collective representations and understandings of the family, the polity, and the theatre. The "metadrama" of *A Midsummer Night's Dream* analogizes the powers of parents, princes, and playwrights, the fashioning of children, subjects, and plays. When Oberon blesses the bride-beds of "the couples three" (5.1.393), he metaphorizes the engendering of their offspring as an act of writing: "And the blots of Nature's hand / Shall not in their issue stand" (5.1.395–96). And when Theseus wryly describes the poet's "fine frenzy" (5.1.12), the text of *A Midsummer Night's Dream* figures forth its own authorship as an act of parthenogenesis:

> And as imagination bodies forth
> The forms of things unknown, the poet's pen
> Turns them to shapes, and gives to airy nothing
> A local habitation and a name.

> (5.1.14–17)

That the play foregrounds the dramatic medium and the poetic process does not necessarily imply a claim for the self-referentiality of the literary object or the aesthetic act. I suggest, instead, that it manifests a dialectic between Shakespeare's profession and his society, a dialectic between the theatre and the world.

The relationship of Shakespeare's play and its production to traditions of amateur and occasional dramatic entertainments is at once internalized and distanced in the mechanicals' ridiculous rehearsal and performance of *Pyramus and Thisbe*. And by the way in which it frames the attitudes of Theseus and the play-within-the-play's courtly audience, *A Midsummer Night's Dream* internalizes and distances the relationship of the public and professional theatre to the pressures and constraints of aristocratic and royal patronage. Its resonances of popular pastimes and amateur civic drama, on the one hand, and of royal pageantry and courtly entertainments, on the other, serve to situate *A Midsummer Night's Dream* in relationship to its cultural antecedents and its socioeconomic context. Through the play of affinity and difference, these resonances serve to distinguish Shakespeare's comedy from both amateur and courtly modes and to define it as a production of the professional and commercial theatre— "As it hath been sundry times publickely acted, by the Right honourable, the Lord Chamberlaine his servants." The much noted metatheatricality of *A Midsummer Night's Dream* is no more apparent and striking than in this process by which the play assimilates its own cultural determinants and produces them anew as its own dramatic effects. When I suggest that the play simultaneously subsumes and projects the conditions of its own possibility, I trust that no one will imagine that I am making a claim for its timelessness and universality. On the contrary, I am attempting to locate it more precisely in the ideological matrix of its original production. The foregrounding of theatricality as a mode of human cognition and human agency is a striking feature of Shakespearean drama. Such theatricality becomes possible at a particular historical moment. By this means, the professional practitioners of what was both an immensely popular and a bitterly contested emergent cultural practice could articulate their collective consciousness of their paradoxical place in the social and cultural order—the location of the theatre and of theatricality at once on the margins and at the center of the Elizabethan world.

◡
•

A KINGDOM OF SHADOWS

The invocation of "genius" normally marks the limit of understanding; it is a mysterious essence, to which we have recourse when the powers of explanation fail us. Yet "genius," too, has historical conditions of possibility, which we should endeavor to specify before we genuflect to the ineffable. My Epilogue endeavors to specify some of the historical conditions of possibility of Shakespeare's genius. Although Elizabethan professional acting companies like the Lord Chamberlain's Men were in many ways representative of an emergent sociocultural and commercial formation, their organization retained features of the artisan guilds. Shakespeare's company was divided into a hierarchy of sharers, hired men, and apprentices; he was one of the sharers, with a direct financial interest in the company's properties, costumes, and scripts. After 1598, he also became one of several "housekeepers" who owned shares in the Globe, and, subsequently, in the Blackfriars.[1] There is an important distinction to be noted between the relationship of players to playhouses that are merely leased space and their relationship to a playhouse that is the collective property of the company—or, more precisely, the property of those sharers in the company who are also housekeepers in

---

1. Gerald Eades Bentley, *The Profession of Player in Shakespeare's Time 1590–1642*, devotes individual chapters to discussions of sharers (25–63), hired men (64–112), and apprentices (113–46). On some possible differences between the acquisition of players' apprentices and other forms of apprenticeship in the period, see Herbert Berry, "The Player's Apprentice," *Essays in Theatre* 1 (1983), 73–80. On the commercial concerns and corporate structure of the Chamberlain's/King's Men, also see Andrew Gurr, "Money or Audiences: The Impact of Shakespeare's Globe."

the theatre. This distinction implies significant differences among players, not only in terms of income and socioeconomic status but also in terms of their collective professional consciousness. To be housekeepers at the Globe, and subsequently at the Blackfriars, was the enviable situation of some of the sharers in The Lord Chamberlain's/King's Men after 1598, but not of the hired men nor of the apprentices. In addition to being a player, sharer, and housekeeper, Shakespeare was, of course, also the principal playwright for his company. Since scripts were bought outright from writers and were the exclusive property of the company, as a part-owner of the company, Shakespeare was in the very unusual position of holding "a reversionary interest in his own plays" (Wickham, *Early English Stages*, 2: 1: 135).

G. E. Bentley identifies Shakespeare as one of only eight "attached or regular" professional *playwrights* who were "primarily dependent upon the theatres for their livelihood." These dramatists "did not easily or frequently shift their company associations, but tended to work regularly for one troupe for long periods," and were regular, consistent, and prolific in their production of scripts (*Profession of Dramatist in Shakespeare's Time*, 30–37). Elsewhere, Bentley identifies Shakespeare as one of only eight professional *players* (exclusive of the genuinely rich Edward Alleyn) who "accumulated respectable estates." All of them were sharers; almost all of them were housekeepers, and half of those were members of the Lord Chamberlain's/King's Men (*Profession of Player in Shakespeare's Time*, 5–6). Shakespeare's is the only name common to these two lists. Bentley points out that The Lord Chamberlain's/King's Men were the only troupe of players with "a continuous existence throughout the period"; that they were "the only company operating two theaters and maintaining over a long period of time the same system of ownership"; and that "none of the other score or more of London theatrical troupes in the period is known to have enjoyed the control of its own playhouse" (*The Profession of Player in Shakespeare's Time*, 12, 15). Shakespeare was, at one and the same time, a sharer and housekeeper in the Lord Chamberlain's company and also its chief dramatist. He was uniquely positioned within a close-knit, stable, and extraordinarily successful joint enterprise. Thus, he was able to enjoy both material and ideological conditions for artistic production that far surpassed those of most Elizabethan literary professionals and patronage poets, as well as those of his notoriously insecure fellow dramatists. Although this conjunction of circumstances cannot fully account for the special qualities of Shakespeare's dramatic corpus, it does suggest that those special qualities emerged and developed within an individually configured framework of determinate historical and material conditions.

The *meta*dramatic or *meta*theatrical dimensions of Shakespeare's plays, which have exercised the ingenuity of a great many academic Shakespeare critics during the past quarter century, are not incidental rhetorical commonplaces nor symptoms of aestheticism. The metaphorical identification of the world and the stage is one of the reflexive dramatic strategies by which Shakespeare shapes a dialectic between his profession and his society. This remarkably pervasive and sophisticated reflexivity articulates a dramatistic conception of social life that is rooted in the historical circumstances of Shakespeare's experience as Elizabethan player, playwright, and theatrical entrepreneur. Precisely because the professional and commercial theatre was so successful an innovation, it was also persistently subject to attack. The players lived and worked in a volatile relationship to the unstable, and sometimes conflicting, socioeconomic categories of the period. Their own anomalousness and vulnerability, and the unprecedented range of social groups to whom they played and from whom they sought approval, reward, and protection, seem to have led them and their plays into shifting identifications, and thus into shifting antipathies. In varying contexts, they both personated and were capable of identifying themselves with sharply differentiated segments of society: with the sovereign, and/or with the aristocracy and gentry, who were their patrons and the elite segment of their audience; with merchants, yeomanry, or artisans, from whose ranks they came and who composed probably the largest sector of their public audience; with liveried servingmen, in which role they officially served their patrons; with women, who were a significant presence in their audiences; with "rogues, vagabonds, and sturdy beggars," a group with whom the itinerant players had been classified; or with outcasts and aliens, the roles into which they had been cast by the anti-theatrical polemicists. The players' precarious and contradictory situation may well have had the effect of heightening their collective consciousness, of strengthening their identification with

their calling. If we can isolate any relatively stable ideological position in the corpus of Shakespeare's plays—if they can be said to
champion, with any degree of consistency, a particular set of interests
within Elizabethan society—it is precisely that of the professional
theatre with which he was identified in a perhaps uniquely comprehensive way.

By representing particular cultural forms and human actions
within fictional frames, Shakespeare's theatre invited its audience to
reflect upon those forms and actions. But the theatre also reached out
to frame and to elucidate the world of the audience by means of its
own cultural form—a dramatistic paradigm of social life, based upon
the interaction of protean players. The heterodoxy enacted in the
plays performed at the Globe is the logical consequence of the Elizabethan theatre's claim to hold the mirror up to nature. And this theatre holds the mirror up to nature precisely by reflecting upon its own
artifice, for not only does it exemplify the contradictions and conflicts
of Elizabethan society and culture but it also makes such contradictions and conflicts the very subject of its plays. The professional players, playwrights, and playhouses of Elizabethan London were abomi-
nations. They represented a profound challenge to traditional modes
of thinking—not only to particular orthodox beliefs and opinions but
also to the dominant paradigm of agency and authority—both because they failed to fit conveniently into existing cultural frameworks
and because they presented an alternative framework, a dramatistic
or theatrical world picture.[2]

2. In the Introduction to the English language edition of his *Shakespeare and
the Popular Tradition in the Theater*, Robert Weimann writes that

> Shakespeare's theater and his society were interrelated in the sense that
> the Elizabethan stage, even when it reflected the tensions and compro-
> mises of sixteenth-century England, was also a potent force that helped to
> create the specific character and transitional nature of that society. . . . The
> sensibilities and receptivity of the audience and the consciousness and art-
> istry of the drama were so mutually influential that a new historical synthe-
> sis seems conceivable only through an increased awareness of the dialectics
> of this interdependence. (xii)

Dialectical, historicist, and materialist work has become central to the study of
Shakespeare in the United States and Britain since the publication of *Shakespeare
and the Popular Tradition in the Theater*; and such work—including mine—has been
enabled by the critical perspective announced and exemplified in Weimann's
landmark book.

When the Lord Chamberlain's Men performed Shakespeare's *As You Like It* at the newly opened Globe at the end of the 1590s, Queen Elizabeth's subjects heard the compelling assertion that "All the world's a stage, / And all the men and women merely players" (2.7.138–39). This declaration was both materially and symbolically affirmed in the very name, shape, and motto of the playhouse in which the play was being performed: The many-sided first Globe playhouse had as its sign the figure of Hercules carrying the globe; and as its motto, *Totus mundus agit histrionem.*[3] The metatheatricality of the Elizabethan drama did not necessarily obscure what Stephen Greenblatt has called the "privileged visibility" of the royal actor. Indeed, as I have argued in part 1, when the public theatre staged greatness—"in the sight and view of all the world dulie observed"— the equivocal privilege of its visibility was exposure to its subjects. When the "absolutist theatricality" of the state was played in the public and professional playhouse, it became subject to appropriation and destabilization. At the same time, in the process of asserting theatricality as a universal condition of social life, the professional players asserted their own privileged visibility within their circumscribed domain; they manifested that the symbolic social space of the professional theatre was the locus of a power and authority distinct from the "absolutist theatricality" of the queen. Within the playhouse, as upon its stage, *all* the men and women were merely players.

Shakespeare's professional milieu was a paradoxical phenomenon, at once on the margins and at the center of the Elizabethan world. Despite a host of opposing and constraining forces, and for a relatively brief time, the Elizabethan players and playmakers were able to forge a popular and professional drama that appealed to city, court, and country alike. They created and satisfied their own audience, their own market. The public playhouses of Shakespeare's London provided the physical basis for a stable acting company, for the improvement of productions and the control of profits. But a playhouse like the Globe was also a new kind of social and cognitive space—a material realization of the *theatrum mundi* metaphor, far more powerful and immediate in its impact upon an audience than any merely

---

3. For a learned discussion of the circumstantial evidence for the sign and motto, see Richard Dutton, "*Hamlet, An Apology for Actors,* and the Sign of the Globe," *Shakespeare Survey* 41 (1988), 35–43.

literary or oratorical commonplace could be. If Shakespeare and his fellows could convince their audiences that the *theatrum mundi* metaphor was both accurate and useful—if all the men and women were, indeed, merely players—then people might go to the playhouses to learn, from experts, how to play.